Simmel and Since

Few contemporaries of Simmel enjoyed a readership larger than his. In the intellectual circles of Berlin at the turn of the century his dazzling and inimitable essays and books on metropolitan life were a *cause célèbre* in intellectual circles. His eclipse after his death in 1918 is therefore one of the most remarkable circumstances of sociology in the twentieth century. In part it is to be explained by his style of analysis which few 'disciples' could measure up to. But Simmel has also suffered from the serious error of labelling him as a 'formal sociologist'. It is a rich irony that one of the most subtle and many-sided of sociological thinkers should have suffered this fate. The 1980s has witnessed a steady growth of interest in Simmel. This is due in no small measure to the work of David Frisby. Through a series of translations, essays and books, Frisby has played a significant role in reclaiming Simmel as a key sociologist of the modern tradition.

This new book ranges from accounts of Simmel's key concepts such as that of 'society' and his neglected contribution to social psychology. It includes chapters on Simmel's work on the metropolis, social space, leisure, aesthetics and modernity. The final chapter considers the relevance of Simmel for present day debates on culture, aesthetics and postmodernity. Scholarly and shrewd, the book will be of interest to students of Sociology and Cultural Studies.

David Frisby is Professor of Sociology at the University of Glasgow.

Simmel and Since
Essays on Georg Simmel's Social Theory

David Frisby

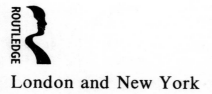

London and New York

First published in 1992
by Routledge
11 New Fetter Lane, London EC4P 4EE

Simultaneously published in the USA and Canada
by Routledge
a division of Routledge, Chapman and Hall Inc.
29 West 35th Street, New York, NY 10001

Printed and bound in Great Britain by
Biddles Ltd, Guildford and King's Lynn

British Library Cataloguing in Publication Data
Frisby, David
 Simmel and since: essays on Georg Simmel's social theory.
 1. Sociology. Simmel Georg 1858–1918
 I. Title
 301.092

Library of Congress Cataloging in Publication Data
Frisby, David.
 Simmel and since: essays on Simmel's social theory.
  p. cm.
 Includes bibliographical references and index.
 1. Simmel, Georg, 1858–1918. 2. Sociology-- Germany--History.
 3. Sociology--Methodology--History. I. Title.
 HM22.G3S4828   1992
 301'.01--dc20   91–15069
                                                            CIP

ISBN   0–415–00975–8
ISBN   0–415–07275–1 (pbk)

Contents

This book was difficult 2 understand and to be honest Simmel was a boring bastard ☺ Have a good day! THANKS!

Acknowledgements

I wish to thank the following for permission to reproduce, where appropriate, in a revised form the essays collected in this volume: Chapter 1 originally appeared as 'Georg Simmel's Concept of Society' in 1990 in M. Kaern, B. Phillips and R. Cohen (eds), *Georg Simmel and Contemporary Sociology*, Dordrecht (Kluwer), pp.39–55 and is reprinted by permission of Kluwer Academic Publishers. Chapter 2 originally appeared in 1984 as 'Georg Simmel and Social Psychology', *Journal of the History of the Behavioral Sciences*, 20, No. 2, pp.107–27, and is reprinted with permission of Clinical Psychology Publishing Co. Inc., Brandon, Vermont. Chapter 3 appears here in English for the first time. An earlier, shorter version appeared in 1988 as 'Soziologie und Moderne: Ferdinand Tönnies, George Simmel und Max Weber' in O. Rammstedt (ed) *Simmel und die frühen Soziologen*, Frankfurt (Suhrkamp), pp.196–221. Chapter 4 appeared as 'Georg Simmel and the Study of Modernity' in M. Kaern *et al.* (eds), *Georg Simmel and Contemporary Sociology*, pp.57–74, and is reprinted by permission of Kluwer Academic Publishers. Chapter 5 appears here for the first time. It is a revised version of a paper read to the twelfth World Congress of Sociology, Madrid, 1990. Chapter 6 appears here for the first time as the reworking of a lecture given to the Department of Sociology, Helsinki University, in October 1989. Chapter 7 appeared originally in a shorter version in 1989 as 'Simmel and Leisure' in C. Rojek (ed), *Leisure for Leisure*, Basingstoke and London (Macmillan), pp.75–91. Chapter 8 is a revised version of a paper given to the American Sociological Association Annual Meeting (Culture Section) in San Francisco in August 1989 and published in 1991 in *Theory, Culture and Society*, 8, No. 3, and is reprinted by permission of Sage Publishers. Chapter 9 appears here for the first time.

Thanks are also due to the Nuffield Foundation for a grant which enabled me to research some of these contributions at Konstanz University in 1987. More recently, a small grant from the German Academic Exchange Service facilitated a further study at Konstanz in the summer of 1990. I am therefore grateful to the DAAD (German Academic Exchange Service) and, as ever, to the Fachgruppe Soziologie, Konstanz University, and especially to Horst Baier, for their hospitality.
Finally, I wish to thank Ann Adamson and Pip Townsend for typing the final manuscript.

David Frisby
Glasgow

Introduction

The essays on Georg Simmel's social theory assembled here are the result of a decade's preoccupation with his work. This commenced with the joint translation (with Tom Bottomore) of Simmel's *The Philosophy of Money* (first published 1978). It continued with monographs in which Simmel's work stands at the centre, notably *Sociological Impressionism* (first published 1981) and *Georg Simmel* (first published 1984). Simmel's work on modernity also forms a significant component of my *Fragments of Modernity* (first published 1986). Reflections on Simmel's social theory also play a more minor role in *Society* (1986, with Derek Sayer). Alongside a number of interpretive essays, most of which are reprinted here in revised form, my concern with Simmel's social theory has been enhanced by participation in the critical German edition of his works (under the general editorship of Otthein Rammstedt) which will eventually comprise twenty-four volumes. This has resulted in my editing (with Klaus C. Köhnke) the critical edition of *Philosophie des Geldes* (1989) and (with H.-Jürgen Dahme) of *Aufsätze und Abhandlungen: 1894– 1900* (1992). In addition, a volume of materials for the contextualisation and interpretation of the former work (again with Klaus C. Köhnke) will appear as *Materialien zur Philosophie des Geldes* (1992).

What is offered in the present volume is a presentation and reworking of themes that have been my concern in the process of becoming acquainted with some, but by no means all, of Simmel's many works. The main focus of the essays offered here is upon social theory but – as one would expect of interpretations of the works of such a wide-ranging author as Simmel – a social theory that extends into many other areas.

The essays are assembled in three sections of unequal length. In the first section, two essays examine some general aspects of Simmel's sociology, namely the diversity of his conceptions of society and his treatment of individual interaction in and as society, as well as an indication of his contribution to social psychology. The main body of essays is contained in the second section and examines various dimensions of Simmel's contribution to a social theory of modernity. This section commences with an attempt to locate his contribution to this topic in the context of his German contemporaries, notably Tönnies and Weber. It is followed by an overview of significant features of Simmel's theory of modernity, the details of which are presented more fully and substantively in my *Fragments of Modernity*. Two succeeding essays take up aspects of the two sites of modernity – the mature money economy and the metropolis – in the hope of revealing neglected dimensions of both. The last two essays in this section examine, respectively, Simmel's contribution to a sociology of leisure (again drawing upon experience of metropolitan existence) and to a social aesthetics of modern everyday life. The final section seeks to examine once more Simmel's contribution to a social theory of modernity and, perhaps more problematically, to a theory of postmodernity. It also highlights, in this context, what proved to be an important project amongst critical social theorists, namely, the development of reflections upon 'the culture of things'. More generally, the last section contains some remarks on the fate of Simmel's social theory since his death in 1918.

In assembling these essays for publication, it is apparent how little of Simmel's corpus of work is actually covered in them. The reader must refer to other works on Simmel for an examination of the many themes not dealt with here. It is indeed difficult to do justice to an author who displays such a variety of rich analyses and insights in a whole range of areas. The present volume is a small contribution to that task. The interpretation of Simmel's work which it contains is therefore one that extends my earlier explorations. Apart from the first two chapters, on foundational aspects of Simmel's sociology, the remainder of the text is largely concerned with his contributions to the study of modernity and possibly postmodernity. The interpretive thrust of these chapters centres around *The Philosophy of Money* and associated texts. There are, of course, many different areas of Simmel's work that are the concern of other scholars.

Part I

Societies and individuals

1   The study of society

What is society, whatever its form? The product of human reciprocal action.

Karl Marx

Society . . . is only the synthesis or the general term for the totality of . . . specific interactions.

Georg Simmel

I

I would like to draw attention to the diversity of Simmel's conceptions of what was once viewed as a foundational question in sociology, without whose satisfactory answer it was often claimed the discipline could not exist: namely, the concept of society. Simmel is one of the first sociologists who sought to secure grounds for the new discipline of sociology without having recourse to the then – and often subsequently – seemingly unproblematical answer: sociology is the study of society. Indeed, Simmel maintained that only by abandoning society as a hypostatized and totalized object could sociology develop successfully as an independent academic discipline.

Simmel's interventions into the grounding of sociology must be seen within the context of the late nineteenth century in which the terrain of the social sciences as a whole was being aggressively contested. This was taking place, on the one hand, in a context in which universal claims were being made to ground large parts of the domain of the human sciences in three competing directions – as being the object of the *Geisteswissenschaften*, as the object of a *Völkerpsychologie* (comprising the study of culture, language and social forms), and as the object of specialized *Sozialwissenschaften*.[1] On the other hand, and at the same time, demarcation disputes within the tighter division of labour between political science (as *Staatswissenschaft*) and economics (as *Nationalökonomie*), between psychology and sociology, and between sociology and history were also under way, with attempts by each discipline radically to exclude the other (e.g. Durkheim's attempted exclusion of psychology from sociology), or to incorporate one into another (e.g. Barth's incorporation of sociology into the philosophy of history). Taking both directions together, and borrowing terms from Mannheim, we can see that there were disputes concerning both foundational sciences (*Begründungswissenschaften*) – and claims to be such sciences – and the specialized sciences (*Spezialwissenschaften*). In addition, there were even more hotly contested disputes within some of the narrower disciplines themselves (most noticeably between the historical and logical (marginalist) schools in economics).

In this latter context, and despite the fact that for a time at least one of his patrons was Gustav Schmoller, Simmel did not particularly concern himself with the so-called *Methodenstreit* (unless one includes his discussions of the problems of the study of history or his review of Stammler's *Wirtschaft und Recht nach der materialistischen Geschichtsauffassung* in 1896).[2] Rather, he was concerned in the 1890s with the grounding of a Moral*wissenschaft*, as opposed to a Moral*philosophie* – the former arguing for the substantive analysis of ethical norms and hence feeding directly into his sociology – and with establishing sociology as an independent discipline.[3]

However, our concern is not directly with this vital chapter in the history of sociology but rather with the delineation of Simmel's shifting conceptions of society. In order to do this, it may be instructive to briefly examine some of the possible antecedents to the conceptions and formulations that constitute Simmel's early notions of society.

This in turn may make it easier to highlight the distinctive nature of Simmel's diverse concepts of society. They comprise: society (*Gesellschaft*) as a totality, society as sociation (*Vergesellschaftung*), society as experience and as everyday knowledge and, finally, society as aesthetic object. These conceptions of society should not be understood as listed in a chronological sequence, nor should they all be deemed to be mutually exclusive. None the less, having delineated the major features of these concepts of society, it may be possible to indicate some of the problems associated with them and to draw out their contemporary relevance.

II

All Simmel's conceptions of society are either directly grounded in or presuppose the concept of interaction or reciprocal effect (*Wechselwirkung*). The concept of interaction or reciprocal effect was already in frequent use in philosophy and elsewhere in the second half of the nineteenth century. Any indication of Simmel's sources must be qualified as possibilities, as provisional, unless a direct connection can be established. In recent discussions, Böhringer has outlined the putative relevance of Gustav Fechner's work for the young Simmel.[4] Certainly in Fechner's work we find a conception of the reciprocal effects (*Wechselwirkung*) of physical and psychological elements upon one another rather than the operation of forces in a single direction. This is a constituent feature of Fechner's logical atomism, whose relevance for Simmel's social theory Böhringer has outlined as follows:

> The dissolution of the substance of the psyche into the functional unity of its elements follows necessarily from Fechner's simple atomism. It enables Simmel to move from *Völkerpsychologie* to a sociology that no longer justified its object by a distinctive substance, but rather wished to describe the formal relationship of complex elements in a functional constellation.[5]

It is certainly true that Simmel knew Fechner's work and that he established early on an ensemble of relational concepts for his social theory, but it is more plausible to argue that these can be found in the *Völkerpsychologie* of Lazarus and Steinthal who were, after all, Simmel's self-acknowledged influential teachers.

We know also that in the late 1880s (in fact in 1886–87) Simmel was lecturing on Hermann Lotze's practical philosophy, in which the concept of interaction [*Wechselwirkung*] also figures. For instance, in volume three of *Mikrokosmos*, whose third section is entitled 'The Connection of Things', Lotze maintains that the relationship between things appears not merely on the surface of objects but also penetrates their very existence.[6] This putative source requires further investigation.

For Simmel's sociology and concept of society more readily verifiable sources are to be found in the work of Spencer, Dilthey and Lazarus. Spencer, for instance, was read intensively by Simmel in his early years, providing him not merely with an elaborate discussion of the concept of differentiation, amongst others, but also with a number of the historical and ethnographic examples and instances which populate his earlier works. More especially, however, the first volume of Spencer's *Principles of Sociology* commences with 'The Data of Sociology' before moving on to 'The Inductions of Sociology', the first of which is 'What is Society?'. But there, in contrast to Simmel, Spencer speaks of 'the reciprocal influence of the society and its units' – thereby already hypostatizing society.[7] For Simmel, however, it is not the relationship of the part to the whole which is central but rather the conviction that the totality of reciprocal influence of units *is* society.

For a time at least, Simmel came under the influence of Dilthey, though it is doubtful that the relationship of the Privatdozent to the Ordinarius was ever a close and harmonious one. None the less, Dilthey's work in the 1870s and 1880s often contains elements of a conception of society and interaction which would appeal to Simmel. In his *Einleitung in die Geisteswissenschaften*, for instance, Dilthey proposes a conception of individual interaction in which 'the individual is an element in the interactions of society, a point of intersection of the diverse systems of these interactions who reacts with conscious intention and action upon their effects'.[8]

But without in any way diminishing the significance of Dilthey's conception here, it is none the less true that a similar constellation is to be found in the work of Lazarus, whose pupils were Dilthey and Simmel. Lazarus (and Steinthal) had already grounded a *Völkerpsychologie* in the early 1860s whose object was to be 'the psychology of societal human beings or human society', in which society is not a 'mere *sum* of all individual minds' but rather the *unity* of a plurality of individuals which lies in the '*content* and *form* or mode of their activity'. Again, even closer to Simmel's later conception of society, Lazarus insists that

> within the large circle of society, smaller circles are formed . . . These circles, however, do not stand side by side but intersect and affect one another in many ways. Thus, within society, there emerges a highly varied . . . relationship of connection and separation (*Absonderung*).[9]

It need hardly be pointed out that the issue of the intersection of social circles was one of Simmel's earliest sociological problematics, indeed one amongst others that were deemed important in Lazarus and Steinthal's programme for a *Völkerpsychologie* (covering language, culture and social forms).

Finally, it should not be assumed that Simmel abandoned these earlier insights gained into a conception of society as interaction of its elements. The theme of connection and separation of interactions that is found in Lazarus's formulation reappears, for example, at the outset of one of Simmel's most famous essays, 'Bridge and Door' (1909), in the following manner:

> The undisturbed transformation of matter as well as energies brings everything in relation to everything else and makes a *single* cosmos out of all individual elements . . . In contrast to nature, it is only given to human beings to unite and to dissolve things and to do this, in fact, in the distinctive manner that the one is always the presupposition of the other.[10]

What Simmel is about to deal with here in terms of connection and separation in society fully accords with his earlier principles upon which he established his conception of sociology and society.

These principles may be readily summarized by extracting from Simmel's early works. He starts out from 'a regulative principle that everything interacts in some way with everything else'. This principle of interaction holds for society too. Secondly, the dynamic element of interactions is often emphasized, as in the statement that 'between every point in the world and every other force permanently moving relationships exist'.[11] Later, Simmel identified both principles as symptomatic of real tendencies in intellectual life, as a 'general tendency of modern thought, with its dissolving of substances into functions, the fixed and permanent in the flux of restless development'.[12] Thirdly, in order to come to terms with this dynamic interaction of a totality, Simmel argued that the only appropriate concepts were relational ones: 'We gain a secure – as opposed to a rigid – position, as soon as we explain what is objective, in both knowledge and action, as a *relational concept*'.[13] Fourthly, any substantive unity that exists or is discerned is itself the result of interaction: 'Where one speaks of the *unity of a form* of whatever type, there one means – since we have no access to the absolute, metaphysical unity – the *interaction of parts*'.[14] Finally, in his most elaborate grounding of sociology prior to the publication of his *Soziologie* in 1908, namely in the essay 'The Problem of Sociology' (extended version in English published 1895), Simmel commences with the anti-individualist proposition that 'we now regard social forces, national [collective] movements, as the real and determining factors out of which the parts which individuals play cannot be evaluated with complete definiteness. The science of human beings has become the science of human society'.[15]

These are some of the key presuppositions from which Simmel elaborates his various conceptions of society. Taken together, they already indicate the centrality of a dynamic interaction that can only be grasped through relational concepts: interaction or reciprocal effect (*Wechselwirkung*), sociation (*Vergesellschaftung*) or the process by which we become socialized and, as Kracauer intimated, a crucial assumption of the fundamental interrelatedness [*Wesenszusammenge-hörigkeit*] of phenomena. In addition, even the concept of form can only be understood in relation to that of content.

We can now turn to the elucidation of Simmel's concepts of society, commencing with society as totality (*Gesellschaft*).

III

In his earliest attempts to ground sociology as an independent discipline, Simmel rejected society as totality as the object of this discipline. He denied that it was 'an absolute entity'; indeed, society is only a secondary phenomenon 'compared with the real interaction of the parts'.[16] However, this early formulation still betrays the false separation of parts and whole that is to be found in Spencer's work. None the less, in keeping with this separation, Simmel maintains that there can be no laws of general social development, since while there may exist laws in relation to particular elements, 'for the whole there exists no law'. Furthermore, there already exists a whole range of social sciences that study aspects and contents of society, and sociology cannot legitimately claim as its object that which is already investigated by other disciplines.

Hence, in Simmel's early writings, the concept of society remains a somewhat empty totalization whose content can only gradually be filled in through the exhaustive investigation of the sum of social interactions. In this sense, then, society is 'only the name of the sum of these interactions . . . It is therefore not a unified, fixed concept but rather a gradual one', that is ultimately 'merely . . . a constellation of individuals'.[17]

Yet in order to understand more fully why it is that society as totality remains a largely negative and incomplete category in Simmel's early works, we need to look at the significance of the contrast between this concept and what for him is a more legitimate object of sociological investigation. He insists that we take seriously the distinction

> between that 'society' which is only a collective name arising from our inability to treat singly the separate phenomena, and that society which determines such phenomena through specific forces

. . . between that which takes place merely *within* society, as within a frame, and that which comes to pass *through* society.[18]

Only the latter is the true object of sociological investigation, namely 'that which in society is "society"'. To anticipate Simmel's argument, the legitimate object of sociology is the study of forms of sociation, of the processes by which we become members of society. This means that only when such forms of interaction and sociation have been

> investigated in all their manifoldness from their primitive shape to their most complicated development can we gradually solve the riddle, 'What is Society?'. For certainly it is not a unified being which lends itself readily to apt definition, but rather consists of the sum of all those modes and forces of association which unite its elements.[19]

In a number of places, Simmel indicates that only when we have fully investigated the modes and forces of sociation can we understand how the unit of society comes about. In fact, Simmel suggests that the study of each of the various forms of sociation itself constitutes the study of 'one of the forms in which "society" comes into being'. It is the totality of these interactions and forms of sociation that 'springing from the most diverse impulses, directed towards the most diverse objects, and aiming at the most diverse ends, constitutes "society"'.[20] Here, in 1896, Simmel views sociology as being concerned with 'the historico-psychological origin' of these forms of interaction, necessitating the investigation of drives and impulses, purposes and ends. This psychological dimension is still evident in Simmel's 'Sociology Lectures' of 1899, transcribed by Park, during the course of the introduction to which Simmel asks:

> What is society as such? Society exists where several individuals (for one another, with one another or against one another) enter into interaction. (This definition is not complete, it is only for our use.) In turn, this interaction always takes place from drives which are *terminus a quo* (e.g. love, hunger, impulse to play, etc.) or *terminus ad quem* (acquisition, defence, nourishment, instruction). The working together of these drives is the unity of human beings which we term society. We know empirically no other unities than interactions of several elements. The 'organism' is a unity and this because all its elements work together. Society is a unity because and insofar as all its individuals interact.[21]

Although Simmel gives due recognition to the 'drives or purposes' as such which stimulate interaction – for which he was charged with adhering to a psychologistic conception of society but which, viewed more positively, led him to investigate sociologically the psychological and emotional foundations of interaction – they constitute merely 'the *material* of society', the content, that becomes truly social only in interaction: 'Sociation is the *form* around which the interests of human beings crystallize'.[22]

In short, society must be filled out by the investigation of the forms of sociation whose totality it constitutes. We can study any 'one of those relations through which a number of individuals become a social group, and "society" is identical with the sum total of these relations'; 'it is only the synthesis or the general term for the totality of these specific interactions'.[23] In other words, the answer to the question 'What is society?' still lies in the future for Simmel. This is still true after his *Soziologie* (1908) provided a structured outline of some of the necessary forms of sociation, and after his *Philosophy of Money* (1900) analysed one form of sociation – exchange – which he took to be both paradigmatic and symbolic of society as a whole.

IV

It is, then, society as sociation (*Vergesellschaftung*) which constitutes the actual object of Simmel's sociological investigations. Again, only when we have fully examined all the forms of sociation – 'the forms in which "society" comes into being'[24] – can we answer the question, 'What is society?'. The interchangeable usage of society and sociation, as in formulations such as 'society or sociation as such', indicates the centrality of sociation for Simmel's sociological project. The sole object of sociology is therefore 'the investigation of the forces, forms and development of sociation, of the co-operation, association and co-existence of individuals', thereby ensuring its status as 'the only science which really seeks to know only society, *sensu strictissimo*'.[25]

However, the gestation of society in individual interactions brings with it the problem that society could be reduced to the study of individuals. Simmel does indeed say 'I see . . . society everywhere, where a number of human beings enter into interaction and form a temporary or permanent unity'.[26] Further, he concedes that one cannot start out from 'a more specific definition of society than that society exists wherever several individuals stand in reciprocal relationship to one another'. However:

If society is to be an autonomous object of an independent

discipline, then it can only be so by virtue of the fact that, out of the sum total of individual elements which constitute it, a new entity emerges; otherwise, all problems of social science would only be those of individual psychology. Yet unity from several elements is nothing other than interaction of the same reciprocally exercised forces of cohesion, attraction, perhaps even a certain repulsion.[27]

Simmel's focus is therefore upon the forms which reciprocal relations between human beings take, including those such as conflict which seem to divide them.

The advantage of this focus upon forms of interaction or sociation is that it allows Simmel to investigate *any* human interaction and to elucidate its significance. There exists no preconceived hierarchy of forms of sociation. Furthermore, the search for the 'laws, forms and developments' of sociation will not readily or rapidly be completed in the discovery of 'a few simple fundamental forms of human association' since 'social phenomena are too immeasurably complicated, and the methods of analysis are too incomplete'.[28] None the less, by the turn of the century, and after several reformulations of the object and methods of sociology, Simmel was satisfied that he had established grounds for the study of society as the study of forms of sociation. This enabled him to declare that 'it is less important to propose a programme than to demonstrate its significance and usefulness'.[29] His *Soziologie* of 1908 is the most sustained testimony to such intentions, with its myriad investigations of forms of sociation and its minimum of methodological prolegomena.

V

In the *Soziologie* and elsewhere we can find indications of a much less fully elucidated conception of society, but one which is both innovative and anticipatory of future developments. It is the notion of society as grounded in the experience and knowledge of its participants, at once pointing forward to a phenomenology of society and to a sociology of knowledge of society. In his 'Sociology of the Senses' (1907), Simmel maintains that sociology initially commenced from the study of the apparent 'structures of a higher order':

States and trade unions, priesthoods and forms of family structure, the nature of guilds and factories, class formation and the industrial division of labour – *these and similar major organs and systems appear to constitute society* and so form the realm of science concerned with it.[30]

However, sociology should equally deal with the less structured constellations of interaction, with 'countless others which, as it were, remain in a fluid, fleeting state but are no less agents of the connection of individuals to societal existence'.

Indeed, there is a more compelling reason for examining 'the delicate, invisible threads that are woven between one person and another'. Not only will it give us a 'deeper and more accurate' understanding of 'the web of society' – an aesthetic image to which we must return later – but the investigation of the seemingly insignificant interactions will more readily give us access to how we experience society in our everyday existence than will the study of 'major organisational systems'. If we confined our attention to the latter, to the 'major formations' in society, then 'it would be totally impossible to piece together *the real life of society as we encounter it in our experience*'. In contrast, the study of the 'microscopic–molecular processes' in interaction has the advantage that they 'exhibit society, as it were, *statu nascendi*'.[31]

Simmel's plea here for the study of the 'delicate, invisible threads' of interaction that bind individuals to one another highlights the following:

> On every day, at every hour, such threads are spun, are allowed to fall, are taken up again, replaced by others, intertwined with others. Here lie the interactions ... between the atoms of society which bear the whole tenacity and elasticity, the whole colourfulness and unity of this so evident and so puzzling life of society.[32]

In contrast to Durkheim, who viewed society as a 'system of active forces' operating *upon* individuals, Simmel here sees society as constituted by interactional 'forces' *between* individuals. This enables him to reflect upon our experience of society in every single social interaction in which we engage. It forces Simmel to take seriously the role of the senses in interaction, the role of emotions and the like that are accessible only to a 'psychological microscopy'. We experience society in every interaction.

If such reflections are then combined with those found in the only totally new piece which Simmel wrote for his *Soziologie* – the excursus 'How is Society Possible?' – then it is plausible to argue that he was working towards a conception of society which regards it as grounded in members' experience and knowledge of it. The quasi-Kantian question which Simmel raises – how is society possible? – is provided with a non-Kantian answer: 'The unity of society needs no observer. It is directly realized by its own elements because these elements are themselves conscious and synthesizing units'.[33] The unity of society is thereby demystified since for each individual 'the consciousness of constituting with the others a unity is actually all there is to this unity . . . [the individual] is absorbed in innumerable, specific relations and *in the feeling and the knowledge* of determining others and of being determined by them'.[34]

In fact, Simmel sees the whole of his *Soziologie* as an inquiry 'into the processes – those which, ultimately, take place in the individuals themselves – that condition the existence of the individuals as society'.[35] 'Society is "my representation" ' because other individuals – others as 'you' – are felt to be both independent of ourselves and yet capable of being represented (though never comnpletely known) by us. This interaction between the 'I' and the 'you' and its third, the 'we', proved to be a productive paradigm for a phenomenological sociology.

But there is a further dimension to which Simmel draws attention in the context of his elucidation of the three 'a priori effective conditions or forms of sociation' – of role, individuality and structure ('the phenomenological structure of society') – namely, 'the epistemology of society', a sociology of knowledge of society. Simmel highlights 'the consciousness of sociating or of being sociated' since 'the consciousness of sociation is . . . the immediate agent, the inner significance, of sociation itself. It is the processes of interaction which signify the fact of being sociated to the individual'.[36] Consciousness of sociation requires 'thought experiments', social abstractions, categories of the other (typifications), the process of knowing that sociation is taking place. Its investigation required the development of a sociology of our knowledge of society, a project that was initiated by some of Simmel's contemporaries (Max Scheler) and students (Karl Mannheim).

Finally, in this context, it is worth pointing to the significance of Simmel's third a priori for society, that of structure, since it indicates a conceptual construction of society that is in fact a necessary counterfactual ideal. It is a concept of society 'which is built up from that of the potentially autonomous individual, as the *terminus a quo* and the *terminus ad quem* of the individual's life and fate. This capacity constitutes an a priori of empirical society. It makes possible the form of society as we know it'.[37] In particular, Simmel suggests that 'the life of society' itself constitutes a counterfactual idea in so far as we interact within it as if there existed 'an unquestionable harmony between the individual and society as a whole', 'as if each of its elements were predestined for its particular place in it'. Thus, despite empirical discrepancies,

> social life exists as if all of its elements found themselves interrelated with one another in such a manner that each of them, because of its very individuality, depands on all others and all others depend on it.[38]

This third a priori of the possibility of society thus operates as a counterfactual ideal and as a regulative idea of society as a totality, as an ideal totality. Hence it forms a connection between the third and first conception of society that was outlined.

VI

The fourth conception of society, that of society as aesthetic object, also returns to Simmel's first concept in so far as society can be conceived as an aesthetic totality. As we shall see, however, this is not the only possibility within the aesthetic dimension of society. In one of the early indications of the significance of society as aesthetic object in Simmel's work, Murray Davis cites one of Simmel's students Arthur Salz who suggests that his teacher 'conceives of sociology as the study of the forms of sociation. But whoever speaks of forms moves in the field of aesthetics. *Society*, in the last analysis, *is a work of art*'.[39] What evidence is there for this?

No one would deny the significance of the aesthetic dimension in Simmel's sociology, which was commented upon extensively by many of his contemporaries and has been discussed in subsequent interpretations of his work.[40] Further, Simmel himself acknowledged the significance of aesthetic valuation alongside ethical and intellectual valuations. Some contemporaries viewed the first dimension as the most important. Rudulf Goldscheid, reviewing *The Philosophy of Money*, maintained that 'behind Simmel's whole work there stands not the ethical but the aesthetic ideal. And it is this aesthetic ideal which determines his whole interpretation of life and thus his whole scientific life activity'.[41] Indeed, a closer look at Simmel's work in the 1890s might suggest a shift in orientation around 1895–6 from ethical to aesthetic concerns in the social sphere, from a substantive ethics and some commitment to socialism to an interest (though not an exclusive one) in the aesthetics of society. Such an interpretation might be substantiated by the essay which Simmel published in 1896 entitled 'Sociological Aesthetics[42], in which he indicates more clearly than elsewhere his conception of society as an aesthetic object. Furthermore, this essay also intimates how society as totality may be conceived as an aesthetic totality and how society as sociation may also be an aesthetic totality. Indeed if we relate back to society as encountered in our experience, the essay also reveals the significance of the aesthetic mode of experience, the abstraction, the distance from the threads of fragmented interactions that is necessary in order to recognize, however fleetingly, the totality. In other words, 'the web of society', the labyrinth of interactions, is the aesthetic mode in which we perceive society as totality; the 'fortuitous fragments of reality', 'the delicate invisible threads' of interaction, are the aesthetic mode in which we perceive society as sociation.

In 'Sociological Aesthetics' Simmel argues that our appreciation of an object 'becomes aesthetic only as a result of increasing distance, abstraction and sublimation', through the creation of a distance which brings us closer to the object. The central category in Simmel's aesthetic is that of symmetry and its opposite, the asymmetrical. Indeed,

> The origin of all aesthetic themes is found in symmetry . . . Thus, the first aesthetic step leads beyond a mere acceptance of the meaninglessness of things to a will to transform them symmetrically. As aesthetic values are refined and deepened, however, human beings return to the irregular and asymmetrical.[43]

This distinctive 'charm of symmetry, with its internal equilibration, its external unity, and its harmonic relationship to all parts of its unified center' can be perceived in society itself, and especially in those utopian conceptions of society that are fascinated by 'the completely symmetrical structure of society'. This accounts for the appeal of socialism, as Simmel conceives of it, since

> the rational organisation of society has a high aesthetic attraction. It aims to make the totality of lives in the whole organisation into a work of art, which at present can hardly be accomplished for the life of an individual. *The more we learn to appreciate composite forms, the more readily we will extend aesthetic categories to forms of society as a whole.*[44]

Simmel contrasts this rational symmetry (which also accounts for the aesthetic appeal of machines) with 'an individuated society, character-ized by heterogeneous interests and irreconcilable tendencies . . . [which] presents to the mind a restless, uneven image, which conti-nuously requires new nervous exertion and effort for its understand-ing'. But this individualistic society is, through its very asymmetry, also 'aesthetically attractive'. There exists 'an aesthetic charm even in this lack of symmetry'. This may be because the aesthetic attraction lies in individual elements themselves rather than the totality. This still accords with Simmel's conception of symmetry since 'in aesthetics, symmetry means the dependence of individual elements on their mutual interdependence with all others, but also self-containment within the designated circle'.[45] Society as totality (interdependence of all elements) and society as each form 'in which "society" comes into being' (sociation) are both indicated here.

However, alongside society as symmetrical or asymmetrical totality and aesthetic object, Simmel draws attention to the fragments of interaction themselves as aesthetic objects:

> For us the essence of aesthetic observation and interpretation lies in the fact that the typical is to be found in what is unique, the lawlike in what is fortuitous, the essence and significance of things in the superficial and transitory . . . Every point conceals the possibility of being released into absolute aesthetic significance. To the adequately trained eye, the total beauty, the total meaning of the world as a whole radiates from every single point.[46]

The most insignificant form of sociation, the cell forms of society as it were, can, viewed aesthetically, constitute the key to the totality of society. And since society as totality is either a gradual conception or a regulative ideal or even a counterfactual idea, it is not surprising that Simmel devotes most of his sociological efforts to understanding the forms of sociation, however insignificant they might be. Again, this accords with the aesthetic dimension in so far as Simmel maintains that the individual will experience 'the secret charm' of aesthetic distance 'even more intensely when art deals with proximate, low and relatively secular material'.[47]

VII

We have already established that Simmel does not deal to an equal extent with the four conceptions of society outlined above. We have also claimed that the concepts, to a greater or lesser extent, are interrelated. For instance, society as a totality in Simmel's early view must await the comprehensive investigation of forms of sociation. The first two concepts of society, in so far as they are suggestive of generality and individuality (as in the third conception, too, of society as encountered in our experience), also raise a crucial problem with regard to the methodological orientation of sociology itself: the problematic relationship between explanation and understanding. Society conceived as a dual nexus of generality and individuality incorporates two modes of scientific procedure:

The nexus by which each social element (each individual) is interwoven with the life and activities of every other, and by which the external framework of society is produced, is a causal nexus. But it is transformed into a *teleological nexus* as soon as it is considered from the perspective of the elements that carry and produce it – individuals.[48]

We might add that from the aesthetic 'perspective', society is also an aesthetic nexus that is experienced both by individuals in interaction and perceived by the sociologist (who is concerned with sociological aesthetics) through distancing him/herself from society as object. The hiatus between these 'perspectives' is not resolved by Simmel in favour of any one of them.

The same absence of a resolution is also present in another methodological sphere. Simmel viewed his sociology as being concerned not with abstract forms of sociation but with their concrete comparative and historical investigation. But without a concrete concept of society, such comparative and historical study is confined to changes in the forms of sociation, which themselves presuppose developmental tendencies in society as a whole. There can be no doubt that important developmental tendencies are present in his social theory: increasing social differentiation, individuation, the domination of formal rationality and the domination of the intellect, the transformation of the teleology of means and ends, the development of objectification and reification and the widening gap between subjective and objective culture. Interestingly they are all to be found in *The Philosophy of Money* in which Simmel comes closest to developing a conception of society as a totality (albeit one in which its ideal form is symbolised by exchange). But in a sense these developmental tendencies are not theorised as part of a general theory of society.

The conceptions of society as members' experience and knowledge of it and as an aesthetic object remained undeveloped in Simmel's work. The former was developed from different beginnings in phonomenological sociology. The latter is intimately tied to our perspective of Simmel. None of his contemporaries were so concerned with this aesthetic dimension and thus none were able to capture so successfully the aesthetic dimension of modernity. If this had been Simmel's only conception of society, then it might well have carried with it the danger of the aestheticization of society itself.

2 Georg Simmel and social psychology

['The Problem of Sociology'] is the latest result of lines of thought that you first awakened in me. For, however divergent and independent my subsequent development may be, I will never forget that, above all others, you forcibly directed me to the problem of the supra-individual.

> Georg Simmel to Moritz Lazarus (5 November 1894)

In the second part of *The Philosophy of Money* he wrote the most beautiful pages on social psychology.

> Karl Mannheim (1918)

In recent decades, especially in social psychology but also in symbolic interactionist sociology in the United States, the contribution of Georg Simmel to the study of small-group interaction has been increasingly recognized. This is particularly true of Simmel's writings on dyadic and triadic relationships, the consequences of which have still not been fully investigated. Simmel's contribution to small-group interaction, the psychology of conflict, reference-group theory, role theory, and other areas has also been given recognition.[1] However, recent research in social psychology and small-group sociology has focused only on those writings that are in translation and on his later works.[2] The result is that his contribution to social psychology has been seen to be derived largely from translations of sections of his Soziologie (1908), the whole of which has still not been translated.[3] The absence of any sense of the development of Simmel's work as a totality has also created the impression that his possible contributions to social psychology are merely an offshoot of his interest in sociology. This is perhaps understandable in the light of Simmel's present-day reputation primarily as a sociologist. His contribution to this latter discipline has come to be assessed in the light of that of his contemporaries, Max Weber, Emile Durkheim, and, to a lesser degree, Ferdinand Tönnies.

The largely unresearched historiography of sociology therefore assumes that Simmel's *Soziologie*, for instance, indicates an interest in sociology on his part that renders his social theory contemporary with that of Weber, but later than that of Tönnies and Durkheim. In fact, Simmel's *Soziologie* represents the culmination of his sociological interests to which little was subsequently added. Indeed, Friedrich Tenbruck has suggested that Simmel's *Soziologie* appeared

> after sociological study was already left far behind him and he had definitely turned his attention toward philosophical and aesthetic questions. The sociological period, announced by the themes of a number of articles in the 1880s, commences with the study *Über sociale Differenzierung* (1890) and reaches its real high point and completion in the *Philosophie des Geldes* (1990). Between these dates there lies a large number of articles which, in changed or enlarged form, in the original formulation or translation, improved, merged with one another, are reworked and finally presented in the collection, *Soziologie*.[4]

If we accept the main thrust of Tenbruck's argument, then Simmel's interest in sociology was, strictly speaking, not contemporary with that of Weber, whose 'sociological' work commenced around 1903–4 with his essays on *The Protestant Ethic*. Instead, it has more in common with the work of Durkheim, who was preoccupied in the 1890s with establishing sociology as an independent discipline (also independent of psychology), and Tönnies (who reviewed Simmel's early work).

However, what Tenbruck's argument does not take into account is Simmel's parallel, if perhaps not so strong, interest in psychology in exactly the same period as he pinpoints Simmel's major interest in sociology. Indeed, one might go further and suggest that rather than Simmel's contributions to social psychology being an extension of his interest in and formulation of a sociological problematic, this sociological project has its origins in Simmel's early interest in psychology. But rather than anticipate this possible line of argument, it is necessary at this point to indicate the extent of Simmel's connections with psychology in Germany during the last quarter of the nineteenth century, beginning with a chronological sketch of Simmel's career and output in relation to psychology and then moving on to a systematic examination of the role of psychology in his social theory.

Before doing so, however, it is perhaps worth noting the extent to which the concept of psychology – like that of sociology – was open to various interpretations in this period. Simmel seems to have used the term psychology rather freely in the title of many of his essays. Apart from early reviews that refer to the work of Gabriel Tarde, Gustav Le Bon and Havelock Ellis, there exists only one psychological tradition with which Simmel had direct contact: *Völkerpsychologie*. Although today this discipline is usually associated with the name of Wilhelm Wundt, it was not Wundt's interpretation that directly influenced Simmel but rather that of Moritz Lazarus and Heymann Steinthal. As we shall see, their earlier program for a *Völkerpsychologie* already presupposed a strong sociological component. Indeed, it was even suggested that this discipline constituted 'an initial stage of sociology'.[5] Questionable though such a thesis may be in terms of the development of sociology in general, it is certainly pertinent to the evolution of Simmel's conception of sociology. And in some respects, at least, this earlier *Völkerpsychologie* came closer to what might be subsumed under social psychology than many other traditions in psychology.

I

Simmel began his studies at Berlin University in the summer of 1876 with an initial interest in history (under Theodor Mommsen). However, he soon moved on to the study of psychology under Lazarus (with whom Wilhelm Dilthey and Wundt had also studied) and ethnology under Adolf Bastian before turning finally to philosophy. Simmel later 'characterised Steinthal and Lazarus, the founders of *Völkerpsychologie*, as his two most important teachers in his student days.'[6] His study on the origins of music, entitled 'Psychological and Ethnographic Studies on Music', was rejected as his dissertation in 1880. One of his examiners – Hermann Helmholz – suggested that Simmel's researches should not be encouraged in this direction. In 1881 Simmel did obtain his doctorate with an earlier prize essay on Immanuel Kant. Among his friends at this time was Paul Radestock, who in 1880 had obtained his doctorate with Wundt.[7] This is quite possibly the basis for the contract Simmel later formed with G. Stanley Hall. In 1883 Simmel submitted further work on Kant for his *Habilitation*, which was finally awarded in January 1885, and he became a Privatdozent at Berlin University, a post he held until 1900. In 1898 the philosophical faculty sought to secure for Simmel the title of *Extraordinarius*. In their submission to the minister of education, the professoriate (among them Dilthey) spoke of his teaching in a variety of areas, including 'sociological psychology'. They went on to highlight that the task that he has set himself especially in so-called sociology lies in the analysis of the psychological forms, dominant processes and structures which are produced and are effective in society. In this respect, his efforts are similar to those of *Völkerpsychologie*. Thus, he pursues the effectiveness of the principle of energy-saving in the psychological sphere, he analyzes the process of social differentiation psychologically, he deals with the psychological side of such social facts as competition or money. In his most comprehensive work too, the two-volume introduction to moral science, he is inclined to focus upon a sociological and psychological derivation of the basic elements of moral consciousness.[8]

Simmel's contemporaries and peers thus saw his major contribution in these early years as being to 'sociology, social ethics and social psychology'.[9] Much later (1915), in Simmel's unsuccessful bid for a chair in philosophy at Heidelberg University, the Heidelberg philosophy faculty pointed to Simmel's major achievements as

the transformation and completely new foundation of the social sciences, through which the philosophy of history has also experienced a transformed, infinitely fruitful orientation. In three major works, *On Social Differentiation, The Philosophy of Money* and *Sociology*, he has grounded social science anew – which hitherto had become a hotbed both of arbitrary and personal caprices and a rigid positivism – he has drawn its boundaries, established its method, formed its concepts and *above all brilliantly carried out its psychological foundation which had always been required but never achieved.*[10]

But these impressive claims for Simmel's work lie at the end of his career. It is necessary to return to his earliest works to see how far his interest in psychology manifested itself.

This interest is apparent from the courses Simmel taught at Berlin University. Apart from the course 'Selected Aspects of Social Science' in the winter semester of 1888–9 – which probably contained some psychological component – Simmel taught courses on psychology (including social psychology) thirteen times between the summer semesters of 1889 and 1909.[11] Thereafter, psychology no longer figured in his teaching programme. This teaching commitment is interesting not merely because it confirms Simmel's interest in psychology but also because it largely parallels his teaching commitment to sociology.[12]

Apart from his teaching program, many indications of Simmel's interest in psychology during these years can be found among his twenty-five books and over 300 articles, reviews, and other pieces. This is apparent as early as the mid-1880s. Simmel's first publications, 'Psychological and Ethnological Studies of Music' and 'Dante's Psychology', both appeared in the *Zeitschrift für Völkerpsychologie und Sprachwissenschaft*, edited by Steinthal and Lazarus.[13] Simmel also reviewed Steinthal's *Allgemeine Ethik* in 1886.[14] In the same year, he anonymously published the article 'On the Psychology of Pessimism' – a theme that preoccupied him in this and the following decade.[15] In 1889 Simmel published a brief 'Notice' in a philosophy journal on the study of psychology in the United States and in particular Hall's new psychology programme at Johns Hopkins University.[16] This short piece also indicates that Simmel was in correspondence with Hall at this time, since the latter informed him that his psychology laboratory was 'like Wundt's but much larger'. In the same year Simmel published 'On the Psychology of Money',[17] the first seed of his *Philosophy of Money* (1900),[18] which contains a wealth of social psychological observations. And in 1890 he published 'On the Psychology of Women' – the first of his many articles on women (including two on the growing women's movement in Germany in the 1890s).[19]

The year 1890 also saw the publication of Simmel's first major work, *Über soziale Differenzierung: Soziologische und psychologische Untersuchungen*,[20] which, as its title suggests, combined sociological and psychological studies of social differentiation – a theme Durkheim took up slightly later in a very different manner in his *Division of Labour in Society*. The first chapter of *Über soziale Differenzierung* also constitutes Simmel's first attempt to demarcate sociology from psychology and other disciplines. Furthermore, in the first half of this decade, Simmel completed two major studies in different areas, both of which contain much material on psychology: *Die Probleme der Geschichtsphilosophie* (1892)[21] and *Einleitung in die Moralwissenschaft* (1892–3).[22]

In the course of the 1890s Simmel also reviewed books for the *Zeitschrift für Psychologie und Physiologie der Sinnesorgane* as well as contributing an article to this important journal entitled 'Outline of a Theory of the Will' (1896).[23] Among the reviews is that of Tarde's *Les lois de l'imitation* (1890)[24] – one of the key texts for the subsequent development of mass psychology – and, in another journal, of Le Bon's *Psychologie des Foules* (1895).[25] Elsewhere, Simmel entered a plea for the recognition of the importance of psychological insights for those dealing with criminality.[26] At the same time, Simmel was increasingly preoccupied with demarcating sociology from psychology, as is evident from the importance he himself attached to his article 'The Problems of Sociology' (1894),[27] – by 1900 translated into French, English, Italian, and Russian. In the substantive sphere, Simmel published an article on the psychology of fashion in 1895,[28] a theme to which he returned several times in the course of the succeeding decade.[29]

The year 1900 saw the publication of one of the most significant of Simmel's works, *The Philosophy of Money*, whose intention was 'to construct a new storey beneath historical materialism' in order to reveal, among others things, the 'psychological . . . preconditions' of economic forms.[30] As one reviewer argued, 'Some passages of *The Philosophy of Money* read like a translation of Marx's economic discussions into the language of psychology',[31] Still within the context of his analysis of the sociological and psychological dimensions of modern life is Simmel's classic essay 'The Metropolis and Mental Life' (1903),[32] in which 'the products of specifically modern life are questioned as to their *inner nature*, as it were, the body of culture as to its soul' by commencing with 'the psychological foundation of the metropolitan type', namely, 'the increase in nervous life, which emerged out of the rapid and unbroken change in external and internal stimuli'.[33]

During the first part of the new decade, Simmel also published many of the essays that make up his *Soziologie* (1908). These include 'The Psychology of Adornment', 'The Sociology of the Senses', and the important essay 'On the Nature of Social Psychology'.[34] After the publication of his *Soziologie* in 1908, Simmel's interest in psychology and sociology exhibited a distinct downturn. But what is important in the present context is that Simmel's contribution to social psychology and interactionist and small-group sociology is very largely derived from the essays contained in his *Soziologie*. Only very seldom are earlier works referred to, with the result that Simmel's connections with psychology in Germany are obscured. Hence, in order to elaborate this line of argument, it is necessary to return to a more systematic examination of some of these earlier works.

II

As Klaus Köhnke reports, 'The problem of the genesis of the early Simmel's thought, like hardly any other problem of research on Simmel, awaits thorough investigation'.[35] He goes on to outline the content of a whole range of hitherto unknown texts by Simmel, many from the 1880s – the period of Simmel's first publications. But anyone investigating the origins of Simmel's social and psychological theory is confronted with a characteristic feature of his writings, namely, the absence of references to other works in the text and the lack of citations. Simmel's early writings therefore confront the investigator with the formidable problem of the hermeneutic reconstruction of the texts and their location in a context to which Simmel himself left behind few clues. These earlier writings seem so untypical of our image of Simmel that access to them is made more difficult by our own preconceptions. But as a starting point we can take Michael Landmann's characterisation of Simmel's early work as commencing with

> pragmatism, social Darwinism, Spencerian evolutionism and the principle of differentation. Fechner's atomism and Spencer's 'definite differentiation' led him . . . to the problem of the individual. Through his teachers Lazarus and Steinthal . . . however, Simmel already early on became acquainted with the 'objective spirit'. The fact that, in this first phase, Simmel exercised little influence and that he himself turned away from it has hardly been investigated at all.[36]

Even if we accept this outline of the origins of Simmel's early work, the detailed confirmation of the influence of these various currents upon Simmel's writings has hardly begun. One such influence may be Gustav Fechner. Hannes Böhringer has attempted to show that in his early writings what Simmel took from Fechner was his doctrine of logical atomism, which enabled Simmel to develop a conception of society that did not move in the direction of either 'the hypostatization of a *Volksseele*', as in much early *Völkerpsychologie*, or a 'substantive anthropology', as in Herbert Spencer's work.[37] Rather, Simmel conceived of society as the interaction of its elements (individuals) rather than as a substance. Simmel also rejected causal laws in favour of regularities of interaction. Here, of course, Fechner's own concept of interaction (*Wechselwirkung*) of elements rather than the operation of forces in one direction may have enabled Simmel to take this step.[38] As Böhringer concludes,

> The dissolution of the substance of the psyche into the functional unity of its elements follows necessarily from Fechner's simple atomism. It enabled Simmel to move from *Völkerpsychologie* into a sociology that no longer justified its object by a distinctive sub-

stance, but rather wished more to describe the formal relationship of complex elements in a functional constellation.[39]

But if Simmel very early on moved away from a substantive *Volksseele* to a conception of society as the ceaseless interaction of its members, then this key concept of interaction was probably not derived from Fechner alone. The concept is also to be found not only in Hermann Lotze's philosophy (and in 1886-7 Simmel was lecturing on Lotze's practical philosophy) but also in Dilthey's early writings and in the context of a conception of society. For instance, in his important essay 'Über das Studium der Geschichte der Wissenschaften vom Menschen, der Gesellschaft und dem Staat' (1875),[40] Dilthey already speaks of 'the play of interactions in society'.[41] Later, in his *Einleitung in die Geisteswissenschaften* (1883), Dilthey conceives of society – 'our world' – as 'the summation of interactions' and the individual as the focal point of these interactions: 'The individual . . . is an element in the interactions of society, a point of intersection of the diverse systems of these interactions who reacts with conscious intention and action upon their effects.'[42]

Perhaps more questionably, it is possible that Simmel was acquainted with the almost totally forgotten work of Gustav Lindner, a member of the Prague Herbart school of psychology whose *Ideen zur Psychologie der Gesellschaft als Grundlage der Sozialwissenschaft* (1871) also starts out from a conception of society as interacting individuals and which places some emphasis upon sociability as a key factor in society.[43] Lindner also produces many valuable arguments for the development of a social psychology out of the *Völkerpsychologie* of Lazarus and Steinthal.

But in order for social interaction to take place, there must be a given diversity of individuals. And here Simmel probably took up Spencer's doctrine of social differentiation developed in his *First Principles*,[44] a translation of which appeared in German in 1875. This work contains not merely Spencer's law of evolution with its emphasis on the transition from homogeneity to heterogeneity, the persistence of force, a theory of continuous motion, the doctrine of relativity – all of which appear under a different guise in Simmel's early social theory – but also the principle of social differentiation and its relationship to social integration. Already in 1888 Simmel was studying 'the forms of differentiation' within social groups and their consequences for the development of individuality.[45]

Finally, and despite the preceding critical remarks, the programme for a *Völkerpsychologie* outlined by Lazarus and Steinthal (1860),[46] contained a conception of psychology which went beyond that of existing 'individual' psychology. Some aspects of this programme relevant to Simmel's later development are also contained in Lazarus's *The Life of the Soul*,[47] especially 'On the Relationship of Individuals to the Totality'.

According to Lazarus and Steinthal, 'Psychology teaches us that human beings are thoroughly and according to their essence societal; i.e., that they are determined by social life.'[48] Human beings are characterized both by the features they have in common with contemporary fellow individuals and by their consciousness. This does not mean that individuals coexist with all their fellow contemporaries and predecessors to the same extent, since 'within the large circle of society, smaller circles are formed . . . These circles, however, do not stand side by side but intersect and affect one another in many ways. Thus, within society, there emerges a highly varied . . . relationship of connection and separation [*Absonderung*]'.[49] Hence, the object of *Völkerpsychologie* is 'the psychology of societal human beings or human society'. But this does not mean that society is a 'mere sum of all individual minds'. Rather, the unity of a plurality of individuals lies in the 'content and the form or mode of their activity'.[50] None the less, what Lazarus and Steinthal have in mind here is not so much social interaction as a *Volksgeist*: 'that which is common to the inner activity of all individuals'.

Individuals interacting with one another create their culture as an *objektiver Geist*. According to Kurt Danziger, Lazarus and Steinthal conceived of this process as occurring

> in a more or less dialectical fashion. Thus, the individuals whose common activity created the objective reality of cultural forms were themselves to be seen as the product of these forms . . . 'Wherever several people live together it is a necessary result of their companionship that there develops an objective mental content which then becomes the content, norm and organ of their further subjective activity' (Lazarus). Social attitudes and cognitive forms are objective in so far as they have a characteristic and durable social distribution, but they exist only through the activity of individual subjects.[51]

In a very similar manner, Simmel designated culture as 'that which the mind has deposited in language, morals, institutions, art and, last but not least, technology too. Culture is *objektiver Geist* in the sense in which he had become acquainted with it from Moritz Lazarus'.[52] The first seeds of Simmel's conception of the tragedy of culture are also present here in rudimentary form.

Steinthal, at least, saw the affinities between Simmel's early sociological work and his expanded programme for a *Völkerpsychologie*.[53] In his preface to the first volume of the *Zeitschrift des Vereins für Völkerpsychologie*, Steinthal incorporated into his programme for a *Völkerpsychologie* not merely those disciplines that had already been singled out some thirty years earlier – 'psychology in the commonly understood sense', ethnology, and history – but a fourth, the 'youngest of all disciplines': sociology. Here Steinthal cited not merely the now almost forgotten contribution of Paul von Lilienfeld but that of Simmel. In particular, Steinthal was impressed by Simmel's *Über sociale Differenzierung* in which 'the author in the introduction indicates very sharply the psychological character of sociology (even though he also avoids the term "objektiver Geist")'.[54] In the book's deliberations, 'there is nowhere any flirting with analogies, but rather one really feels oneself to be on the firm ground of an exact observation of psychological relationships and phenomena'.[55]

Yet, in this first major study, Simmel attempts not only to outline the tasks of sociology but also to demarcate this discipline from psychology. Here he maintains that sociology must ask, without having fixed, a priori answers, 'What is a society? What is an individual? How are reciprocal psychological effects of individuals upon each other possible?' Otherwise, sociology 'will fall into the error of the older psychology: one must first of all have defined the nature of the soul before one can scientifically recognize psychological phenomena'.[56] This does not mean that Simmel gives no answer to these questions in the course of his studies. Indeed, they are the basic questions that preoccupy him. Yet they are questions that cannot be answered a priori or merely on the basis of conceptualizations.

But if Simmel seems here to turn away from earlier aprioristic psychology, this does not mean that he grounds sociology in the a priori of society. He is concerned that sociology do justice to the complexity of individuals and their interactions with one another. If the individual is 'furnished with an almost incalculable wealth of latent and effective forces', then this raises immense problems for the study of such individuals. But the problem is that much greater 'where reciprocal effects of such entities upon one another are present and the complexity of the one to some extent multiplies with that of the other' and 'makes possible an immeasurability of combinations.' From this Simmel infers that if it is the task of sociology to describe the forms of human communal existence and to find the rules according to which the individual, in so far as he or she is the member of a group, and groups relate to one another, then the complexity of this object has a consequence for our science which places it in an epistemological relationship – which I must extensively ground – alongside meta-physics and psychology.[57]

The two latter disciplines are characterized by the fact that both produce contrary propositions which have the same probability and verifiability. Simmel concludes that what is lacking in psychology is 'the unequivocalness of a scientific rule'. The general concepts of psychological functions are so general and the 'wealth of nuances' in each psychological function so great that to subsume a complex phenomenon under the same single concept usually leads to a failure to distinguish why different causes produce the same effect: 'Indeed so many processes simultaneously play a part in our psyche, so many forces are simultaneously effective in it, that the establishment of a causal connection between simple psychological concepts . . . is always completely one-sided'.[58] This leads Simmel to reject psychology as a natural science:

This is the reason why psychology cannot arrive at any laws in the natural scientific sense: because in view of the complexity of its phenomena, no isolated, simple effective force [*Kraftwirkung*] can be observed in the mind. Rather, each is directed by so many supplementary phenomena that it is never possible to establish with complete certainty what in fact is indeed the cause of a given effect or the effect of a given cause.[59]

However, this argument does not lead Simmel to reject psychology as a discipline. It remains a precursor of exact knowledge that seeks to organise the mass of complex phenomena it deals with.

Nor does it lead him to assert the superiority of sociology. Indeed, Simmel views sociology as facing the same problem of the complexity of its object, which 'completely prevents its separation into simple parts and its basic forces and relationships'. This prevents sociology, too, from generating 'laws of social development. Undoubtedly, each element of a society moves according to natural laws. Yet for the whole there exists no law; as in nature, so equally here, there is no higher law above the laws that govern the movement of the smallest parts.[60] In a similar manner, Simmel argues against sociology taking as its starting point an overarching, reified conception of society. This decisively differentiates Simmel's sociology from that of many of his predecessors (August Comte, Spencer) and contemporaries (Albert Schäffle) and, incidentally, renders it much more accessible and amenable to social psychology. For Simmel the only genuine reality is the individuals who make up society:

> If society is merely a . . . constellation of individuals who are the actual realities then the latter and their behavior also constitutes the real object of science and the concept of society evaporates . . . What palpably exists is indeed only individual human beings and their circumstances and activities: therefore the task can only be to understand them, whereas the essence of society, that emerges purely through an ideal synthesis and is never to be grasped, should not form the object of reflection that is directed toward the investigation of reality.[61]

Simmel here seeks to guard against both a conception of society as an autonomous entity and a thoroughgoing individualistic foundation for sociology that reduces social reality to isolated atoms.

In order to secure sociology from this latter danger, Simmel has to indicate some object of study that is not merely individuals as such. And here we move to the heart of Simmel's sociology. He starts out from 'a regulative world principle that everything interacts in some way with everything else, that between every point in the world and every other force permanently moving relationships exist'.[62] We cannot extract a single element out of this ceaseless interaction and say that it is the decisive one. Rather, we must assert that what unites individual elements in some objective form is interaction: 'There exists only one basic factor which provides at least a relative objectivity of unification: the interaction [*Wechselwirkung*] of the parts. We characterize any object as unified to the extent to which its parts stand in a reciprocal dynamic relationship.'[63] Is this how Simmel conceives of society?

Sociology is concerned 'with empirical atoms, with conceptions, individuals and groups that function as unities'. It does not commence from society since society is

> only the name for the sum of these interactions . . . It is therefore not a unified, fixed concept but rather a gradual one . . . according to the greater number and cohesion of the existing interactions that exist between given persons. In this manner, the concept of society completely loses its mystical facet that individualistic realism wishes to see in it.[64]

Society is thus composed of the ceaseless interaction of its individual elements, a conception that forces Simmel's sociology to concentrate upon human *relationships*, namely, social interaction.

Four years later, we find Simmel again seeking to clarify the distinctive nature of sociology in his essay 'The Problem of Sociology' (1894),[65] which again takes up the relationship between sociology and psychology. Simmel sees this is an important task since 'the attempt has been made to reduce all sciences to psychology' – a reference perhaps not only to Lindner's attempt at a psychology of society but, more important, to Wundt's argument in his *Methodenlehre* (1883) that psychology must be regarded as the basis of the human sciences.[66] The grounds for this reduction of all sciences to psychology, according to Simmel, is the contention that they are all the products of the human mind. But this fails to distinguish between the science of psychology and the functions of the psyche. In the same manner, sociology too could be conceived of as the study of everything that occurs in society. Simmel, however, is concerned to restrict the task of sociology in the following manner:

> Just as the differentiation of what is specifically psychological from objective matter produces psychology as a science, so a genuine sociology can only concern itself with what is specifically societal [*das Specifisch-Gesellschaftliche*], the form and forms of sociation [*Vergesellschaftung*] as such, as distinct from the individual interests and contents in and through which sociation is realized.[67]

Such interests and contents constitute the content of other distinctive disciplines, whereas sociology is concerned with 'the forms of sociation'.

Sociology's task is therefore to study 'sociation of the most diverse levels and types' and to abstract from social interaction the forms of sociation that are less varied than their content since 'the same form, the same type of sociation can enter into the most diverse material'. In other words, like other sciences that proceed by abstraction, sociology

> extracts the purely social element from the totality of human history – i.e., what occurs in society – for special attention; or, expressed with somewhat paradoxical brevity, it studies that which in society is 'society'.[68]

If this is sociology's task, what methods does Simmel advance for realizing this goal? Simmel's answer to this question is unambiguous in its emphasis upon a grounding in psychology:

The method according to which the problems of sociation are to be investigated are *the same as in all comparative psychological sciences*. As a foundation there exist *certain psychological presuppositions* that belong to them without which no historical science can exist: the phenomena of seeking and giving help, of love and hate, of avarice and the sense of satisfaction in communal existence, the self-preservation of individuals with the same interests, on the one hand, through competition, on the other, through combination, and a series of other primary psychological processes must be presupposed in order that one can at all understand how sociations, group formations, relations of individuals to a whole entity, etc., came about.[69]

Given that Simmel many times asserted that this essay was programmatic for his sociological investigations, it is not surprising that he had already taken up or was to take up all these phenomena in his sociological and psychological studies. Even more remarkable is that at the time of the publication of this essay, Dilthey was also preparing a programme for a comparative psychology (in 1895 he prepared a paper 'On Comparative Psychology' which he withdrew from publication).[70] Although Dilthey's early work certainly influenced Simmel and although Dilthey subsequently excluded Simmel's sociology from his strictures against modern sociology, there was little contact between the two (even though they were within the same faculty at Berlin University) and evidence of some hostility on Dilthey's part.[71]

Simmel continues his programmatic statement of his method by arguing that just as economic history applies economic abstractions to historical material, so there exists a science of society 'because certain specific structures within his historical complex are to be related back to *psychological states and actions* which only proceed out of the reciprocal effects of individuals and groups upon one another, out of social contact'.[72] Sociology thus proceeds in two directions: either by cutting a cross section through a historical development in order to examine its social formation or by cutting a cross section through 'individual developments' in order to see what relationships or forms of sociation they have in common.

It should be added here that, alongside Simmel's somewhat paradoxical demarcation of sociology from psychology which still retains its ground in psychological presuppositions, he also demarcates sociology from a philosophy of history that seeks 'to subsume historical facts in their totality, both external and psychological, under "general concepts" '. Instead, 'sociology as a specific science . . .

confines itself completely within the course of events and their immediate psychological significance'.[73] Indeed, 'the sole object of sociology' is 'the investigation of the forces, forms and developments of sociation, of the co-operation, association and co-existence of individuals [*des Mit-. Für-und Nebeneinanderseins der Individuen*]'.[74] Nor does it include ethnology within the province of sociology on the mistaken assumption that what occurs 'within' society is the same as what occurs 'through' society. Sociology is to be concerned with those 'specifically social forces' that determine social phenomena.[75]

In the course of the 1890s, Simmel often came back to the problem of demarcating sociology from psychology as when he argued, for instance, that 'if society is to be an autonomous object of an independent science, then it can only be so through the fact that, out of the sum of individual elements that constitute it, a new entity emerges; otherwise all problems of social science would only be those of individual psychology'.[76] But if Simmel seems to be guarded in his response to individual psychology, he is more ambiguous in relation to 'mass' or collective psychology, as revealed in his brief reviews of the works of its then main proponents, Le Bon and Tarde.

Simmel praises Tarde's *Les lois de l'imitation* (1890),[77] 'which offers very significant pointers for social psychology', and he is impressed by Tarde's argument that 'imitation is a kind of hypnotic suggestion' operating upon the individual within social groups. Tarde has 'provided social psychology a major service in that he has demarcated imitation as pure form from the content in which it is presented and has thereby made possible, at least problematically, the search for functional regularities' that would otherwise be difficult to find in the mass of diverse material.[78] Simmel is impressed by the role of imitation in socialization and, referring to a theme of his own, maintains that imitation may well be like competition which possesses 'typical forms and developments' relatively independent of its content. In short, Tarde indicated one of the key features 'in which individual psychology must be enlarged by a return to the processes in the social group'.[79] Indeed, the theme of imitation soon appears in Simmel's first of many incursions into the study of fashion with his ambiguously titled article 'On the Psychology of Fashion: A Sociological Study' (1895).[80]

But if Simmel was impressed with Tarde's early work, he was much less captivated by Le Bon's *Psychologie des Foules* (1895), a work that 'in itself is not particularly significant'.[81] Its description and classification of social psychological processes seldom extends 'to their causes and hidden constellations' while the key concept of the crowd is insufficiently differentiated. Although Simmel viewed Le Bon's work as a basis for collective or mass psychology, it is not in this review but in his article 'Mass Criminality' (1897) that Simmel expresses his reservations as to the distinctive nature of this discipline.[82] Simmel maintains

> The fact that the psychological action of a crowd appears as a unified action carried out by a crowd lies in the fact that the *result* of this action presents itself as unified . . . The unified external result of many subjective psychological processes is interpreted as the result of a unified subjective process, namely a process in the collective psyche. *The unified nature of the resulting phenomenon is reflected in the presupposed unity of its psychological cause.* What is illusory about this inference, however, upon which the whole of collective psychology rests in its general distinction from individual psychology, is now apparent: the unity of collective actions, which only lies in the observable result, is accordingly obtained surreptitiously by means of the inner cause, of the subjective agent.[83]

Simmel's argument against a collective or mass psychology is thus similar to his own strictures against a hypostatized notion of society as a cause of social action.

In the same year in which this critique was written, Simmel did praise the work of one writer – Friedrich Nietzsche – for the depth of his 'psychological analysis', 'such as has not been achieved hitherto in German psychology'.[84] Simmel does acknowledge, however, that

> this psychology does not yet possess the status of science and is hardly to be distinguished methodologically from psychology in a poetic work. Yet the inner realities that form its problematic are indeed presented, and so long as the available beginnings of an exact psychology are so very far away from their solution, then only the narrow-minded arrogance of a scientific bureaucracy can reject the instalments that are offered . . . in the form of artistic intuition.[85]

Only a few years later, and perhaps with reference to this 'scientific bureaucracy', Simmel expressed himself even more strongly on the 'ominous' preoccupation with technique that has

> infected even the purely intellectual branches of knowledge; in the historical sciences, as in that of experimental psychology, investigations, essentially worthless and, as regards the ultimate end of all

research, most unimportant, frequently enjoy a quite disproportion-
ate degree of recognition, provided only that they be carried out by
means of perfect methodical, technical processes.[86]

Unfortunately, as is so often the case in his work, no reference is
provided to indicate the object of Simmel's critique. It does, however,
leave one in little doubt as to Simmel's attitude towards most
experimental psychology.[87]

If Simmel seldom mentions experimental psychology, this is, in
part, an indication of his lack of interest in this field of research. But
his own determination to establish sociology as an independent
discipline often clashed with the wealth of social psychological investigations that it appears to contain, and with many contemporary
judgements – such as that of Tönnies – that 'the real significance of his
studies lies in the penetrating psychological analysis'.[88] It is not
surprising, therefore, to find that among the essays that make up his
Soziologie (1908), Simmel attempts to delineate the discipline with
which he had also come to be identified, namely, social psychology.
Similarly, the first chapter of his *Soziologie* takes up once more, in a
revised form, 'the problem of sociology' as an independent discipline.

Simmel's problem in effecting this demarcation lies not merely in his
acknowledgement of the 'psychological presuppositions' from which
sociological analysis commences but also in his concentration upon
seemingly insignificant social phenomena that are apparent in face-to-
face, small-scale social interactions. Indeed, Simmel often asserts that
these interactions form the basis or foundation for sociation as such
and for larger, more complex social configurations. In the first version
of his 'Sociology of the Senses' (1907),[89] Simmel maintains that just as
'the science of organic life' now concerns itself with 'the smallest
agents, the cells' of human life, so too has social science recently come
to concern itself with 'the beginnings of microscopic investigation'.[90]
But without denying either the existence or the significance of any
'structures of a higher order', Simmel is interested not merely in these
structured interactions but in 'countless others which, as it were,
remain in a fluid, fleeting state but are no less agents of the connection
of individuals to societal existence'.[91] Elsewhere, Simmel is more
explicit as to the limitation of sociology in relation to the study of
'these major formations' that have been its traditional concern. If we
merely started out from them 'it would be entirely impossible to piece
together the real life of society as we encounter it in our experience'.
We should concern ourselves too 'with microscopic–molecular processes within human material' since they 'exhibit society, as it were,

statu nascendi.[92] His explicit concern is therefore the 'fortuitous fragments' of social interaction:

> On every day, at every hour, such threads are spun, are allowed to fall, are taken up again, replaced by others, intertwined with others. Here lie the interactions – *only accessible through psychological microscopy* – between the atoms of society which bear the whole tenacity and elasticity, the whole colorfulness and unity of this so evident and so puzzling life of society.[93]

Hence, this investigation produces a 'deeper and more accurate' understanding of society than does 'the mere treatment of major, completely supra-individual total structures'.[94] In so far as Simmel argues further that the explanation of the smallest interactions is necessary in order to explain the major constellations of society, he ultimately traces his sociological problematic back to the interaction of individuals.

Simmel was aware of this difficulty in the first chapter of his *Soziologie* where he admits that 'this turn in the discussion seems to make the investigations planned here to be nothing other than chapters of psychology, at best social psychology'. Indeed, he concedes that 'all societal processes and instincts have their seat in minds and that sociation is, as consequence, a psychical phenomenon'. We should recognize 'psychic motivations – feelings, thoughts, and needs – . . . not merely as bearers of . . . external relations but also as their essence, as what really and solely interests us'. Furthermore, 'the aspects of the socio-historical life that we can understand are nothing but psychic concatenations which we reconstruct by means of an instinctive or methodical psychology'.[95]

However, in order to secure a place for sociology, Simmel reiterates his earlier argument (of 1894) that 'the scientific treatment of psychic data is not thereby automatically psychological' since the 'one reality' of social scientific study can be considered 'from a number of different viewpoints' and can be rendered into 'a plurality of mutually independent scientific subject matters'. Hence, although 'the givens of sociology are psychological processes whose immediate reality presents itself first of all under psychological categories . . . these psychological categories . . . remain outside the purpose of sociological investigation. It is to this end that we direct our study to the objective reality of sociation.[96] The 'theory of sociation' thus 'appears to be the only basis for a science that is entitled to the unqualified name of 'science of society'.[97] It is, among other things, directed to answering the question, 'How is society as such possible, as an objective form of subjective minds?[98] This however, is not the place to seek Simmel's answer to this question.

What Simmel does indicate is the legitimate existence of psychology as individual psychology. But, as we have seen, Simmel rejects any notion of a collective psychology. He also rejects any notion of collective consciousness, of 'a *Volksseele*, a consciousness of society, a spirit of the times' as 'real productive forces'. This he condemns as 'mysticism'. Hence, as he makes clear in his essay 'On the Nature of Social Psychology' (1908),[99] such entities could not form the basis for a social psychology that he would recognize as a legitimate discipline. Its problematic is outlined as follows:

> What modification does the psychological process of the individual undergo if, under specific influences, he moves through the societal environment? Yet this is a part of the general psychological task which . . . is an individual psychological one. Social psychology is perhaps co-ordinated as a subordinate section with the physiological, which investigates the determination of psychological processes through their connection with the body, just as the former does through their connection with other psyches.[100]

This extremely narrow demarcation of social psychology seems to suggest once more that, in the end, Simmel is inclined to recognize only individual psychology as psychology. Yet later in the same essay Simmel seeks once more to define social psychological phenomena as those deriving from the fact that

> the similarity of many individuals, by means of which we may obtain a type, an average, a more or less unified image, cannot come into existence without reciprocal influence. The object of investigation always remains the psychological individual, the group as a whole, for these categories of observation too, can have no 'soul'.[101]

Such homogeneities derive only from the interaction of individuals.

In one of the few recent discussions of Simmel's demarcation of sociology and psychology, Heinz-Jürgen Dahme concludes, with reference to social psychology's and sociology's study of regularities of behaviour and so forth, that

> while statistical figures, interpreted social psychologically, bring out qualities of individuals, viewed sociologically they bring out features of interactions, qualities of systems. With this demarcation Simmel sought once more to establish the possibility of an independent sociology, although he knew that in any particular concrete

individual study the boundaries between social psychological and sociological analysis are always fluid. He therefore never seriously concerned himself with avoiding social psychological statements in sociological investigations.[102]

The paradox contained in this summary of Simmel's intentions is that his own outline of sociology's tasks, rooted as it is – and as he readily acknowledged – in psychological presuppositions, taken together with the wealth of insights into face-to-face interactions that are contained in his substantive studies, must lead one to conclude that Simmel's demarcation of sociology from psychology is contradicted by his own substantive work. This is true not merely of the content of his social theory but, very often, of its essayistic form, of which he was a master and through which he could develop his thoughts in a whole series of unrestricted directions.

III

Although not the task of the present study, some indication should be given of where Simmel's contribution to social psychology lies. A full account would require a separate study of Simmel's psychology, which has hitherto never been undertaken. It should be apparent that his contribution to social psychology does not lie primarily in his explicit statement on the nature of social psychology. Nor does it lie especially in his various attempts to demarcate sociology from psychology. Indeed, many sociological critics of his work in fact complained that Simmel has provided a psychologistic foundation for sociology. This criticism received one of its early formulations in the work of Othmar Spann,[103] who maintained that Simmel's 'psychologistic concept of society' was based on his 'definition of societal interaction as the interaction of *psychological* entities'. Instead, Spann argued that a 'specifically *social* criterion for interaction' could be derived only from an adequate conception of society that is not grounded in the interaction of psychological entities. Spann was not alone in voicing this criticism. In an incomplete assessment of Simmel's work, Weber referred to Spann's 'perceptive criticism' of Simmel's sociology prior to the publication of his *Soziologie*, though he qualified this judgement by stating that 'in relation to the earlier work which Spann criticized, Simmel's recently published *Soziologie* shows some notable, but not *fundamental*, modifications'.[104]

But viewed from the standpoint of social psychology, Simmel's attempt to ground sociology in 'the interaction of psychological entities' is appealing.[105] Social psychologists might share with Simmel an antipathy towards a preoccupation with societal structures and systems as if they were concrete entities. They might too recognize in Simmel a social theorist who, more than any other of his time, sought to locate social analysis at the level of human interaction, however insignificant its instances might appear at first sight. Through analysis of the forms of sociation, Simmel was also in a position to examine the universal features of human interaction.

Furthermore, the basic principles of Simmel's sociology might themselves prove attractive to social psychologists in search of a nonreified framework for their own research. Reduced to its basic elements, and at the risk of some simplification, Simmel's social theory is grounded in the following propositions. He starts out from 'a regulative world principle that everything interacts in some way with everything else'. This implies that relationships between things are in permanent flux: 'Between every point in the world and every other force a permanently moving relationship exists'.[106] Indeed, one of his students, Siegfried Kracauer, detected in Simmel's social theory a 'core principle' of 'the fundamental interrelatedness [*Wesenszusamm-engehörigkeit*] of the most diverse phenomena'.[107] All of these principles point to a feature of the world that preoccupies Simmel, namely, the relationships between phenomena. Not surprisingly, therefore, Simmel applies the concept of interaction to social life and indicates that its basis lies in the interaction (*Wechselwirkung*) or reciprocal relationship between its elements. These elements are conscious individuals who interact with one another for a variety of motives, purposes and interests. This is the source of the psychological presuppositions that Simmel acknowledges in his social theory. However, in order to discover the general features of human interaction, Simmel maintains that the researcher must proceed, as in all sciences, on the basis of a methodical abstraction. For Simmel this constitutes the separation of the form from the content of social interactions, the forms by which individuals and groups of individuals come to be members of society. The goal of his sociology is, therefore, the study of the forms of being part of society, namely, sociation (*Vergesellschaftung*). Referring to his *Soziologie* around 1908 or 1909, Simmel says that on this basis he

> secured a new concept of sociology in which I separated the forms of sociation from the contents, i.e., the impulses, goals, material content that, only by being taken up by the interactions between individuals, become societal; in my book, therefore, I have under-

taken the investigation of these types of interactions as the object of a pure sociology.[108]

As indicated earlier, Simmel also assumes that the more complex social formations are merely extensions of the simplest interactions between human beings. There is no reified notion of society in Simmel's sociology. And since his key concepts are all relational ones, it is not surprising that Simmel conceives of society as a labyrinth or web of interactions.

As we have already seen, the simplest interactions are to be studied as the basis of a 'psychological microscopy.' In his substantive studies, Simmel analyses such elementary social phenomena as the social dimension of our senses,[109] sociability as an instance of sociation in its purest form,[110] mealtimes,[111] writing a letter,[112] and so forth. Further, he takes up the problem of our experience of time in essays on adventure,[113] spatial dimensions of interaction,[114] and mass in the sense of quantitative changes in group size (including dyadic and triadic interaction) that produce qualitative changes in the form of human interaction.[115] In his major works, such as *The Philosophy of Money* and *Soziologie*, we have a social analysis not merely of human rationality – including instrumentalism – but human emotions such as greed, avarice, the blasé attitude to the world (all of which Simmel relates to the development of monetary relationships in modern society),[116] shame,[117] gratitude,[118] and so on. And all this is without regard to the more well-known contributions that Simmel made to social psychology in the fields of reference group theory, role theory, and so forth. Not surprisingly, therefore, Simmel's work has been claimed by both sociologists and social psychologists as making significant contributions to their disciplines.

It can be argued that one of the reasons for this is that Simmel's social theory started out in its earliest formulations within a framework derived, in part, from *Völkerpsychologie*. Simmel continued to insist upon the psychological presuppositions necessary for a sociology that centred on social interaction, even when he was busy demarcating sociology from psychology and even when he had developed a programme for sociology that went far beyond the *Völkerpsychologie* of Lazarus and Steinthal.

Part II
Into modernity

3 German sociologists and modernity

Modernity has found here a dynamic expression: the totality of fragmentary, centrifugal directions of existence and the arbitrariness of individual elements are brought to light.

Thomas Masaryk on Simmel's *Soziologie*

We have known for some time that not America but present day Germany, the Germany of Wilhelm II, must be the land of unlimited possibilities! Perhaps one can more precisely term it, the land of unlimited impossibilities.

Georg Korn (1906)

I

The history of sociology's relationship to modernity presents us with a paradox. In its struggle consciously to assert itself as an independent academic discipline in the second half of the nineteenth century and especially around the turn of the century, sociology often took as its object of study that of which it was a product – modernity. It might even be suggested that those who not merely analysed its features but also experienced and expressed its central features in their writings (i.e. actually belonged to the modernist tradition) were the most successful in carrying out this task. This, it has been argued elsewhere, was true of Simmel who came closest to expressing and analysing the modes of experiencing the 'new' and 'modern' life-world.[1] But the study of modernity itself reveals a fractured history. If we take as axiomatic that the conceptualization of modernity presupposes a theory of modernization and, in turn, if we note that the original formulation of *modernité* by Baudelaire included a theory of modernism, then we can see how the study of modernity possesses a fragmented history. Sociology now abounds in theories of modernization which refer largely to the transformation of political, economic and social systems or sub-systems. Sometimes, as Habermas has argued with respect to the recent neo-conservative social theories of Bell and others, these are combined with a denunciation of the culture of modernism in order to assert the existence of post-modernism, post-industrialism and post-capitalism.[2] For its part, modernism – understood largely as a series of aesthetic movements – has been confined to the attentions of those who deal with art and culture. The result is that modernity itself is either subsumed under modernization or modernism or it disappears altogether as an object of investigation. For instance, to take up a distinction which Habermas applies in his overview of modernity, those social theories which are most successful in dealing with the modernization of social systems are often least successful in either analysing the 'life-world' or indicating sufficiently the mediations between the two.[3]

In order to examine the origins of this splintered conception of modernity, it is necessary to return briefly to some of its original conceptualizations in the mid-nineteenth century before turning to the relevance of the works of Tönnies, Simmel and Weber for the study of modernity. The former task involves an overview of modernity as understood by Baudelaire and Marx. The latter is examined in some detail with regard to Tönnies and Simmel and merely sketched out for Weber.

II

In his writings on aesthetics, Baudelaire recognized modernity as both a quality of modern life and a new object of artistic activity. Both rely upon the concept of the *new* which is itself *transitory*. This newness coincides with Habermas' notion of what is modern as that which 'assists in the objective expression of a spontaneous, self-renewing contemporaneity of the spirit of the times'. But, as Habermas points out, this newness can only be recognized in its juxtaposition with a classical past. Hence Baudelaire's conception of modernity as 'the ephemeral, the fugitive, the contingent' is instantly set in opposition to 'the eternal, the immutable'. Benjamin maintained that in his poetical writings this polarity is given a specific location: the city of Paris in its decrepitude as antiquity; the masses as modernity. Yet this is no simple aesthetic antinomy since for Baudelaire the transitory, fleeting element itself contains its opposite: eternity. Not surprisingly, therefore, he highlights the task of 'the painter of modern life', of modernity, as being 'to distil the eternal from the transitory'.

If we compare this task with that of key sociologists around the turn of the century then, at first sight, we seem to confront a similar problem in which the attempt to distil what is new, what is modern in modern society can only be performed in terms of a juxtaposition with its opposite. To take the examples in historical sequence, a reading of Tönnies' early work gives us the opposition of *Gemeinschaft* and *Gesellschaft*, in Durkheim's case the opposition of societies based upon mechanical and organic solidarity, for Simmel the contrast between a non-money economy and a developed (capitalist) money economy, and for Weber all previous 'traditional' societies compared with a society based on modern western rationalism (modern western rational capitalism). With pessimistic hindsight, it has been fashionable in modern sociological discourse to read all these polarities as if they were grounded in a philosophy of history thesis of the inevitable transition from one to the other, in such a way that the source of their dynamic – be it functional differentiation, rationalization, etc. – not merely produced only negative consequences but obscured the complexities of the 'present' societies and any countervailing tendencies operating within them. To take but one example, to which we shall return later, Tönnies emphasized time and time again not merely that features of *Gemeinschaft* and *Gesellschaft* exist side by side in contemporary society but – and this is a crucial thesis of modernity theories – that *Gesellschaft* is itself a transitory social formation. Similar problems arise in a static interpretation of the opposition of the old and the new in other classical sociological theories of modern society.

This transitory nature of the new in notions of modernity was associated with crucial changes in time consciousness in such a way that the study of modernity could become 'a reconnaissance into an unknown realm, that carries with it the risks of sudden, shocking confrontations' (Habermas).[4] One implication was to see society and social relations in a state of flux, in motion, in ceaseless movement. This, it has been argued recently, is a central feature of Marx's social theory which renders him 'the first and greatest of modernists' (Berman).[5] Berman's argument is that Marx has been recognized only as a major contributor to theories of modernization but not of modernity.[6] Yet, he maintains, crucial aspects of modernity and critical reflection upon them, are contained in Marx's work.

Certainly there is evidence for an analysis of the internal dynamic of modernity in Marx's account of the 'unleashing' of productive forces, production relations and social relations in general, the 'life' of the commodity and the stripping away of illusions. Some are already summed up in his early (1848) characterization of the 'new' historical configuration of capitalism:

> Constant revolutionizing of production, uninterrupted disturbance of all social relations, everlasting uncertainty and agitation, distinguish the bourgeois epoch from all earlier ones. All fixed, fast-frozen relationships, with their train of venerable ideas and opinions, are swept away, all new-formed ones become obsolete before they can ossify. All that is solid melts into air, all that is holy is profaned and human beings at last are forced to face with sober senses the real conditions of their lives and their relations with their fellow human beings.[7]

This vision of a 'revolution en permanence' (Proudhon) is an impossible one for those who seek to dominate such a society. Any society which requires for its dynamic the revolutionizing of production as a permanent (or even periodic) process requries at the same time the stabilization of some social relations that are necessary for this mode of production. Alongside a need for the permanent adaptability of individual personalities (not merely by virtue of work discipline) there is a corresponding necessity to maintain crucial relationships between capital and labour. Hence, one possibility which Berman considers is that ' "uninterrupted disturbance, everlasting uncertainty and agitation", instead of subverting this society, actually serves to strengthen it.'[8]

The role of the social sciences, confronted with this revolutionizing of 'the instruments of production, and thereby the relations of production, and with them the whole relations of society',[9] could be to search for the 'laws of motion' of this society in permanent flux. It could also be to seek out the sources of stabilization and integration in such a society. Marx's option to uncover the dynamic of capitalist society and apply that knowledge within that society, within 'the vanguard of movement', was not the only one available. Lorenz von Stein, for example, because of the complex of movements in modern society, could assert that 'the life of European society is such an infinitely multifarious, restless to and fro', whose movements themselves were caught 'in the threads that lead through the labyrinth of movement' in such a way that 'most see nothing of the motion of things and the law of this life'. One of the ways out of this 'labyrinth of movement' for Stein lay in a 'System of Statistics', 'whose foundation is the fact of moving energy'.[10]

Whereas in 1848 Marx could assert that the fundamental relations in society had been rid of their 'religious and political illusions', or that 'the bourgeoisie has stripped of its halo every occupation hitherto honoured and looked upon with reverent awe' and has 'torn away' the 'sentimental veil' from the family, he was less certain two decades later that social relations had been stripped of their illusions. This became the task of a critical social science, especially in relation to the 'secret' of 'fetishism of the commodity' and its 'mysterious character' by attempting to 'decipher the hieroglyphic' of value. As Benjamin was later to recognize in his 'prehistory of modernity', the commodity form not merely symbolizes social relations of modernity; it is a central source of their origin. The 'phantasmagoria' of the world of commodities is precisely a world in motion, in flux, in which all values are transitory, relations are fleeting and indifferent. But though this world of commodities appears to be transitory, it goes together with 'the continuous reproduction of the same relations – the relations which postulate capitalist production'.

Yet when all this is conceded, Marx's social theory remains one which is critical of modernity. Indeed, if we follow Habermas' characterization, it does not share all the features of a theoretical manifestation of modernity. When Habermas maintains that 'in the over-evaluation of the transitory, the fleeting and the ephemeral . . . there is expressed just as much the desire for an untarnished, still intact present', this does not apply to Marx's account of modernity which neither expresses this secret desire for present-day society nor poses an 'abstract opposition to the past'. The capitalist society which Marx analysed was, for him, doomed to be transitory. In so far as European socialist movements retained this perspective in the late nineteenth century they became the 'spectre' that 'haunted' sociology's own analyses of modernity.

III

In the opening pages of his *Gemeinschaft und Gesellschaft*, Tönnies announces that *Gesellschaft* exists as a transitory social formation: 'Society is only a transitional and superficial phenomenon'.[11] Further, whereas 'community is old, society is *new*, as a phenomenon and as a name'. One goes into the latter 'as into a *strange* country', which must be understood as a 'mechanical aggregate and artefact'. And lest we imagine that *Gemeinschaft* and *Gesellschaft* are merely 'normal concepts' or typifications, Tönnies himself in a subsequent article (1899) declared that 'in his treatment of the process of *Gesellschaft*, the author had *modern* society in mind, and thereby made use in an appropriate manner of the uncovering of its "economic law of motion" by K. Marx'.[12] In a very emphatic sense, Tönnies' social theory – despite its use of historical theories of law, etc. – has its origins in the present, as he makes clear at the very end of *Gemeinschaft und Gesellschaft* where he states that in order to understand 'the currents and struggles' of the present age

> we will take as our actual, even necessary, starting point, in contrast to all history deduced from the depths of the past, the amount of time in which the present spectator enjoys the inestimable advantage of observing the movements as they are occurring with the eyes of his own experience and, even though chained to the rocks of time, perceives the approaching tones and fragrance of Oceanus' daughters.[13]

In this respect, Tönnies' analysis can be understood as a form of analysis of the present (*Gegenwartsanalyse*).

If this is the case, then we need to ask what these 'new' societal processes were which Tönnies saw as constituting *Gesellschaft*. At first sight, given the initial declaration that *Gesellschaft* is a transitory form that is already driven towards socialism as an 'empirical cultural form', and given Tönnies' acknowledgement to Marx's 'economic law of motion' in *Capital*, it would appear that Tönnies' delineation of 'modern' society has strong affinities with that of Marx. Is this the case?

In his early outline of *Gemeinschaft und Gesellschaft* (1880) Tönnies declares his intention to apply his concepts (e.g. of *Gemeinschaft* and *Gesellschaft* as already sketched there) to 'the historical and contemporary reality of human collective life' in such a way that they can express 'the facts of experience'. Tönnies had already associated the concept of *Gesellschaft* with relationships of 'indifference', 'hostility' and contractual exchange relations. The latter is one of the crucial forms in which 'this concept strives toward realization'.[14] Indeed, in a later article (1899), Tönnies insists that 'the elementary fact of *Gesellschaft* is *the act of exchange*, which presents itself in its purest form if it is thought of and performed by individuals who are alien to each other, have nothing in common with each other, and confront each other in an essentially antagonistic and even hostile manner'.[15] Still later, and with reference to the origins of *Gesellschaft*, Tönnies declared that 'the decisive factor in the emergence of *Gesellschaft*, that is, *the causative factor* in the tremendous revolution that culminates in *Gesellschaft*, is economic in nature, namely, trade. In my opinion, trade in its development is nothing but the capitalistic system.'[16] This emphasis on 'exchange' anticipates Simmel's argument that exchange is a social phenomenon *sui generis*. It also indicates a break with Marx's account of modern society with its emphasis upon production.

But in order to explore more fully Tönnies' own account of modern society we need to turn to *Gemeinschaft und Gesellschaft* and to some of his essays in the succeeding decade in which, building on this early work, he outlines a theory of rationalization which became one of the central theses of modernization theory, and which came to dominate sociological theory for many subsequent decades.

Tönnies starts out by defining the concept of *Gesellschaft* in an almost Hobbesian manner as 'the artificial construction of an aggregate of human beings' all of whom are isolated from one another and exhibit a tension towards all others. Indeed, the negative attitude to others represents a 'normal' relationship. Initially – and again still following Hobbes – all goods in society exist separately and are enjoyed exclusively by their owners. In this respect value equals possession in a *Gesellschaft*. And where 'the exchange of commodities becomes general or societal' qualitative differences are ignored.

But rather than remain merely with the *concept* of *Gesellschaft*, Tönnies seeks to 'show what relationship the real structure of the *Gesellschaft* bears' to its concept.[17] And here, whilst not discarding Hobbes' 'market model of society' (Macpherson), Tönnies appears to rely more heavily upon Marx and contemporary economists. In society as a whole, the continuous exchange of commodities rests on the dependency of each producer of a commodity upon all other producers and 'this condition represents the dependence of the individual on the *Gesellschaft*'. In turn, exchange presupposes a contract, itself 'the resultant of two divergent wills, intersecting in one point'. Bourgeois society, with its 'most important rule, that everyone can do legally within his realm that which he wishes, but nothing outside' or in its extended form as a series of conventions relating to individual freedoms, is thus

an aggregate by convention and law of nature, . . . a multitude of natural and artificial individuals, the wills and spheres of whom are in many relations with and to one another, and remain nevertheless independent of one another and devoid of mutual familiar relationships.[18]

This may be modified by the formation of 'treaties and peace pacts', even to the point at which 'competition is limited and abolished by coalition'.

In an analogous manner, we can understnd 'all conventional society life' whose supreme rule is politeness. It consists of an exchange of words and courtesies in which everyone seems to be present for the good of everyone else and everyone seems to consider everyone else as his equal, whereas in reality everyone is thinking of himself and trying to bring to the fore his importance and advantages in competition with the others.[19]

Conventional society is thus understood largely in terms derived from economic society. All the 'creative, formative and contributive activity of human beings' which is 'akin to art' belongs, as it were, to *Gemeinschaft* as a concept. Its opposite is commerce, with its merchants (the 'intermediaries of exchange') and its bankers (the 'intermediaries of intermediation'). They, 'the merchants or capitalists . . . are the natural masters and rulers of the *Gesellschaft*. The *Gesellschaft* exists for their sake' whereas 'all noncapitalists . . . are either themselves like inanimate tools . . . or they are legally nonentities'.[20]

Assuming that societal forms of relationships are the dominant ones in modern society, are there any countervailing tendencies to 'the process of formation of the *Gesellschaft* and the destruction of *Gemeinschaft*'? Certainly, contemporary tendencies such as growing urbanization could only accelerate this trend, since for Tönnies the city is typical of *Gesellschaft* in general and its highest form is the metropolis. But Tönnies did discern a growing common consciousness of both the proletariat and women which might create 'a more-humane consciousness' against convention which maintains only 'the appearance of morality'. A further possibility is that 'the state, as the reason of *Gesellschaft*, could decide to destroy *Gesellschaft* or at least to reform and renew it'. But, Tönnies continues cryptically, 'the success of such attempts is highly improbable', especially as 'the state is hardly directly concerned with morality'.[21] This state confronts the masses as an alien force as does 'the metropolis' and 'societal conditions', which are 'the ruin and the death of the common people'. They might achieve class consciousness and through class struggle 'destroy the society and the state which it seeks to reform. And since the whole culture is overturned in societal and state civilization, thus culture itself in its changed form is sent to its doom.'[22] This outcome is in contrast to another implicit possibility contained within the historical movement of *Gesellschaft* itself '(state and international) *socialism*', 'already inherent in the concept of *Gesellschaft*'. Its success, however, 'would necessarily dissolve the entire *Gesellschaft* and its civilization'.[23] Several decades later, in subsequent editions of

Gemeinschaft und Gesellschaft, Tönnies discerned the development of collective elements in society in the form of co-operatives (1912) and the call for co-operative production (1922). And against those who saw his diagnosis as too bleak he replied that his 'pessimism refers to the future of the present civilization, not to the future of civilization itself' (1899).

Already implicit in the development of *Gesellschaft* and the arbitrary will is another process which heralds a central thesis in modernization theories, namely rationalization. In 1895, in 'Historicism and Rationalism', Tönnies briefly set out the implications of the process of rationalization for science and society. His main contention there is 'that society and state tend intrinsically towards rationalism . . . and that the same rationalistic trend belongs to the essence of science'.[24] In the case of the social sciences, 'the "historical" approach represents . . . the transition to a new type of rationalistic approach toward the fact of social life', whose characteristic feature there and elsewhere is 'a principle of domination'. The historically existing rationalistic tendencies, for their part, are 'always revolutionary'. They manifest themselves in 'the forces that represent social reason *per se*: society, state, science', that is, 'in the economic, political and intellectual spheres'.[25]

At the societal level, the process is 'essentially one of rationalisation . . . It elevates the rational, calculating individuals . . . An establishment in trade or commerce is comparable to a mechanical construction.' In other words, it involves 'the unleashing and promotion of production and trade' in terms of precise calculation of means. The rational process is epitomized in 'the businessman' who 'degrades everything – objects and men alike – to the level of means'. And within the process of production rationalization signifies 'the commercialization of production', 'the transformation of the social division of labour' into objectified processes that pave the way for 'a total national economy planned by society', and 'the transformation of the internal division of labour' with its artificial fragmentation of the 'divided' worker and the degradation of machine labour. The overall consequence of this pervasive rationalization is to prepare for the social order's own abolition (large-scale enterprises, decline of enterprise spirit, levelling of labour force and absence of competition within it, etc.).

With regard to the process of rationalization within the economic sphere, Tönnies' argument already points towards Max Weber's rationalization thesis, and, with its emphasis on the division of labour, perhaps also points towards Simmel's argument on the causes of the separation of objective from subjective culture. In this context, and in the light of the preceding analysis, there is little doubt that Tönnies was preoccupied with the task of understanding the 'new' element of 'modern' society. Further, he saw this as a crucial task of his sociology (as in the article of 1899). But are the other elements of a social theory of modernity also present in Tönnies' analysis?

Certainly society itself, as *Gesellschaft*, is seen as a transitory phenomenon. By implication, contractual relations within a dynamic capitalist society are also fleeting. Their basis is an egoistic calculation of individual gain that reduces human relations to functional ones. In terms of a transformed time consciousness, however, Tönnies does not subject the reader to 'the shock of the new'. His evolutionary perspective and his early commitment to socialism militate against this. And, as one of his contemporaries argued, Tönnies was unable to grasp the significance of Nietzsche 'because he approaches him from the standpoint of a modern, socialistically tempered evolutionist who accepts without question the real development with its technical climactic, its democratisation of power, eudaemonistic goals as the just and desirable'.[26] What Simmel here praises Nietzsche for, amongst other things, is his sensitivity to psychological processes, to the way in which he was able to analyse the subterranean world of modern society. To return to Habermas' argument on theories of modernity, perhaps we can say that although Tönnies provides us with an account of the 'new' modern society in terms of some of its central mechanisms, the manner in which people experienced them in their own life-world was seldom broached with any degree of success.

IV

One of the ironies of Simmel's critique of Tönnies is that only a few years earlier Simmel had himself espoused ideas on socialism not dissimilar to those of Tönnies. Yet by 1900 Simmel was already sceptical of socialism's tendency 'towards the complete rationalisation of life, towards its direction by means of a high unified principle'[27] and had begun to stress instead its aesthetic appeal. It is worth noting in passing that the association of socialism and rationalization, already present in Tönnies' work too, could easily lead to an abandonment of socialism as a feasible possibility precisely because it implied merely greater rationalization. It thus presaged its rejection as an historical option two decades later by Weber, since its potential for harmful rationalization of all spheres of life was possibly even greater than that of advanced capitalism.

Be that as it may, there can be little doubt that Simmel provided a fin de siècle social theory of modernity that could not be matched by his contemporaries. Indeed, Berman maintains that Simmel 'intimates, but never really develops, what is probably the closest thing to a twentieth-century dialectical theory of modernity',[28] though what he has in mind is largely the outcome of Simmel's theory of the inevitable clash between subjective and objective culture. His contemporaries did recognize his 'interpretation of the time from the modernist perspective' and 'scented the instinct for the times' in his theory of modern society. But before moving on to his analysis of the modes of experiencing modernity it is worth looking briefly at one of the few occasions on which he provides us with a 'diagnosis of the times' shortly after the publication of *The Philosophy of Money* in an article titled 'Tendencies in German Life and Thought since 1870' (1902).[29] There, Simmel seeks to locate important tendencies in 'the spirit of the times', often in a manner which suggests a biographical identification with them.

One fundamental process 'during the last seventy years' – which had preoccupied Simmel since its first announcement in *Über sociale Differenzierung* – had been 'the increased externalization of life that has come about, with regard to the preponderance that the technical side of life has obtained over its inner side, over its personal values'.[30] In other words, the central tendency has been the domination of objective over subjective culture. But rather than see this process in a unilinear manner, Simmel maintains that the various periods of development in Germany 'stand in very complex relations to this tendency' which will include 'the degree in which they embody it or compel reactions against it'. After German unification and the Franco-Prussian War, political and economic forces encouraged the development of 'a practical materialism' and 'the *material* enjoyment of life' whose consequence 'from the psychological point of view . . . was an externalization of interests' – including not merely improved immediate surroundings but also 'the adornment of buildings', 'the greater amount of travel', etc. The economic growth of the *Gründerjahre* (the decade or so after German unification) stimulated the subordination of all things to material interests, resulting in the domination of technique as 'the sole concern of most producers and consumers whilst forgetting that *technique* is a mere means to an end'. Technical perfection was extolled 'as though the electric light raised man a stage nearer perfection, despite the fact that the objects more clearly seen by it are just as trivial, ugly, or unimportant as when looked at by the aid of petroleum'.[31] In the arts, however, Simmel

points to new techniques, as in painting (impressionism) which have
been beneficial.

However, this 'rapid development of external civilization' facilitated
by large-scale industrial development 'has assisted the outbreak of the
greatest popular movement of the century, namely, the rise of the
Social Democrats'. Their 'idealized picture of the future . . . is an
essentially rational one in the highest degree: extreme centralization,
nicely calculated adjustment to each other of demand and supply,
exclusion of competition, equality of rights and duties'. Alongside the
genuine 'ethical impulses of justice and sympathy' on the part of 'the
more highly educated', Simmel discerns more confused motives for an
interest in socialist ideas:

> Many persons are actuated by a diseased longing to experience new
> sensations, and they feel the power of attraction that everything
> paradoxical and revolutionary is always capable of exerting upon
> numerous members of a nervously excitable and degenerate society.
> With this is often connected a fantastic and effeminate mental state,
> a vague desire for unity and universal brotherhood; in other words
> . . . – we might call it parlor socialism – a coquetting with socialistic
> ideals whose realization would be mostly unendurable to these very
> dilettanti.[32]

But Simmel sees the interest in socialism having declined among non-
working class groups once the Social Democrats became 'a reform
party on the basis of the existing social order'.

Simmel sees the interest in social issues as emanating from another
source, in part in the philosophy of Schopenhauer embodying the
notion that there is no final end in life, only the human will. Hence,
'the lack that men felt of a final object, and consequently of an ideal
that should dominate the whole of life, was supplied in the eighties by
the almost spontaneous rise of the idea of social justice'. This also had
its origin in 'the decline of Christianity which had supplied a *final
object* to life', 'above everything relative, above the fragmentary
character of human existence, above the limitless structure of means
and means to means'. This 'yearning after a final object' in a context
which 'no longer renders possible its attainment' produces

> specifically modern feelings, that life has no meaning, that we are
> driven hither and thither in a mechanism built up out of mere
> preliminary stages and means, that the final and absolute wherein
> consists the reward of living, ever escapes our grasp.[33]

In the 1880s, Simmel maintains that this absence was filled with the idea of social justice and a sense of serving society as a whole, a sense 'that the individual was but the crossing-point of social threads and that he, by a devotion to the interests of all, merely discharged an obligation of the most fundamental character'.

Yet Simmel also detected 'the rise of an opposite ideal, that of individualism, which about the year 1890 began to compete with the socialist ideal'. Possibly speaking for himself – at least in the early 1890s – Simmel refers to those 'who are in every way individualists by conviction . . . and who at the same time belong to the social-democratic party, because they regard socialism as a necessary transition stage to a just and enlightened individualism'. This conviction is sometimes stimulated by serious doubts as to 'the physical and spiritual excellence of the higher classes' who 'seem in many cases to be so decadent, so exhausted and neurasthenic as to be unable to bear the future upon their shoulders'. In this context, Simmel even speaks of an 'internal migration' of 'the proletarian elements' into such positions in order that society may preserve itself.

A primary source of this new 'enlightened individualism' was the philosophy of Nietzsche which gained popularity in the 1890s, often amongst those who saw in his ideas 'the justification of an unrestrained egoism, and who considered that they gave an absolute right to develop in the highest degree the personality of the individual in defiance of all social and altruistic claims'. It was particularly attractive to the new youth movement and those who sought a false individuality. At the end of the first part of this article, Simmel draws attention to the inevitable conflict between the maintenance of the highest values of mankind and 'the cry for a levelling' as 'a reaction against the dismemberment of society, against the established division of labour'. Somewhat cryptically, Simmel notes that the reconciliation of the two goals 'may require diametrically opposed measures'.

Thus, alongside differentiating tendencies in modern society, there have simultaneously arisen 'levelling tendencies' manifested, for instance, in the women's movement, to which Simmel elsewhere devotes considerable attention. A further tendency is the growing centralization of church and state and a consequent search by individuals for some secure area 'beyond all the oscillations and the fragmentariness of empirical existence' in order to escape from 'life's complexity and constant unrest'. Here, at the heart of the modernist experience, Simmel argues that for many people

this longing assumes an aesthetic character. They seem to find in the artistic conception of things a release from the fragmentary and painful in real life . . . Unless I am deceived, however, this sudden increase in fondness for art will not long endure. The transcendental impulse, disillusioned by a fragmentary science that is silent as to everything final, and by a social–altruistic activity that neglects the inner, self-centred completion of spiritual development, has sought an outlet for itself in the aesthetic; but it will learn that this field also is too limited.[34]

In other words, Simmel reiterates what was implicit in *The Philosophy of Money*, namely that an aesthetic retreat from reality cannot be a final one. None the less, Simmel still maintains as a goal the capacity

to experience in the individual phenomenon, with all of its details, the fullness of its reality. To this end, . . . a certain retreat from the phenomenon is necessary, a transforming of it which renounces the mere reflection of what is given in nature, in order to regain, from a higher point of view, more fully and more deeply its reality.[35]

This implies a rejection of naturalism in art and also in the historical sciences which, Simmel argues, have passed beyond 'the history of princes and of particular leading persons' as immediate historical facts. Instead, interest has shifted to 'the history of the masses', to 'the totality of social forms and . . . their evolutions'.

This brings us back to Simmel's theory of modernity and the methodological problems associated with its study. The preceding, detailed survey of his 'diagnosis of the times' has been highlighted in order to show that for Simmel the interest in the 'new' in modern society did have a historical location. The economic and social location of modernity – as one of Simmel's central preoccupations around the turn of the century – is to be found in *The Philosophy of Money* and other writings which surround it. Since Simmel's theory of modernity will be outlined in more detail later, only its crucial elements will be highlighted here.

In the sense given to modernity by Baudelaire, it has been argued that Simmel is the first sociologist of modernity. Further, it might be argued that only 'the painter of the passing moment' was able to capture modernity. If modernity as a distinctive mode of experiencing (social) reality involves seeking society and the social relations within it as (temporally) transitory and (spatially) fleeting, then this implies, conversely, that traditional, permanent structures are now absent from human experiences. In other words, to borrow a phrase from Tönnies 'l'évolution sociale prend la forme d'une *désagrégation spontanée*'.[36] The equivalent conception in Simmel's account of modernity is that reality is experienced in flux. In other words, the shock of 'movement' in production, society and history first experienced with the French Revolution and subsequently in the revolutions of the nineteenth century, though at first bounded by actual 'social movements', could be experienced a century later as movement as such, as permanent flux:

> In reality itself things do not last for any length of time; through the restlessness with which they offer themselves at any moment . . . every form immediately dissolves in the very moment when it emerges; it lives, as it were, only by being destroyed; every consolidation of form into lasting objects . . . is an incomplete interpretation that is unable to follow the motion of reality at its own pace.[37]

As we have argued earlier, this makes more difficult the search for the 'laws of motion' in this reality. Instead, the modernist is tempted to search out 'the ideal system of eternally valid lawfulness', to distil the eternal from what is transitory, to try to capture the dialectic of the permanent and the transitory. This might explain the intention behind Simmel's snapshots *sub specie aeternitatis* or later Walter Benjamin's search for 'dialectical images' of modernity, indeed for 'dialectics at a standstill'. Of course, for Simmel, the social phenomenon *par excellence* which embodies both the labyrinth of movement and the dialectic of flux and permanence is money, since 'there is no more striking symbol of the completely dynamic character of the world . . . It is, as it were, an *actus purus*.' Symbolising the transitory and the fleeting it is 'the most ephemeral thing in the external–practical world'.

If everything is in flux and transitory, then social reality no longer exists as an ordered totality. The starting point can only be the fragment which might still reveal 'the totality of meaning' of social reality. This direction for social theories of modernity is chosen not merely by Simmel but by Bloch, Kracauer, Adorno and, above all, Benjamin. But if we no longer experience social reality as a coherent whole, what are the implications for the individual?

Here, Simmel points to the possibilities of partial withdrawal from social reality in *The Philosophy of Money*, including the inward retreat and, as we have seen in his 'diagnosis of the times', the search for an aesthetic totality. Since these options are considered elsewhere as part of Simmel's substantive theory of modernity, it is worthwhile reflecting on the methodological consequences of focusing in this way upon modes of experiencing modernity. One important feature which stands out is the attention that is devoted to the 'inner life' of human beings, to the *psychology* of modernity. This is an important emphasis given sociology's attempts at the end of the nineteenth century to demarcate itself as an independent discipline not merely from history and philosophy, but also from psychology. Simmel, who started out in the *Völkerpsychologie* of Lazarus and Steinthal,[38] retained a sensitivity to psychological processes that proved essential to his analysis of the modes of *experiencing* modernity. Simmel was not merely a master of the sociology of fleeting encounters and interactions; he was also a key figure in the development of a sociology of emotions and intimate interaction, as Birgitta Nedelmann has persuasively argued,[39] and, one must add, of a psychology of emotional life. This was an urgent task for the social theorist of modernity who saw 'the essence of modernity' as 'psychologism, the experiencing and interpretation of the world in terms of the reactions of our inner life and indeed as an inner world, the dissolution of fixed contents in the fluid element of the soul, from which all that is substantive is filtered and whose forms are merely forms of motion'.[40] All the central features of modernity which Simmel analyses in the 'outer world', as it were, are expressed and manifest themselves in the 'inner' life of individuals.

V

By way of contrast, and all too briefly, the difficulties involved in extracting a social theory of modernity from the work of Max Weber will be considered. There is little doubt that Weber provides us with one of the most impressive, if incomplete, theories of modernization which centres on his account of the development of modern western rationalism and its consequences, amongst which is modern western capitalism. Several writers have pointed to the difficulties of clarifying rationality in its variants of the instrumental, substantive, formal and conceptual (Levine, Kalberg).[41] In addition, Levine has argued that one can detect in Weber's work a 'distinction between subjective and objective manifestations of rationality' that not merely echoes Simmel's subjective and objective culture distinction but which might form the basis for a central thesis in the dialectics of modernity.

But when we turn to one of the most recent attempts to outline Weber's theory of modernity, we find that Habermas acknowledges a number of difficulties that were not apparent in his earlier article, 'Modernity – an Unfinished Project'.[42] On the one hand, Habermas maintains that Weber's theory of rationalization offers 'the most promising beginning for the explanation of social pathologies, which appear as a result of capitalist modernization'. Yet 'the pathologies of modernity' arising out of the rationalisation process are considered solely from the standpoint of a theory of the rationalization of systems of action that is itself confined to the standpoint of purposive rationality. As such this theory is incapable of analysing the 'moral–practical and aesthetic–expressive aspects' of modernity. A further problem arises for a historically specific theory of modernity, for a 'diagnosis of the present', in so far as 'the capitalistic form of modernization is identified with societal rationalization as such'. Habermas concludes that Weber's theory must be reconstructed in order to overcome these limitations.

Habermas carries out this reconstruction in part in order to question commonly accepted assumptions as to the inevitable consequences of the rationalization thesis: 'Neither the secularisation of world images nor the structural differentiation of society possesses *per se* unavoidable pathological side-effects'.[43] Instead, Habermas seeks to reconstruct Weber's central theses on bureaucratization as 'a key phenomenon for the understanding of modern societies', and rationalization as the key to the emergence of capitalist society in order to examine once more Weber's diagnosis of the present.

The new type of purposive–rational organizational form is grounded in the rational calculations of production within capitalist enterprises and in public administration by legally trained officials. In both cases, the objectification of social relations in organizations produces depersonalized, 'rationally functioning machines' in such a way that the dead machine in manufacture and the living machine in bureaucratic organization combine as 'the iron cage'. The formally organized spheres of action are distanced dramatically from the life-world: 'Organisations gain autonomy via a *neutralizing demarcation over against the symbolic structures of the life-world*; confronted with culture, society and the personality, they thereby become fundamentally *indifferent*'.[44]

The crucial factor in the emergence of capitalist society is 'the differentiation of the economic system from the structure of domination of European feudalism'. The latter is reorganized in the form of the modern state. In turn, this uncoupling of economic and state administration is traced back to a purposive–rational orientation to action. The central problem then becomes that of social integration into this new orientation which permits the implementation of technical and organizational knowledge to production and, in principle, any other sphere of social life.

Habermas sums up Weber's diagnosis of the present somewhat schematically under the headings of loss of freedom and loss of meaning for individuals. In the former case, rather than seeing the individual's loss of freedom as arising out of the rationalization process *per se*, Habermas argues that it actually arises out of an 'uncoupling of system and life-world' in such a way that orientations to action in the latter are conditioned by the former. With the lack of private orientation consequent upon the decline of inner motivation from a generalized work ethic, the private sphere increasingly lacks any focus for orientation. Weber speaks of 'specialists without spirit' and 'hedonists without heart'. In the public sphere, legitimation of political authority demands increasingly the exclusion of the ethical sphere from the political. What originally gave meaning to the life-world is either fragmented or removed entirely.

In short, Habermas implicitly indicates a theory of modernity in Weber's work which, as a disjunction of social system and life-world and in its contemporary diagnosis, comes to resemble Simmel's separation of objective and subjective culture. The problem of individual orientation, in a similar way, is also acute. But neither in Habermas' reconstruction nor in Weber's own account of modernity is there that level of attention to modes of experiencing the 'new' in modern society that is found in Simmel's work.

VI

The preceding account of the treatment of modernity – announced as a theme by Baudelaire in the mid-nineteenth century and echoed in some of Marx's writings – in the social theories of Tönnies, Simmel and, more briefly, Weber should suggest that it could be extended to other sociologists and social theorists at the turn of the century. The most notable omission is, of course, Durkheim in France. When Habermas speaks of Weber's treatment of 'pathologies of modernity', this could easily be extended to the much more explicit attempt by Durkheim to provide a 'pathology of the present' that is to be found most notably in his *Division of Labour in Society* and *Suicide*. In Germany, one of the most neglected but relevant figures is Werner Sombart, whose social theory of modernity has hardly been examined yet.

With respect to the search for a social theory of modernity that addressed changes in modes of experience, it has been argued that only Simmel provides us with the possibility of extracting such a theory from his works without too much reconstruction. All the major sociologists at the turn of the century sought to define the 'new' element of modern society which, more often than not, became the crucial component of their theory of modernisation. But a broader historical perspective on theories of modernity suggests that they have been most successful where the study of modes of experiencing modern society or its life-world has been informed by that movement which in the cultural sphere expressed the 'newness' of modern life most forcefully, namely modernism. Later in the twentieth century, the most significant instance is that of Benjamin's 'prehistory of modernity', which retained its links with Baudelaire, Marx and even Simmel.

In the light of Habermas' dimensions of modernity it then becomes evident that those social theories which remained too firmly anchored in the past were unable to express the crucial changes in time consciousness implied by modernity and therefore were unable to express 'the shock of the new'. Similarly, the fragmentation of social experience implies that novel ways of approaching the study of modernity, that do not subsume modes of experiencing it under an all-embracing modernisation theory, are necessary. Otherwise, the disjunction between social system and life-world remains unresolved.

4 Simmel and the study of modernity

The superior power of the culture of objects over the culture of individuals is the result of the unity and autonomous self-sufficiency that the objective culture has accomplished in modern times.

The Philosophy of Money

The subjectivism of modern times has the same basic motive as art: to gain a more intimate and truer relationship to objects by dissociating ourselves from them and retreating into ourselves, or by consciously acknowledging the inevitable distance between ourselves and objects.

The Philosophy of Money

I

If it is true that all major social theorists and sociologists since the mid-nineteenth century have sought to delineate and sometimes explain the origins of that which is 'new' in modern society, then why might we wish to single out the endeavours and contribution of Georg Simmel in delineating the study of modernity? If we turn to classical social theorists and sociologists, then we do indeed find important attempts to investigate modernity. Marx, for instance, highlights three dimensions of modernity: the revolutionary new destruction of the past, the ever-new destruction of the present and the ever-same reproduction of the 'socially necessary illusion' of the commodity form as a barrier to a qualitatively different future. Marx's investigation of modernity goes in search of the laws of motion of capitalist society that will explain the phenomenal and illusory forms in which that society appears to us, especially in the sphere of circulation and exchange of commodities. What is largely absent in Marx's analysis is the detailed investigation of the phenomenal forms, of 'the daily traffic of bourgeois life', of 'the movement which proceeds on the surface of the bourgeois world', of how individuals actually experience modernity in everyday life.

Indeed, if we define modernity as the modes of experiencing that which is new in modern society (which is broadly how Baudelaire viewed modernity when he introduced the concept of 'modernité' in 1859), then we find that the classical sociologists did attempt to delineate that which is new in modern society but largely failed to analyse modernity as modes of experiencing the new. Durkheim approaches this object only in asides and notes in *Suicide* and elsewhere, where he refers to 'the different currents of collective sadness', the 'collective melancholy' in modern society, but his putative aversion to psychological explanations left unexamined the experiential dimensions, for example, of the 'suicideogenic currents' in modern society. Instead, modernity's origins are investigated as the transition from mechanical to organic solidarity and, especially, the latter's 'abnormal' forms. Somewhat earlier, Tönnies had opted for the transition from *Gemeinschaft* to *Gesellschaft*, in order to apply these concepts to 'the historical and contemporary reality of human collective life' in such a manner that they can express 'the facts of experience'. However, despite Tönnies early illumination of the process of rationalization in modern society – a theme to be found later in Simmel and, especially, Max Weber – the examination of the modes of experiencing the new in modern society is replaced by a not always clarified theory of will-formation. The problematic of the process of rationalization and the search for the origins of modern western rationalism (and its socio-economic formation, modern western rational capitalism) is, of course, the site of Weber's investigation of modernity. Here, as we have seen in Chapter 3, Habermas had argued that this theory of rationalization offers 'the most promising beginning for the explanation of the social pathologies, which appear as a result of capitalist modernization'. However, it is suggested that Weber's theory of modernity, focusing upon the disjunction of social system and life-world (ostensibly not dissimilar to Simmel's separation of objective and subjective culture), also fails to analyse sufficiently the life-world itself and, in particular, the 'moral–practical and aesthetic–expressive aspects' of modernity.[1]

In Simmel's case, were we to focus merely on his delineation of the transition to modern society, we could not be anything but less than satisfied with the transition from a simple to a mature money economy (which, as Weber and, later, Mannheim pointed out, conflates a mature money economy with a mature capitalist money economy). However, Simmel's investigation of the two crucial sites of modernity

– the mature (and by implication) capitalist money economy and the metropolis – yields an analysis of the consequences of both for individuals' modes of experiencing the social and natural world that, compared to many of his contemporaries, comes closest to a sociological and psychological study of the life-world of modernity as it is experienced in everyday life. The reasons why this is so must now be examined in the course of an outline of the major dimensions of Simmel's delineation of modernity.

II

Let us commence our overview of Simmel's study of modernity with one of the few definitions of modernity with which he provides us. It occurs in his essay 'Rodin', expanded for the volume *Philosophische Kultur* (1911), in which Simmel – as one of the very first German critics to have brought out the significance of Rodin's sculpture to the German public (followed by Rilke, amongst others) – praises Rodin's work as both aesthetically heightening the tensions of modern life and, at the same time, releasing us from that tension. This is Simmel's conception of the function of the work of art, which intimates that one of the reasons for the depth of his delineation of modernity is his connection to some of the modernist aesthetic currents of his day. Simmel announces, then, in this context, that

> the essence of modernity as such is *psychologism*, the experiencing and interpretation of the world in terms of the *reactions of our inner life*, and indeed as *an inner world*, the *dissolution of fixed contents* in the fluid element of the soul, from which all that is substantive is filtered and whose *forms are merely forms of motion.*[2]

What does this definition of modernity indicate to us? If we connect the somewhat obscure notion of psychologism with that of subjectivism, which Simmel had already seen to be an important tendency in modern society in the 1890s, then we can see that what is implied here is that modernity is identified with the dissolution of our contact with the external world through concrete practice. Indeed, it suggests that modern experience has been transformed, in Benjamin's terms, from concrete and conscious historical experience (*Erfahrung*) into individual, lived-out inner experience (*Erlebnis*). It implies, further, the dissolution of actual content in the inner psychological and emotional world itself and the preponderance of fluid forms of inner experience. The experience and interpretation of the external world as an inner world points to an important dimension of what has been identified not merely with modernity but also postmodernity: namely, instead of a concrete reality, images of reality; instead of cognition, emotion; instead of an 'objective' world of intellectualism, an inner world of neurasthenia. This may seem a somewhat extreme interpretation but is justified if we recall the decisive features of individual experience highlighted by Simmel in his analysis of the two sites of modernity – the mature money economy and the metropolis – namely, the increase in nervousness and the preponderance of an inner world as a retreat from excessive external stimuli.

What are the implications of this conception of modernity for Simmel's own analysis of it? First, Simmel's treatment of the symptoms of modernity does focus upon inner experience and the dissolution of stable forms of experiencing time, space and causality (as transitory, fleeting and fortuitous or arbitrary experience which accords with Baudelaire's original definition of modernity). In so doing, he provides us with the beginnings of a sociology of the emotions: love, greed, avarice, trust, gratitude, ennui, the blasé attitude – some of which, such as ennui, are directly identified with modernity ('Ennui, the dulling monotony of days and years. It is the absence of the idea of evolution which condemns the world and mankind to being always the same, without solace'[3]) and the blasé attitude ('There is perhaps no psychological phenomenon that is so unreservedly associated with the metropolis as the blasé attitude. The blasé attitude results first from the rapidly changing and closely compressed contrasting stimulations of the nerves').[4]

Second, the whole of Simmel's sociology focuses upon the forms of social interaction (of sociation), however fortuitous and fleeting they might be. He insists that sociology 'can no longer take to be unimportant consideration of the delicate, invisible threads that are woven between one person and another'.[5] His concern with the 'fortuitous fragments of reality', with 'what is apparently most superficial and insubstantial', is not confined to vignettes of fleeting interactions (such as the rendezvous). The whole of his analysis in *The Philosophy of Money*, investigating *the* site of modernity, is guided by 'the possibility . . . of finding in each of life's details the totality of its meaning'.[6]

This suggests a further important implication for Simmel's approach to the study of modernity: that the fractured and dissolved totality of modernity can only be apprehended from the individual element, from the fragment. Such a standpoint presupposes that there is a perspective capable of creating a unity out of the fragmented world of modernity. In 'Sociological Aesthetics' (1896), for instance, Simmel reveals that perspective to be the aesthetic mode of interpretation since

> the essence of aesthetic observation and interpretation lies in the fact that the typical is to be found in what is unique, the law-like in what is fortuitous, the essence and significance of things in the superficial and transitory . . . Every point conceals the possibility of being released into absolute aesthetic significance. To the adequately trained eye, the *total* beauty, the *total* meaning of the world as a whole radiates from every single point.[7]

If a sociology of modernity commences its analysis with 'what is fortuitous', with 'the superficial and transitory', then it cannot be either an orthodox project or one which does not rely upon other disciplines and perspectives. Simmel insists that 'the very standpoint of a single science, which is also based on the division of labour, never exhausts the totality of reality'.

Furthermore, if the study of modernity is to commence with modes of experiencing social reality and social relations as transitory and fleeting, then it must confront the problem that social reality is experienced in flux, not merely as the shock of the new or even the shock of movement, but as permanent flux:

> Through the restlessness with which they offer themselves at any moment . . . every form immediately dissolves in the very moment when it emerges; it lives, as it were, only by being destroyed; every consolidation of form into lasting objects . . . is an incomplete interpretation that is unable to follow the motion of reality at its own pace.[8]

Faced with this, the modernist is tempted to distil the eternal from the transitory, to capture the dialectic of the permanent and the transitory. This might explain the intention behind Simmel's 'snapshots *sub specie aeternitatis*'.[9] For him, the social phenomenon par excellence which embodies both the labyrinth of movement and the dialectic of flux and permanence is money as the 'symbol of the completely dynamic character of the world . . . It is, as it were, an *actus purus*'. As symbol of the transitory and fleeting, it is 'the most ephemeral thing in the external–practical world'.[10]

Methodically, Simmel is able to confront the fragments that reveal themselves in society in flux since the notion of substance is dissolved to that of threads which hold society together (whose most powerful symbol is money) and conceptually all his crucial concepts are relational ones (interaction (*Wechselwirkung*), sociation (*Ver-*

gesellschaftung)). The emotional and sensory threads are to be dealt with by a 'psychological microscopy', in the realm which captures 'human beings in the stream of their life'. Thus, whatever the judgement that may be passed upon Simmel's delineation of modernity, there can be little doubt that his methodological presuppositions did equip him with an ensemble of means for presenting modes of experiencing that which is new in modern society which his sociological contemporaries often lacked.[11]

III

Simmel's investigation of the two interrelated sites of modernity – the metropolis and the mature money economy – focuses upon the effects of their development for everyday experience and for our inner life. The two sites of modernity are both conceived as complex networks, webs and labyrinths of social interactions. Whereas the metropolis is, as it were, the point of *concentration* of modernity, the mature money economy (which also has its focal point in the metropolis) is responsible for the *diffusion* of modernity throughout society. Taken together, the two sites signify respectively the *intensification* and *extensification* of modernity.

On both sites, the acceleration and accentuation of long-term developmental tendencies manifest themselves. These are the increase in social differentiation (in part the result of an increased division of labour), the increase in functionalization of social relations, and the widening gap between subjective and objective culture (with reduced social space for the former and increased social space for the latter). The latter, to which we must return later, is summarised by Simmel as 'the atrophy of individual culture and the hypertrophy of objective culture'.[12] A concomitant feature of this process is the growing tendency for both the objective and the subjective culture to be autonomous spheres, the former possessing a 'unity and autonomous self-sufficiency' and the latter being created out of 'the subjectivism of modern times' with its impulse towards 'dissociation' and 'retreat' from objective culture. The reification of these two spheres can never be complete. Indeed, the interaction between objective and subjective culture is a major source of the fragmentation of individual experience in so far as the process of fragmentation present in objective culture permeates the subjective culture of individuals.

We could go further and suggest, as Simmel does, that there is a tendency, never fully completed, for the culture of human beings to become the culture of things. This tendency manifests itself both in the metropolis and the mature money economy. As such it constitutes an innovative dimension in social theory which examines both the cultural and aesthetic veil of the universe of things and the consequences for human 'inner life' of the development of cultural life within the context of a universe of things. Simmel explores in an imaginative manner the interface between human beings and the objects with which they are surrounded. In their often very different ways, the investigation of the culture of things is one of the important features to be found in the works of Lukács, Bloch, Kracauer, Benjamin and Adorno (and, of course, the first three were erstwhile students of Simmel).

Let us turn, first, to the objective culture of the metropolis, the showplace of modernity which extends its effects far into its hinterland. Within 'the genuine showplace of this culture' of objectified material entities and relationships, within the constantly changing, disintegrating and reconstituting social and cultural space of the metropolis, there are found the possibilities for an increase in 'the material enjoyment of life' resulting from 'the most developed economic division of labour'. The latter, most often located within the metropolis (and in this context we should not forget that Berlin by the turn of the century was the largest source of finished manufactured goods in Germany), 'has transformed the struggle with nature for livelihood into a struggle with other human beings for gain'.[13] This struggle manifests itself not merely within the sphere of production but also within those of circulation, exchange and consumption. Not surprisingly for a social theorist who asserts that 'exchange is a sociological phenomenon *sui generis*', it is these latter spheres that largely claim Simmel's attention, such as 'the motley disorder of metropolitan communication', the levelling effect of the money economy which 'dominates the metropolis', and the consequences of the creation of a 'mass' of consumers with its attendant 'fifty cents bazaar' and 'the production of cheap trash'. Similarly, with respect to the sphere of consumption, it should not be forgotten that the world of fashion is firmly located within the metropolis: 'In contrast to all narrower milieus, metropolitan centres become the nourishing ground of fashion'.[14] The metropolis is thus the focal point of the universe of things or artefacts created by human beings. It is the site at which 'life is made infinitely easy for the personality in that stimulations, interests, *fillings in of time and consciousness* are offered to it from all sides. They carry the person, as if in a stream, and one needs hardly to swim for oneself'.[15] Yet the very passivity which Simmel stresses here on the part of the individual consumer of things (commodities, distractions, amusements, etc.) already signifies one source of 'the atrophy of individual culture'. This is not the sphere of concrete action and creativity but rather of *passivity* and *adaptation*.

The structures which surround the individual in the metropolis are also not conducive to a fruitful interaction betwen the two. Rather,

> in buildings and educational institutions, in the wonders and comforts of space-conquering technology, in the formations of communal life and in the visible state institutions, there is offered such an overpowering wealth of crystallised, impersonalised mind, as it were, that the personality cannot maintain itself when confronted with it.[16]

This is the reified universe of objectifications of human activity which is matched by an equally estranged world of interaction, by reifications in motion, by the shocks of abstract confrontations. In the latter case, individuals must respond to the shock of 'the rapid and unbroken change in external and internal stimuli' experienced 'with every crossing of the street, with the speed and diversity of economic, professional and social life', as 'the rapid crowding of changing images, the sharp discontinuity in the grasp of a single glance, and the unexpectedness of onrushing impressions'.[17]

This 'particularly abstract existence' of the metropolis has one of its sources, of course, in the very complexity of the labyrinth of interactions themselves which require functionality, precise differentiation, intellectuality, exactitude and calculability – in fact the very features highlighted by Simmel as essential for the operations of the mature money economy. What appears to the individual as 'the tumult of the metropolis' with its myriad criss-crossing of abstract interactions and impressions and 'the brevity and infrequency of meetings which are allotted to each individual', in short what appears as a *chaos* of impressions and interactions, in fact results from the '*calculating exactness* of practical life' that is necessary in order that 'the agglomeration of so many persons with such differentiated interests' are able to 'intertwine with one another into a many-membered organism'.[18]

In this context, what is the nature of the forms of individuality created in the metropolitan setting? Simmel provides us with a typification of metropolitan individuality that results from 'the adaptations of the personality' to the objective culture of the metropolis. Its psychological foundation is 'the increase in nervous life' resulting from the bombardment of the senses by changing, dissociated, external stimuli. Protection against this 'uprootedness' from a stable relationship to the environment, and against the latter's 'discrepancies', is provided by the intellect, as the highest psychological organ, in the form of a defence mechanism, 'as a preservative of subjective life against the violent oppressions of the metropolis'.[19] The intellect creates a necessary distance, abstraction and inner barrier from 'the jostling crowdedness and the motley disorder of metropolitan communication'.[20] Its social counterpart is the predominance of intellectuality (including calculation) in the metropolis. Psychologically, its counterpart is neurasthenia (including nervous tensions unable to be released) and psychological distance. In turn, its pathological forms common to the metropolis are agoraphobia and hyperaesthesia. Socially, this distance takes the form of indifference, dissociation and the blasé attitude. The need for self-preservation in the metropolis can take the further form of an 'external reserve' towards others, producing an 'aversion', 'strangeness' and 'repulsion' which, in more extreme circumstances can 'break into hatred and struggle at the moment of a closer contact'.[21]

These are the 'elementary forms of socialisation' in the metropolis which are, as it were, the price that is paid for 'a kind and measure of personal freedom' that only exists in this location. But even this freedom has its obverse where, 'under particular circumstances, one nowhere feels so lonely and lost than in the metropolitan crowd. For here, as elsewhere, it is in no way necessary that human beings' freedom be reflected in their emotional life as a sense of well-being.'[22] However, for Simmel, there is no other psychological phenomenon which, above all others, is 'so unreservedly associated with the metropolis as the blasé attitude' which 'results first from the rapidly changing and closely compressed contrasting stimulations of the nerves', from 'a life in boundless pursuit of pleasure . . . [which] agitates the nerves to their strongest reactivity for such a long time that they finally cease to react at all', resulting in 'an incapacity to react to new sensations with the appropriate energy'.[23]

But, as Simmel constantly emphasises, the blasé attitude and those associated with the metropolis have their roots ultimately in the money economy whose focal point is the metropolis. What, then, of the objective culture of the mature money economy? Here too it is the alienated forms of existence that become the objective forms within which we exist. The sphere of *production* is no longer conducive to 'the harmonious growth of the self'; the 'subjective aura of the *product* also disappears' in mass production; 'subjectivity is destroyed and transposed into cool reserve and anonymous objectivity' in *exchange* relations; within the sphere of *consumption*, 'objects complete the final state of their separation from people. The slot machine is the ultimate example of the mechanical character of the modern economy.'[24] This objectified, reified world too presents itself to us 'at an ever increasing distance'. The barriers that we erect to protect ourselves from this world – the reserve, indifference and 'the specifically metropolitan excesses of aloofness, caprice and fastidiousness' – are ultimately ineffective against the experience of modernity as the discontinuity and disintegration of the modes of experiencing time, space and causality (including the teleology of means and ends).

Yet just as there is a tension in Simmel's account of modernity in the metropolis between rigid objectified forms on the one hand and the dynamic flux of relations within the metropolis on the other, so too in his delineation of the mature money economy, money features as both the reification of social relations of exchange and as the symbol of the dynamic flux of commodity circulation. Money as the universal equivalent is the universal nexus which links everything to everything else and which is the symbol for what holds society together, though in its reified form. The maturation of the money economy and its permeation of all spheres of life produces a seemingly autonomous world since money is

> the reification of the pure relationship between things as expressed in their economic motion. Money stands between the individual objects related to it, in a realm organised according to its own norms which is the objectification of the movements of balancing and exchange originally accomplished by the objects themselves.[25]

The apparently autonomous realm of circulation and exchange emerges out of the discontinuity of that which has been fragmented. Extreme differentiation produces the fragmentation of individuals; the commodification of everything produces a levelling of value and indifference to value; the destruction of the teleology of means and ends in the money economy results in the domination of the most indifferent means.

Of course, these developments constitute an essential dimension of *The Philosophy of Money* which, in each chapter, deals with a dichotomous aspect of the transformation of basic social relations by the money economy. Thus, the possibility of subjective and objective *value* is resolved in favour of a subjective theory of value, thereby arguably rendering value valueless and, at all events, relative; the discussion of value as *substance* is oriented towards its transformation into a relational concept in which substance is rendered insubstantial and money relations appear as the reification of exchange relations; money's effects upon the *teleology* of ends and means indicates the lengthening and widening of the teleological chain but only through the elevation of money to a pure instrument, to the most indifferent means (and an absolute end) and through the reduction of quality to quantity; individual *freedom* is enhanced by monetary relations but only at the price of the reduction of individual relations to functional relations (and thereby acting as a barrier to genuine individuality); *personal value* as actual and substantive is reduced in the money economy to money value or to labour value (as part of the explicit critique of Marx's labour theory); the *style of life* presents itself to us as an objective totality but is in fact composed of a fragmentary, fleeting universe of the world of circulation and exchange.

The universalization of monetary exchange coincides by implication with the universalization of commodity exchange and circulation and it is within this broader context that Simmel iluminates the transformation of modern experience and individuality. Also within this wider context – i.e. a philosophy of the commodity form and not merely of the universal equivalent – we can see that Simmel makes important contributions to the investigation of the phenomenal life of the commodity. These are apparent in his works from the mid-1890s onwards and include not merely his general discussion of money in modern culture (1896)[26] but also his contributions to the discussion of leisure and consumption, exhibitions, style and, of course, fashion. Two examples must suffice – exhibitions and fashion – to indicate the affinity between the commodity form and modernity.

Anticipating Walter Benjamin's later presentation of the phantasmagoria of commodities in world exhibitions, Simmel views such exhibitions in part as compensation for the tedium of one-sided participation in the production process. As a form of sociation and distraction, the plethora of concentrated exhibits 'produces a paralysis in the capacity for perception, a true hypnosis . . . in its fragmentation of weak impressions there remains in the memory the notion that one should be amused here',[27] amused and distracted by a 'wealth and colourfulness of over-hastened impressions [that] is appropriate to over-excited and exhausted nerves'.[28] Furthermore, such exhibitions reveal the fleeting life of the commodity in the transitory nature of the architectural forms that enclose them. There is an important aesthetic dimension to the mode of presentation of commodities in world exhibitions and the like which seeks to give the galaxy of commodities 'new aesthetic significance through the arrangement of their coming together – just as the ordinary advertisement has advanced to the art of posters'. The aesthetic veil or aura which surrounds the commodity is an essential stimulus to its circulation and is facilitated by what one might term the shop-window quality of things that is evoked by exhibitions. Commodity production . . . must lead to a situation of giving things an enticing external appearance over and above their usefulness . . . one must attempt to excite the interest of the buyer by means of the external attraction of the object.[29]

An associated process that also reveals the 'aesthetic super-additum' or the 'aesthetic productivity' of commodity presentation is present in the modern phenomenon of fashion which is closely tied to the production process. The circulation and exchange of commodities requires the production of an ever-new face of the commodity, an ever-new fashion that is absolutely present for the moment of appearance. The acceleration of commodity exchange requires the conscious production of ever-new faces for the commodity. The commodity clothed in the latest fashion cries out for its purchase *now*, in the present. Fashion, Simmel maintains, 'always stands at the watershed of the past and future and thus . . . gives us a strong sense of presentness as do few other phenomena'.[30] This accelerating ever-new and ever-transitory present that is a feature of fashion is succinctly summarised by Hauke Brunkhorst:

Fashion is the 'concentration of social consciousness upon the point', in which 'the seeds of its own death also lie'. Without an objective reason, a 'new entity' is 'suddenly' there, only to be instantly destroyed once more. Fashion is 'an aesthetic form of the drive to destruction', a totally 'present' 'break with the past'. In it, the 'fleeting and changeable elements of life' stand in place of the 'major, permanent, unquestioned convictions' that 'increasingly lose their force' in modernity.[31]

The complement to the 'feverish change' of fashion is that 'each individual fashion to a certain extent emerges *as if it wishes to live for eternity*'.[32]

Even this brief selection and indication of some of Simmel's illuminations of the modes of experiencing that which is new in modern society should enable us to delineate in a summary form the changes in modes of experience that constitute modernity. With some simplification, it is possible to view the experience of modernity as the discontinuous and fragmentary experience of time, space and causality as, respectively, transitory, fleeting and fortuitous. Such a preliminary delineation is to be found earlier in Baudelaire's definition of modernity. In Simmel's work, too, we find time experienced as an eternal present (fashion, the adventure) and emphasis upon the fleeting moment. Space is dealt with by Simmel in a complex manner involving both boundaries, distance and the removal of boundaries (the money nexus overcoming spatial boundaries). Conceptually, that which is associated with causality is transformed into the absence of historical necessity (Troeltsch argued that Simmel transformed 'history into a somewhat free game of fantasy. This was the most basic essence of modernity'[33]), the inversion of the teleology of means and ends (the universalization of money transactions in the exchange and circulation spheres destroys ends or purposes and creates the centrality of means and technique) and the centrality of the fortuitous on the surface of everyday life. Perhaps less persuasively, we can see as consequences of the mature money economy the disintegration of mass into indeterminacy, the concrete into the abstract and substance into fragments.

The implications of these modes of experiencing modernity for the individual are an increasing fragmentation of experience and, faced with the growing significance of the objective culture (with its dialectic of both increased differentiation and levelling), a tendency towards extreme subjectivism. Simmel viewed the currents of modern culture as moving in two contradictory directions: on the one hand, towards a levelling of individuals and values and the production of even more comprehensive social circles and, on the other, the development of the most individual aspects of the human subject. In the latter context, this does not coincide with the creation of greater possibilities for the expression of human individuality in a positive sense. Instead, Simmel refers time and time again to 'the exaggerated subjectivism of the times', to the fact that 'subjectivism and individuality have accelerated almost to breaking point'.[34] As such, he is referring to one side of the dialectic of subjective and objective culture, whose increasing separation from one another not only strains that dialectical relationship but also, for Simmel, constitutes, variously, a 'crisis of culture', a 'tragedy of culture' and even a 'pathology of culture' (in which there are some parallels with Durkheim's investigation of pathological forms of individualism which he terms 'excessive individualism').

This widening gap between an expanding objective culture and a putatively contracting or at least seriously compromised subjective culture becomes the foundation for a universal cultural theory of alienation in Simmel's later writings. The social space for the development of a genuine individuality is rendered problematic by virtue of the growing autonomy of the objective culture (increasingly viewed as domination by the technology of means and anticipating later cultural critiques of Horkheimer, Adorno and Marcuse) and the increasing subjectivism that dominates subjective culture either in the hope of individuals dissociating themselves from the objective culture (the internal retreat) or by recognizing the inevitability of the distance between the two spheres (the tragic vision). It is a conflict that is not readily resolved by Simmel since he has persuasively argued that the objective culture created by human subjects has not merely achieved a form of autonomy and self-sufficiency but has thoroughly penetrated the subjective culture itself. Indeed, Simmel at times failed to grasp the consequences of his own argument concerning the internalization of a reified culture in alienated forms of existence. Böhringer has recently summarised this unresolved problem as follows:

> Money . . . objectifies the 'style of life', forces metropolitan people into 'objectivity' 'indifference', 'intellectuality', 'lack of character', 'lack of quality'. Money socializes human beings as strangers . . . money also transforms human beings into *res absolutae*, into objects. Simmel's student, Georg Lukács, correctly noticed that this objectification (in his words: reification and alienation) did not remain external, cannot, as Simmel maintained, be the 'gatekeeper of the innermost elements', but rather itself becomes internalized.[35]

Certainly, on occasion, Simmel maintained that it was possible to erect barriers to the objectified world, as when he suggests that money's success in 'imposing a distance between ourselves and our purposes' creates a situation in which 'the individual mind can enrich the forms and contents of its own development only by *distancing* itself still further from that (objective) culture and developing its own at a much slower pace'.[36] Similarly, he speaks of the attempt 'under favourable circumstances, [to] secure an island of subjectivity, a secret, closed-off sphere of privacy'[37] as an objective possibility. How such an attempt can avoid being seriously compromised by the internalization of the features of the objective culture is unclear. Like many of his successors, Simmel views the aesthetic sphere as one source of reconciliation of these two cultural spheres. As early as 1895 Simmel was proclaiming that 'an essential element of any great art is that it unifies oppositions, undisturbed by the necessity of an either/or',[38] a feature which he later saw embodied in Rodin's work as the symbol of modernism. Outside the aesthetic sphere, and perhaps Simmel's individual law too, we have to recognize that 'personal development, although it pertains to the subject, can be reached only through the mediation of objects'.[39]

IV

Simmel's delineation of modernity focuses upon modes of experiencing the immediate present in modern society as differentiated and discontinuous. The two sites of modernity – the metropolis and the mature money economy – are both rooted in the exchange and circulation processes (of commodities, individuals, values, etc.). By reconstructing Simmel's social theory of modernity, we can reveal a constellation of themes in many of his writings which provides a new focus, a new interpretation of his work. This is important in at least two respects. First, our traditional conception of Simmel has been that of a formal sociologist who made a surprising number of contributions to a disparate range of themes in sociology. This conception is derived largely from those essays which constitute his major *Sociology* (1908): on the significance of number, conflict, domination, extension of the group, intersection of social circles, etc. Some of these have been operationalized and most have been viewed as his important contribution to fields of *micro-sociology*. In this respect, Simmel's sociology was incorporated into the corpus of North American sociology. (As an important aside, here, it should be pointed out that the significance of the fact that more items of his work were translated into Russian between 1893 and 1926 than into English in the same period has hardly been investigated.)[40] Second, if Simmel's theory of modernity was basically completed by the turn of the century and if it is embodied principally in his most systematic work *The Philosophy of Money* (1900; 1907),then what light does this work, and those surrounding it, throw upon this former interpretation? It suggests that Simmel did develop an important theory of *modern society* that is equally significant for understanding his sociological and social theoretical project. It suggests, further, that we view a substantial body of his work in social theory as being related to this wider thematic ensemble. This would include contributions to the sociology of experience (including the adventure, leisure experience), the stranger (and social distance), the intersection of social circles, the metropolis (and a wider sociology of space, as well as fashion and exhibitions), emotional life (greed, avarice, gratitude, shame), sociology of the senses, the aesthetics of modern life, and women and modernity (the women's movement, prostitution, female culture – and Simmel's argument that the *objective* culture is predominantly male).[41]

But alongside a new interpretation of Simmel's work (and its historical location), we can also indicate its relevance for contemporary themes in sociology and social theory. As a social theorist, philosopher and aesthete (in a positive sense), Simmel was intimately connected with and theoretically concerned with some of the avant-garde movements of his day. This makes his discussion of *modernity* in particular of striking relevance for debate on *postmodernity* today (in part as a result of common ancestry in Nietzchean themes). Even if it is maintained that postmodernity constitutes such a radical break with modernity that delineations of the latter no longer suffice for understanding postmodernity, we must still concede that Simmel opened up an analysis of modernity that was developed in different ways by his students and successors: by Lukács, Kracauer, Bloch (amongst his students) and by Benjamin and, more questionably, Adorno. Within the more restricted confines of sociology as an academic discipline, Simmel opened up specific areas of sociological analysis – often within the context of his theory of modernity – that are only now being fully developed. This is true of a sociology of spatial relations, leisure, the emotions and the aesthetics of modern life. Within his delineation of modernity, we should also emphasize his contribution to 'the culture of things', indeed to the modes of experiencing that which is new in modern society.

In fact, some recent work on 'the culture of things' and commodities has taken up a number of Simmel's insights, particularly in the field of anthropology. Thus, in a stimulating examination of the expansion of material culture and its consequences for the study of mass consumption, Daniel Miller argues that Simmel's work contains 'the most convincing analysis of modernity consistent with the concept of objectification' developed by the author.[42] As we shall see, the analysis of the relationship between 'the culture of things' and the sphere of consumption that is signalled by Simmel in various places constitutes further grounds for his relevance, not merely to a theory of modernity, but also to postmodernity.

5 Some economic aspects of *The Philosophy of Money*

He concludes with the style of life, whereas I conclude with the Austrian currency.

G. F. Knapp, 3 August 1906

The explanation of social formations is a task that the theory of value is no longer able to achieve with its means. Economic theory is certainly not capable of completely mastering this, rather only a theory of society which takes into account factors other than the merely economic.

Friedrich von Wieser, *Der Natuerliche Werth* (1889)

I

Anyone attempting to examine the economic foundations of *The Philosophy of Money* is immediately confronted with a number of difficulties. The first is Simmel's own disclaimer in the preface that 'not a single line of these investigations is meant to be a statement about economics'.[1] This statement is reinforced in the self-advertisement for the book when it first appeared in 1900. There, in its opening sentence, Simmel declares that it is 'a book, in which I attempt to indicate the intellectual foundations and the intellectual significance of economic life'.[2] Hence, it does not deal directly with economic theory *as such*. This reading is again confirmed in the 'Preface'. The economic phenomena of value, exchange, production and the like 'which economics views from one standpoint, are here viewed from another'. Simmel questions 'the apparent justification for regarding them simply as "economic facts" '.[3] As with other one-sided, discipline-specific treatments of phenomena so too, for instance,

the fact that two people exchange their products is by no means simply an economic fact. Such a fact – that is, one whose content would be exhausted in the image that economics presents of it – does not exist. Moreover, and just as legitimately, such an exchange can be treated as a *psychological fact*, or one that derives from *the history of morals*, or even as an *aesthetic fact*. Even when it is considered to be an economic fact, it does not reach the end of a cul-de-sac; rather, in this guise it becomes the object of philosophical study, which examines its preconditions in non-economic concepts and facts and its consequences for non-economic values and relationships.[4]

Simmel's approach to his subject matter is therefore not confined to a single disciplinary orientation; rather it is interdisciplinary.

The second problem, which Simmel himself has already intimated, is the nature of a 'philosophy' of money. His 'philosophy of money', as already indicated, examines both 'its preconditions in non-economic concepts and facts' and 'its consequences for non-economic values and relationships'. Therefore, Simmel asserts, 'if there is to be a philosophy of money, then it can only lie on *either side* of the economic science of money'.[5] The first part of the book examines the first side, the preconditions for the possibility of money, or, as Simmel puts it, money's relation to 'the conditions that determine its essence and the meaning of its existence'. The second part of the book deals with 'the historical phenomenon of money', which means for Simmel, largely though not exclusively, money's 'effects upon the inner world – upon the vitality of individuals, upon the linking of their fates, upon culture in general'. Hence, this treatment of money's relation to 'the developments and valuations of inner life stands just as far *behind* the economic science of money as the problem area of the first part of the book stood *before* it'.[6] It is the first part of the book, then, which should deal philosophically with the economic principles and presupposition of money and the second part with its effects. Though this is largely the case, the second part deals also with the labour theory of value (Chapter Five, Section Three) where Simmel claims that 'without pronouncing on which of the proposed unifications of value is the sole legitimate one, I wish to assert that *the labour theory of value is, at least philosophically, the most interesting theory*'.[7]

Simmel's preface to *The Philosophy of Money*, which is vital to an understanding of the volume as a whole, has thus indicated that we can examine exchange (and money exchange) as an *economic* phenomenon, as a *psychological* phenomenon, as an *ethical* phenomenon and as an *aesthetic* phenomenon, as well as, more generally, as a *historical* and, above all, as a *philosophical* phenomenon. Certainly, to

take but one of these aspects, there are at least forty places in the text
in which he deals with its *aesthetic* dimension. If we look back at the
history of this text, we find that the earliest indication of its
problematic is to be found in Simmel's 1889 essay 'On the Psychology
of Money'.[8] As late as June 1895, writing to Célestin Bouglé, Simmel
announces that 'at present I am working on a "Psychology of Money"
that will hopefully be completed by next year'.[9] The psychological,
ethical, aesthetic, historical and cultural dimensions of money are
presented in an overview in a lecture delivered in October 1896 to the
Society of Austrian Economists (whose potential audience would
include Carl Menger, Friedrich von Wieser and Eugen von Böhm-
Bawerk) entitled 'Money in Modern Culture'.[10] The first known
indication of a 'philosophy' of money is contained in a letter to Georg
Jellinek in June 1897 (to accompany an offprint of Simmel's article
'The Significance of Money for the Tempo of Life'[11]) which states: 'I
take the liberty of sending you here a work of mine that appeared
recently – an extract from a future "Philosophy of Money" '.[12]
Thereafter, the work was viewed by Simmel as a philosophy of money.

A third problem associated with an investigation of the economic
foundations of Simmel's text is highlighted in its first two chapters,
which contain the grounding of his discussion of exchange and money
exchange. A theory of exchange and of money's significance for
exchange would not be possible without a theory of value. It is,
therefore, with reflection upon theories of value that the text commences. In general terms, Simmel examines the interaction of subjective and objective theories of value. It is these two chapters – and
especially the first – which caused Simmel the greatest difficulty, a fact
that is indicated by a comparison of the 1900 and 1907 editions of *The
Philosophy of Money* which reveals the most substantial changes to
the text in these chapters.[13] The difficulties surrounding his theory of
value are also highlighted in his correspondence with Heinrich Rickert
during 1898. Simmel informs Rickert that work on his theory of value
is making him 'quite depressed', since, he says,

> I have reached a dead end in my work – in the theory of value! – and
> can progress neither forwards nor backwards. The concept of value
> seems to me to contain not merely the same *regressus in infinitum* as
> that of causality, but also in addition a *circulus vitiosus* because, if
> one follows the connections far enough, one always finds that the
> value of A is grounded in that of B or that of B only in that of A. I
> would already be quite satisfied with this and explain it as a basic
> form of representation, that cannot in fact be removed by logic – if it

were not for the fact, just as real, that absolute and objective values lay claim to recognition.[14]

Simmel goes on to indicate that he wishes to retain a relativist theory of value that can also solve the problems raised by absolute theories. The nature of Simmel's own theory will be examined below.

A further problem in Simmel's text, which is one associated with most of his other works, is that few authors are cited (with reference to economics, Adam Smith once, Proudhon once and Karl Marx four times) and there are no notes to the text. Existing correspondence, too, gives no indication of Simmel's sources. This means that Simmel's own work seems to provide us with no precise intimation of his knowledge of particular economic theories, apart from the important exception – the labour theory of value – which he explicitly names. Are there perhaps any clues to be found in the intersection of social and academic circles in which Simmel moved? Further, are there any clues to be gleaned from contemporary economists' reviews of *The Philosophy of Money*?

II

Simmel did not study economics at Berlin University but philosophy, history, *Völkerpsychologie*, ethnology and Italian. However, we know that one of his patrons at Berlin University, certainly until the turn of the century, was Gustav Schmoller, a leading member of the Historical School of economics. And Schmoller's review of *The Philosophy of Money* reveals that Simmel gave a lecture to Schmoller's seminar in May 1889 on the psychology of money, which Schmoller published in his *Jahrbuch* later that year.[15] Indeed, apart from *The Philosophy of Money* and earlier articles incorporated into the final work, the only piece which Simmel published directly on economics was a review of Schmoller's own work in 1900.[16] Simmel's early *Ueber sociale Differenzierung* appeared in 1890 in a series edited by Schmoller.[17] Therefore, it seems unlikely that Simmel was unacquainted with some of the writings of the Historical School, as reviewers of *The Philosophy of Money* occasionally detected.

Also in Berlin in the 1890s was the monetary economist Georg Friedrich Knapp with whom Simmel was acquainted, and who is reported to have described *The Philosophy of Money* as 'weavings of gold in the tapestry of life'.[18] In Knapp's foreword to his own *Staatliche Theorie des Geldes* (1905), he relates giving a series of lectures on the state and money in the winter semester of 1895. 'Soon afterwards', he continues, 'the sociologist Georg Simmel came forth with his *Philosophy of Money* . . . ; but this profound work does not really deal with money as such, but rather with the sociological side of the money economy'.[19] Yet Knapp is unlikely to have been a source for Simmel's theory of value, however much their functional theories of money have in common. The same may also be true of Simmel's long-time friend and sometime neighbour Ignaz Jastrow, editor of economic policy journals and certainly acquainted with contemporary debates in applied economics.[20]

More interesting is the origin of Simmel's knowledge of the labour theory of value that is subjected to acclaimed critique in *The Philosophy of Money*. The critique, and the work in general, is considered by Simmel to be part of his attempt to deepen historical materialism, though the latter is fundamentally criticized in the last chapter of the second, totally revised edition of *Problems of the Philosophy of History* (1905; first edition 1892).[21] However, we do know that Simmel not only published extensively in socialist journals and newspapers in the first half of the 1890s (including *Die neue Zeit* and *Vorwärts*) but also was acquainted with some of its intellectual circles in Berlin.[22]

When we turn to the reviews of *The Philosophy of Money* by economists, we find a somewhat disparate response, a response that is, in part, a manifestation of the heated debates in economics and political economy in this period. Do these reviews give any indication as to how Simmel's contemporaries viewed the economic foundations of *The Philosophy of Money*?

Schmoller's extensive review does not specifically highlight Simmel's contribution to economic theory, but rather draws out its cultural implications. Indeed, Schmoller is convinced that 'Simmel does not wish to deliver a new economic theory of money',[23] but rather in the first chapter presents 'the psychological principles of a theory of value that is characterized by the presentation of the process of the psychological objectivation of value conceptions', whilst in the second chapter 'the author's economic interpretation of money' is grounded in 'a developmental historical doctrine of money'.[24] In this respect, and despite specific criticism, Schmoller views Simmel's orientation as located in the tradition of the Historical School.

More negatively, Menger's review of *The Philosophy of Money* is highly critical of this position in economic theory. Indeed, Menger sees the work as suffering from

a fundamental defect. In this work, the author only focuses upon historical economics, whose insufficiency with regard to the needs of science and life . . . he correctly senses and, in part, clearly recognises. In contrast, in the sphere of economic theory, he appears to be insufficiently well orientated. Otherwise he could not overlook the fact that it does indeed belong to the tasks of economic theory and the theory of money to investigate the essence of money and its functions . . . A special philosophical analysis . . . is therefore not required.[25]

Menger is convinced that the results of such an analysis are already contained in economic theory itself.

A more positive and judicious examination of Simmel's economic theory is provided by George Herbert Mead's review.[26] Mead draws a contrast between 'the subjective world of impulse and feeling' that conditions our desire for objects and an objective world of values, 'of law and order in which alone "things" as distinct from feelings can exist. What gives them their character as "things" is their relation to each other abstracted from the impulses and feelings.' Hence, within this objective realm 'the essential relation . . . is exchangeability'. By focusing on value in exchange, Mead argues that Simmel's theory of value is decisively opposed to that of marginal utility theorists. Since, he argues,

utility . . . is a presupposition of all economic activity . . . it cannot be made the standard of value . . . The standard of value must be found in the objective equations between things that are exchanged in this economic world. This is a statement of interest in view of the futile character of the psychological calculations of the utilitarians, on the one hand, and the Austrian school, on the other.[27]

Furthermore, in contrast to Menger, Mead maintains that Simmel's study 'demonstrates . . . not only the legitimacy, but the value of approaching economic science from the philosophical standpoint'.

Other reviews of *The Philosophy of Money* by economists do not always reveal a great deal of information on Simmel's economic theory. Wilhelm Lexis, for example, whilst taking up Simmel's critique of 'labour money' and the labour theory of value, merely notes that his own theory of value 'remains . . . on the foundations of predominant doctrines'.[28] In a review of contemporary theories of value, von Bortkiewicz suggests parallels between Simmel's theory of value and that of Friedrich von Wieser.[29] And it is interesting to note here that Werner Sombart reviewed von Weiser's *Der natürliche*

Werth (1889) in the same volume of Schmoller's *Jahrbuch* in which Simmel's essay on the psychology of money appeared.[30]

If Mead's interpretation is broadly correct, then Simmel's theory of value and exchange cannot be readily identified with the marginalist school, however much there might exist affinities with the latter. Similarly, the reviews of *The Philosophy of Money* by contemporary socialists, such as Conrad Schmidt, do not see any obvious affinities between Simmel's economic theory and the labour theory of value of Marx. Taken together, contemporary reviews suggest an interpretation of Simmel's economics as located between those of Menger, on the one side, and Marx, on the other.

If we turn from actual reviews to more general discussions of the theories of value and money in contemporary economic literature, we find that although Simmel's work is occasionally mentioned, there is not infrequently ambiguity as to where his theory of money is to be located. In a survey of theories of money, Hoffman associates Simmel's theory of money with those who reject the autonomous value of money such as 'Hume and his followers and most recently Simmel', in which money 'exercises its function as a standard value'.[31] In a study of Adam Müller's theory of money (developed in the early nineteenth century), Stephinger traces Müller's influence in contemporary theories such as those of Brentano, Knapp, Sombart and Simmel, and states that 'some of Simmel's sociological viewpoints are in a certain sense anticipated by the reflections of Müller, who, through his basic formula of person-thing, emphasized the significance of the human factor over against that of objectification by the English economists'.[32] The strongest claims for Simmel's theory of money are made in surveys such as Döring's which refers to the 'pathbreaking' influence of Simmel's 'brilliant *Philosophy of Money*' – along with Knapp's *State Theory of Money* – in bringing out the importance of the insignificance of the substance of money for its essence. Döring goes on to argue that as a result of *The Philosophy of Money*

> a reference to Simmel is unavoidable because it, like only the *State Theory of Money* subsequently, has had a highly fruitful influence on views upon the nature of money. In the more philosophical reflection upon money, Simmel lays emphasis upon the transformation of money from a substance to a function . . . For him, modern transactions tend towards an exclusion of value as substance . . . Hence the *Philosophy of Money* and the *State Theory of Money* must be characterised as those theories of money that have the greatest influence upon all subsequent monetary theorists, insofar as

they view the function of money as independent from all monetary substance.[33]

The major influence here intimated by Döring is not necessarily reflected in subsequent developments in the economic theory of money. However, equally grand claims are made in a survey of money and value theories by Kiichiro Soda in his *Geld und Wert* (1924)[34] which commences with the judgement that 'in the realm of theories of money, German economics has three guiding lights: namely, Knies, Simmel and Knapp'.[35]

What all these reports and reviews by Simmel's contemporaries indicates is that all felt it necessary to engage critically with the economic theory expounded in *The Philosophy of Money* and that some saw Simmel as making an articulate contribution to a functional theory of money (which was elaborated roughly at the same time, in a more orthodox economic manner, by Knapp). More generally, despite Simmel's own disclaimer, most economist critics would concur with Altmann's view that 'if in the introduction to the work Simmel says that not a single line of the whole book should be interpreted economically, this can only mean that it should not be interpreted *merely* economically'.[36] This suggests that despite Simmel's argument to the contrary, we should re-examine the economic theory of value and exchange that is to be found in the early chapters of *The Philosophy of Money*.

III

A recent series of investigations of the social-philosophical foundations of economic action[37] has drawn attention to four dimensions of economic relations that implicitly or explicitly are contained in theories of economic action, value and exchange. The four dimensions can be viewed as relationships between, first, human beings and the cosmos (including nature); second, human beings and other human beings; third, human beings and things; and, finally, between things and things. The culmination of neo-classical economic theory is a concern with the thing–thing relationship, which permits rational calculation and mathematic presentation of economic outcomes, and is associated amongst other things with the law of indifference (Jevons). In other words, ultimately, 'the economic system is an analytical abstraction, an ideal thing–thing world'.[38]

The neo-classical theory of value formation, focusing as it does upon subjective value (the maximization of individual utilities), requires for its plausibility an array of assumptions concerning rational economic actors, today associated with rational choice models of human behaviour. To take but one of the neo-classical theorists, von Weiser, we find that 'whoever explains value in fact explains the behaviour of those who appreciate value'.[39] Similarly, for Menger, the value of a good is the significance that a particular good acquires for us. The value of goods is derived from the value of individual needs. To human beings originally only the human dimension was important. In contrast, however, things are originally indifferent for us and are only significant in so far as a relationship is observable between them and human interests. Indeed, our natural indifference to things is so great that it requires considerable coercion for us to view them as important. Goods that in themselves are indifferent acquire value from the value associated with their utility. The value of a good, although it has its origin in use, does not reflect that use. Therefore, we need to explain how quantities of utility are transformed into quantities of value. The marginalists view value as the calculatory form of utility, in an economic world in which 'the highest principle of all economy is utility'.[40] Still present in such theories of value is a distinction between use value and exchange value for individual economic actors. The use value of goods to be acquired will vary according to different amounts of individual need, whereas the exchange value of money will largely vary according to the amount of individual wealth possessed. Money is always valued *subjectively* for its exchange value; its exchange value is the anticipated use value of the things that can be acquired for money. But the early marginalists also had a conception of exchange value in an *objective* sense, a transactional value (*Verkehrswert*) in which *price* is decisive. To subjective value there corresponds a specific *feeling* dependent upon a satisfaction of needs by possession of goods, a definite level of interests; in contrast, to objective value there corresponds nothing but a definite price, a definite amount of payment. The *measure* of the former lies in the *levels of desire*, in the latter in *quantities of money*, in the figures of price sums. Price, for von Wieser, is a social fact, but one that does not indicate the social valuation of goods.

There are echoes of these rudimentary elements of a marginalist theory of value in Simmel's discussion in the first two chapters of *The Philosophy of Money*. But, as some reviewers detected, there is also present a *critique* of neo-classical theory, sometimes in an implicit form that raises a series of issues not dealt with by the marginalists. To be sure, there are present elements of a subjective theory of value but the radical consequences of economic exchange relations, the reification of social relations, the shift in focus from individual social *action* to *social interaction* (which is exchange) and to its reified form, money exchange, are also emphasized by Simmel.

Recalling the first dimension of economic relations, that between human beings and the cosmos, including nature, we find that Simmel commences *The Philosophy of Money* with an analysis of the universal significance of the value of objects. Valuation is 'the whole world viewed from a particular vantage point', the creation of a scale of value of objects 'from the highest, through indifference to negative values'.[41] The world of objects, 'the whole world', is being, is reality. There thus exist two realms, those of reality and value, in which 'reality and value are, as it were, *two different languages* by which the logically related contents of the world, valid in their ideal unity, are made comprehensible to the unitary soul'.[42] The 'language' of value within which Simmel's discourse on value is expressed is initially that of subjectivity. Value, for Simmel, 'is never a "quality" of the objects, but a judgement upon them which remains inherent in the subject', even though he recognizes that the concept of value cannot be sufficiently understood merely reference to the 'subject'.

However, when we examine Simmel's 'economic' theory of value, it is presented largely in terms of the human subject, albeit with reference to the subject's desire for objects. Thus, 'we *desire* objects only if they are not immediately given to us for our use and enjoyment; that is, to the extent that they resist our desire'.[43] It follows, therefore, that 'objects are not difficult to acquire because they are valuable, but we call those objects valuable that *resist* our desire to possess them'. Value 'is attributed to the objects of subjective desire'.[44] Value-formation develops through the '*distance* between the consumer and the cause of his enjoyment'. The distance between that which I desire and my own desire varies according to the amount of resistance and my ability to overcome it, just as desires themselves can be increasingly differentiated. Such variation and differentiation of value formation does not negate a central premise, namely that 'in the case of those objects whose valuation forms the basis of the economy, *value is the correlate of demand.* Just as the world of being is my representation, so *the world of value is my demand*'.[45] The satisfaction of demand, of desire, has a price which is sacrifice.

However, once we move away from the solipsistic presuppositions of a single subject and an economic object, we find that other subjects desire the same object, or that another consumer does not desire the object which I have on offer. The resolution and transcendence of subjective desires and demands is effected through *exchange*, where 'value becomes supra-subjective, supra-individual, yet without becoming an objective quality and reality of the things themselves'.[46]

Exchange is at the very heart of Simmel's economic theory of value. It is not merely that the process of exchange renders value 'supra-subjective, supra-individual'; rather, exchange is the realm of values 'more or less completely detached from the subjective–personal substructure'. The exchange of values appears to us as 'something objectively appropriate and law-determined', as 'an automatic mechanism', as 'an objective realm' in which an individual may participate only as 'a representative or executor of these determinants which lie outside himself'.[47] This world of semblances in the exchange process 'frees the objects from their bondage to the mere subjectivity' of individuals. Exchange as mediation creates 'an intermediate realm between *the desires that are the source of all human activity* and the satisfaction of needs in which they culminate'.[48] Simmel thus returns from the objective nature of equivalent exchange to 'the interchange between sacrifice and acquisition within the individual' which is 'the basic presupposition and, as it were, the essential substance of exchange between two people'. This is true for Simmel whether we are referring to a subsistence or a market economy. Hence, 'it is of great importance to reduce the economic process to *what really happens in the mind of each economic subject*'.[49] Such a reduction to subjective value creation enables Simmel to claim that

> exchange is just as productive and value-creating as is production itself. In both cases one is concerned with receiving goods for the price of other goods in exchange, in such a way that the final situation shows a surplus of satisfaction as compared with the situation before the action. We are unable to create either matter or force; we can only transfer those that are given in such a way that as many as possible rise from the realm of reality into the realm of values. This formal shift within the given material is accomplished by exchange between people as well as by the exchange with nature which we call production.[50]

It follows from this emphasis upon exchange as the key to value-creation that the economy itself is 'a special case of the general form of exchange – a surrender of something in order to gain something'.[51] The motive for exchange is the balance between subjective sacrifice and gain (satisfaction). Exchange as the source of value creation means that exchange is the economy, as when Simmel states 'exchange, i.e. the economy, is the source of economic values'.[52]

The marginalist theory of economics also focused upon the concepts of utility and scarcity and these too are dealt with by Simmel, and again from the standpoint of individual subjects. Initially, 'the first requirement for an economic object to exist, based on the disposition of the economic subject, is utility. To this scarcity must be added as a second determining factor if the object is to acquire a specific value'.[53] However, Simmel goes on to maintain that the concept of utility really means 'the desire for the object'. The focus upon subjective desires and the psychological processes associated with the act of equivalent exchange suggests to Simmel that the rational objective equivalence which we appear to see in exchange hides the fact that 'the exchange of possessions from purely subjective impulses has only later taught us the relative value of things'.[54] In this and other respects, Simmel is sceptical of the automatic association of economic relations with objectivity and equivalence as far as their origins is concerned.

There is a further, important respect in which Simmel challenges marginalist economic theory, namely in exploring the preconditions of exchange without making them a logical consequence of utility theory. For Simmel,

> exchange is a sociological phenomenon *sui generis*, an original form and function of social life. It is in no way a logical consequence of those qualitative and quantitative aspects of things that are called utility and scarcity, which acquire their significance for the process of valuation only when exchange is presupposed. If exchange . . . is precluded, then no degree of scarcity of the desired object can produce an economic value.[55]

Of course, exchange has much wider sociological implications for Simmel, in so far as it is viewed as a primary form of sociation, as an ideal form of sociation, as a feature of all social interactions, and, in money exchange, as the reification of economic relations.

However, it is not merely these sociological dimensions of exchange which the marginalist economic theorists would have looked askance at. In *The Philosophy of Money*, Simmel makes the link between exchange relations and money by means of a philosophical justification for a relativistic world view. Indeed, 'the concept of economic value . . . is . . . part of a theoretical world view, in terms of which the philosophical significance of money can be understood'.[56] That worldview is one of relativism: 'The fact that every conception is true only in relation to another one . . . indicates a relativism in our behaviour that also extends to other areas'.[57] This is true of the economic sphere in which 'the value of things, interpreted as their economic interaction, has its purest expression and embodiment in money'.[58] Money – as universal equivalent – possesses the ability 'to replace every specific economic value . . . because it is not connected with any of these values but only with the relations into which they may enter'.[59] Money is able to do this because it is interchangeable and lacking in quality. It is an indication of *the projection of a relationship into an object*, it is *a symbol of a relationship*.

When Simmel comes to discuss the significance of money in the exchange process, it is as if he moves from an earlier discourse (language) of marginal economic theory to a discourse that has more in common with Hegel (and Marx). In this discourse,

> money represents pure interaction in its purest form; it makes comprehensible the most abstract concept; it is an individual thing whose essential significance is to reach beyond individualities. Thus, money is the adequate expression of the relationship of human beings to the world, which can only be grasped in single and concrete instances, yet only really conceived when the singular becomes the embodiment of the living mental process which interweaves all singularities and, in this fashion, creates reality.[60]

The symbol of the particular and the universal is the symbol of the particular and the relative. Pure exchangeability is pure relativity. The value of objects in their exchangeability is

> a fact that Marx formulates as the elimination of use-value in favour of exchange value in a society based upon commodity production – but this development seems unable to reach its consummation. Only money . . . has attained this final stage; it is nothing but the pure form of exchangeability.[61]

As a pure form of exchangeability, money need not be embodied in a particular substance. Indeed, the second chapter of *The Philosophy of Money*, although entitled 'The Value of Money as Substance', is devoted to a critique of precisely the view indicated in its title and, as many of Simmel's contemporaries detected, seeks to demonstrate that the significance of money lies in its *function*.

Simmel provides an account of the shift from the intrinsic value of money to its functional and symbolic value that is both philosophical and historical. In doing so, he retains at times his subjective presuppositions, as when he argues that the 'scheme of the private economy of an individual is obviously not only an analogy of the general economy; its general application determines average prices. The continuous subjective balancing precipitates the objective relation between commodity and price.'[62] On other occasions and at various points in his argument, Simmel indicates much broader presuppositions for his orientation. Money is, on the one hand, part of the comprehensive development of dissolving substance into 'free-floating processes'. On the other hand, however, money

> has a special relationship with concrete values, as that which symbolizes them. Furthermore, money is influenced by the broad cultural trends, and it is at the same time an independent cause of these trends. We are interested in this interrelation here in so far as the form of money is determined by the conditions and needs of human society.[63]

This more dialectical form of argument can be seen in Simmel's discussion of the relationship between exchange and society, money and exchange, and, later, the relationship between means and ends, quantities and qualities. Further, the argument that forms of money are determined by social forms and, later, that forms of exchange determine social forms provides the basis for an implicit critique of marginalist economic theory and, in a sense, of much of Simmel's own early arguments on value with which he had so much difficulty. The richness of Simmel's text derives in part from such ambiguities and contradictions.

Simmel wishes to explore the social consequences of a developed exchange and money economy, thereby extending his focus 'beyond' economics. Indeed, he wishes to claim that economic phenomena must be examined sociologically. This is clearly already evident in the second chapter of *The Philosophy of Money* where he argues that

> the exchange of the products of labour, or of any other possessions, is obviously one of the purest and most primitive forms of human socialization; not in the sense that 'society' was already perfect and then brought about acts of exchange but, on the contrary, that exchange is one of the functions that creates . . . a society, in place of a mere collection of individuals.[64]

Exchange is then 'a form of sociation', 'the purest sociological occurrence'. Its reified form is money exchange, the replacement of human–human or human–thing relations with thing–thing relations. Money is 'the reified function of being exchanged'; it is 'the reification of the pure relationship between things expressed in their economic motion'; it 'stands . . . in a realm organized according to its own norms'; it is 'an absolute intermediary'. This mediation is, however, only possible on the basis of other social factors such as trust, embodied in guarantors, the largest of which is 'the central political power'. Indeed, 'the modern centralized state . . . came into being partly as a result of the prodigious growth of the money economy'.[65] Yet if its guarantors are socially and politically located, its *function* is not since it is 'the purest reification of means, a concrete instrument which is absolutely identical with its abstract concept; it is a pure instrument'.[66]

In subsequent arguments in *The Philosophy of Money*, Simmel seeks to demonstrate that the development of the money economy is associated with the development of specific personality types that culminate in the blasé person. In subtle ways, the money economy's extension is associated with the development of individual freedom as well as the relativization of all that is human. It would go far beyond present concerns to outline Simmel's contribution to a sociology of money. That contribution is summarized by Schmoller as a concern with

> the question as to what money and the money economy have made of the thoughts, feelings and intentions of individuals, of societal constellations of social, legal and economic institutions. His theme is the retroactive effect of the most important institution of the modern economy – money – upon all sides of life, of culture.[67]

In so doing, Simmel only partly follows the Historical School of economics with a detailed historical institutional analysis.[68] Rather, as another reviewer Rudolf Goldscheid detected, 'some passages of *The Philosophy of Money* read like a translation of Marx's economic discussions into the language of psychology'. But although the work 'forms a very interesting correlate to Marx's *Capital*' and although there are 'a multitude of very interesting parallels between Marx's theory of capitalism and Simmel's theories concerning the relativism of money . . . it is an error of Simmel's book that it confronts Marx too little'.[69]

There are indeed some affinities between parts of Simmel's economic analysis and that of Marx, most noticeably in the discussion of the consequences of the division of labour in the final chapter. On the one hand, there are close parallels with the discussion of 'Alienated Labour' in Marx's *Paris Manuscripts* whilst, on the other, the context for Simmel's discussion is a theory of culture. Further, apart from occasional reference to Marx's terminology in the course of the text, there is the critique of the labour theory of value contained in the last section of the fifth chapter, in which Simmel proclaims: 'I wish to assert that the labour theory of value is, at least philosophically, the most interesting theory'.[70] Earlier he had pointed out that the notion that 'the essential feature of value is the socially necessary labour time objectified in it has been used . . . to provide a measure of the deviation of value from price. But the concept of this uniform standard of value does not answer the question of how labour power itself became a value.'[71] For Simmel, this is only possible through exchange, 'by entering into a relation of sacrifice and gain'. Later, in a discussion of 'labour money' – itself the subject of critique by Marx – and, more generally the labour theory of value, Simmel questions the measurement of labour power solely in terms of units of simple labour power as an inappropriate reduction of all forms of labour to manual labour. Simmel calls for greater precision in the examination of what constitutes labour. More specifically, he argues that the value created by mental labour cannot be reduced to units of simple labour power or to money wages (rent for scarce skills is one marginalist alternative), and therefore suggests a search for a more comprehensive unit of labour. This problem is examined today in many debates on the nature of complex labour, and the distinction between abstract and concrete labour.

At a more general level, it is possible to argue that what Simmel focuses his attention upon in major sections of his work is the sphere of circulation and exchange of money and other commodities. In this respect, it has some affinities at least with sections of Marx's then unknown *Grundrisse* which is concerned with the significance of the sphere of circulation and exchange, as well as the excavation of 'the daily traffic of bourgeois life'. It is in this sphere of circulation and exchange that most of Simmel's analysis remains, with the advantage of a sociological, cultural and psychological exploration of some of the phenomenal forms in which capitalist society appears to us.

IV

Any attempt at an overview of Simmel's economic presuppositions in *The Philosophy of Money* must conclude that, as is so often the case in other areas of his work, the precise location of these assumptions is difficult to assess.[72] Simmel does commence his analysis of value formation with a series of assumptions that are indeed very similar to the marginal theorists of the last quarter of the nineteenth century: Menger, von Wieser, Walras, Jevons, etc. Stanley Jevons, for instance, defines economics in the following manner: 'Pleasure and pain are undoubtedly the ultimate objects of the calculus of economics. To satisfy our wants to the utmost with the least effort . . . in other words, *to maximize pleasure*, is the problem of economics'. A commodity is thus 'any object, substance, action or service, which can afford pleasure or ward off pain'.[73] Simmel too starts out with subjective demand, the search for satisfaction and the necessary sacrifices involved. Yet there is an important shift in marginal utility theory from its subjective, personal presuppositions to the measure of utility in exchange through a law of indifference. Again, to quote Jevons, a theory of exchange requires *the law of indifference*, which states that 'when two objects or commodities are subject to no important difference as regards the purpose in view, they will either of them be taken instead of the other with perfect indifference by a purchaser. Every such act of indifferent choice gives rise to an equation of degrees of utility, so that in this principle of indifference we have one of the central pivots of the theory.'[74] A further assumption made in marginalist theory is *the state of equilibrium*. Although, as Jevons says, 'the real condition of industry is one of *perpetual motion and change*', 'it is only as *a purely statical problem* that I can venture to treat the exchange',[75] in fact, to treat the ratio of exchange as *a differential coefficient*.

Despite commencing from marginalist assumptions, Simmel highlights different dimensions of the law of indifference, the state of equilibrium and differential coefficients. Simmel intimates that indifference to value and personality types associated with such indifference (especially the blasé personality) characterize the mature money economy. Second, unconcerned as he is with continuing the development of an 'economic' theory of exchange in later chapters of his study, Simmel highlights the world of circulation and exchange of commodities, money and people as one of dynamic flux, a relativistic world view in which there is no state of equilibrium. Finally, it is a presupposition of calculability that personal qualities are reduced to quantities; indeed, the reification of exchange relations as manifested in mature capitalist money exchange relations is a presupposition for calculation itself. The reification (*Versachlichung*) of social relations as relations between things with seemingly natural properties pinpoints a fundamental opposition in Simmel's work between personal character (*Persönlichkeit*) of relations and the thing-character (*Sachlichkeit*) of relations. A large part of Simmel's later analysis is concerned with the consequences of a shift from person–person or person–thing relations to thing–thing relations.

There is another way of looking at how Simmel goes beyond his initial marginalist assumptions. In the course of a recent study by Jean-Joseph Goux, *Symbolic Economies*,[76] the author examines the semiotics of value in the marginalist movement, 'which makes all economic value depend . . . upon the degree of anticipated satisfaction. Instead of adopting the perspective of laborious production, of servile negativity, . . . the marginalist takes the side of the desirous, *jouissant* consumer and evaluates all "goods" against the satisfaction expected.' The subjective and pyschological measures of value that are presupposed in this theory draw attention to the fact that 'the fields of political economy and psychoanalysis have in common a number of terms, if not concepts: demand, desire, investment, *jouissance*, consumption (*consomation*), and others'.[77] Simmel's analysis in *The Philosophy of Money* (although published in the same year as Freud's *Interpretation of Dreams*) and elsewhere does not go in the direction of psychoanalysis but rather a sociology and social psychology of emotional states, personality types and 'moral sentiments' associated with the mature money economy.

We have already indicated another deviation from marginalist assumptions in the emphasis Simmel places upon exchange not merely as an economic phenomenon but as 'a sociological phenomenon *sui generis*'. The concept of interaction or reciprocal effect (*Wechselwirkung*) lies at the centre of his social theory. It enables Simmel to develop a conception of society as a constellation of interactions, as dynamic, individual and supra-individual, as a system of internal relations. Such a conception contradicts the subjectivist presuppositions of marginalism, indeed of Simmel's own economic starting point in *The Philosophy of Money*. In this and other respects his work contains a sociological and philosophical critique of its own economic presuppositions.

In part, this tension within the economic theory of *The Philosophy of Money* derives from the author's 'basic intention' in this work 'to construct a new storey beneath historical materialism', not by the *rejection* of historical materialism but by a critical engagement with it and by preserving elements of its explanatory value. The 'infinite reciprocity' which Simmel posits between ideal and economic conditions means that 'every interpretation of an ideal structure by means of an economic structure must lead to the demand that the latter in turn be understood from more ideal depths, while for these depths themselves the general economic base has to be sought, and so on indefinitely'.[78]

6 Social space, the city and the metropolis

In any case, we moved house again on April 1st – I believe because the landlord wanted to raise the rent.

Hans Simmel

It is hardly possible to treat of the mental life of the metropolis in a sparser and more biased way than he [Simmel] did in his lecture of that title at the Gehe Foundation in Dresden.

Dietrich Schaefer

I

It has been the fate of many of Simmel's essays to lead a life of their own, far away from their original context. At the same time, other essays treating similar themes are often either not dealt with at all or are examined in completely different constellations. The present investigation seeks to bring together three complexes of work that are usually seen in isolation from one another. In some cases, they have hardly begun to be examined at all.

Simmel's contributions to a sociology of space have seldom been investigated in any detail, and have hardly ever been related to his more famous essay on the metropolis, despite the fact that the two essays which constitute his contribution to the *Soziologie* (1908) on 'The Sociology of Space' both appeared originally in 1903, the same year as the publication of 'The Metropolis and Mental Life' (more accurately 'Metropoles and Mental Life').[1] The two essays dealing with social space were entitled 'On Spatial Projections of Social Forms[2] and 'The Sociology of Space'.[3] In turn, Simmel's essay on the metropolis – described by Louis Wirth in his bibliography for Park and Burgess's influential volume *The City* (1925) as 'the most important single article on the city from the sociological standpoint[4] – has never been placed in the context of his other essays on cities, notably on Rome (1898),[5] Florence (1906)[6] and Venice (1907).[7] These three essays present a very different conception of the city and emphasize in particular its aesthetic dimensions.

The best known of all these essays is, of course, 'The Metropolis and Mental Life', often examined as a virtuoso piece of analysis. Many of its themes emerge out of *The Philosophy of Money* (1900) – especially the final chapter on 'The Style of Life' – and Simmel himself acknowledges this in his essay. The autonomous existence of the metropolis essay and the fact that Simmel spent most of his life in Berlin has also led to its obvious thematic identification with Berlin – and the only metropolis mentioned by Simmel in the essay is indeed Berlin, in the imaginary context of all its clocks telling different times. However, Simmel's first major essay which did not appear anonymously or under a pseudonym that explicitly names Berlin is his 'Berlin Trade Exhibition' (1896),[8] an essay which also introduces some themes that are developed in the later piece. Here, too, mention should be made of 'Berlin Art Letter' (1896),[9] which deals explicitly – though anonymously – with the Berlin National Gallery. There are also a number of other essays which take Berlin as their starting point (as in 'Infelices Possidentes'[10]) and others which, although they do not always explicitly mention Berlin, can be regarded as relating to the metropolis. This is also true of Simmel's opening remarks in 'The Philosophy of Landscape' (1910)[11] on the possibility of the metropolis as a landscape.

II

Before proceeding to an examination of Simmel's analyses of social space, the city and the metropolis, it may be fruitful to indicate his own experience of them. Simmel was born in 1858 'in the house that formed the north-west side of the intersection of the Leipzigerstrasse and Friedrichstrasse. Then still to the west of the old city centre, these two streets were later to become the most characteristic and important commercial streets; one could not, as it were, be 'even more' of a local of Berlin than when one was born [there]'.[12] Simmel was born at what was to become the point of intersection of the social circles of consumption and circulation. At all events, he remained in Berlin until, at the age of fifty-six, he finally secured in 1914 a chair of philosophy at Strasbourg University, a move which he always regretted. Shortly before leaving Berlin for Strasbourg he wrote that his home would always be 'Berlin, Westend'.

Simmel spent the majority of his life in one of the fastest growing cities in Germany after 1870. He experienced the elevation of Berlin from a city to a metropolis – symbolically identified with the Berlin Exhibition of 1896. By the turn of the century, Berlin's population was two million inhabitants. It was then and continued to be one of the centres of migration from Eastern Europe and later from Russia. The University of Berlin was already attracting large numbers of students from both Central Europe and Russia, as well as from North America.

Simmel himself became a significant figure in intellectual and cultural circles, certainly after 1900. Earlier, he went without question to its university where, from 1885 until 1914 he taught philosophy, sociology, aesthetics and social psychology. By the end of the first decade of the twentieth century, his lectures were attracting hundreds of students, often to the chagrin of many of his colleagues. At the same time, Simmel was himself at the intersection of a variety of intellectual circles in Berlin in which philosophers, artists, poets, economists and students might interact. It is not yet known whether he was ever a member of a political party, but in the early 1890s at least he also moved in socialist circles, publishing in their journals and attending their social gatherings.

It is clear from the extent of Simmel's interaction in a variety of cultural and intellectual circles that he was completely at home in the cosmopolitan intellectual environment of the West end of Berlin. Unlike many of his contemporaries who were not enamoured with cities – such as Tönnies who hated Berlin – Simmel identified with the intellectual circles in which he circulated. And in contrast to many of his contemporaries, he displayed little interest in attempts to escape metropolitan existence permanently, to artistic and other communal retreats in the countryside; Worpswede or Sils Maria were not for Simmel. Instead, he was thoroughly at one with a cosmopolitan, metropolitan, intellectual existence. His cultural milieux would include the Stefan George circle, the artistic circle of Reinhold and Sabine Lepsius, Rilke, Max Liebermann, Henry van de Velde, Harry Graf Kessler, the political circle around his sometime neighbour Ignaz Jastrow, self-created circles including his sometime favourite students, such as Georg Lukács, Ernst Bloch, Gertrud Kantorowicz, Margarete Susman, and so on.

Simmel's image of the metropolis is that of a web or network of intersecting spheres of the division of labour, distribution, communications, the money economy, commodity exchange, intellectual and cultural circles. What is largely absent from the image of the metropolis, viewed from its West end is its industrial dimension. What Simmel describes in his essay on the metropolis and elsewhere is the capital city, the focal point of the money economy, not the industrial city, which would have produced a very different conception of the metropolis. The capital city is the city of metropolitan culture, state bureaucracy and, in the case of Prussia, a substantial military presence, as well as its commercial interactions and social distractions. The Berlin of an expanding industrial economy, with often advanced industries, and with its industrial suburbs of Moabit and the like, is absent. It follows from this that what is also absent is a social class analysis of the metropolis, at least in the essay on the metropolis. Industrial conflict and the development of trades unions is present in other essays. In turn, what is also largely absent is the heavily contested public political space of the metropolis, which only receives occasional attention, for instance, in the essays on social space. An interesting exception is Simmel's extensive discussion of the emergent women's movement challenging the patriarchal domination of the public sphere.[13]

However, what makes Simmel's analysis of the metropolis so relevant to the study of modernity is its emphasis upon the sphere of circulation and exchange, not merely of money and commodities but also social groups and individuals, a dynamic intersection of social circles. This sphere of circulation and exchange is, however, a sphere in which value differences are often obscured, in which class divisions are rendered opaque and do not always immediately manifest themselves. Such a concentration might also make Simmel's discussion of the metropolis relevant to the delineation of postmodernity where, in some accounts, his essay is also referenced.

It should be emphasized here that under circulation should be subsumed not merely commodities but also individuals. Perhaps not untypically, Simmel himself circulated in Berlin as far as his residence was concerned. When his son Hans relates that 'we moved house again on April 1st', it was symptomatic of the Simmels' relatively frequent changes of residence. From Simmel's incomplete correspondence, we find the following addresses: Magdeburgerstrasse (1878); Landgrafenstrasse (1886); Kleiststrasse (1891); Lutherstrasse (1892); Wormserstrasse (1894); Lützowerplatz (1894); Hardenbergstrasse (1894); Lindenallee (1902); Nussbaumallee (1905); Königin-Elizabethstrasse (1911).

Also typical of Simmel's own circulation, and in keeping with the mores of the metropolitan bourgeois intelligentsia, was evidence of frequent travel, often abroad. Simmel's 'uncle' Julius Friedländer, between 1875 and 1887, was the owner of Schloss Königsegg on the island of Reichenau, Lake Constance, and the young Simmel spent many vacations there. Later, most summers and sometimes in the spring Simmel went to Switzerland or Italy. On at least one occasion, in 1898, he visited St Petersburg , and he made a number of trips to Paris (where he met Rodin), Prague, Vienna, and so on. Within Germany there were frequent visits to Heidelberg and the Max Weber family and their intellectual circle as well as to Frankfurt and Munich. Around the turn of the century, according to his son Hans, Simmel

> accepted ever more frequent invitations to give lectures in the most varied cities – single lectures or a series – sometimes in student circles, more often before a general audience. He greatly loved this activity of a 'wandering priest'. He found it exciting; on the return journey he sometimes already worked on his next lecture. He often said that, 'if one comes on a very short visit, whether one meets old friends or quite new people, they all seek to be very nice to one, they show one, as it were, their favourable side.[14]

Simmel's son's memoirs contain a wealth of references to his father's Berlin existence and some of his aphorisms. Still within the context of circulation, we find that one of the house removals was to the newer part of Berlin, Westend. Hans relates that,

> In the real 'old Westend' we found nothing suitable, but rather had to move into one of the newly built streets adjacent to it, where we again lived 'third floor', but this time with a lift – even though still without electric light because of the high price of electricity! We had an extensive view from the balcony of the apartment and, in addition, a better connection to the city, since the subway was only two minutes away. Here it occurs to me that my father once related a dream that is so absolutely typical of him that it is worth writing down. He said, 'I have dreamt that synthetic time has been discovered. At first, one could only produce it by the minute, just as one can also only produce artificial diamonds in very small crystals. Now, for instance, when one comes to the subway, and the train [Zug] wishes to depart at this very minute, then one takes one's time box [Zeitzeug] out and strikes a time match [Zeitholz] – one gains a minute and can still catch the train'.[15]

This constellation of the new Westend, to the north west of the extended Kurfürstendamm, with the new underground railway stations, the interaction of time and space, provides a minor instance, a snapshot, of Simmel's milieu.

Living in the relative security of Berlin's Westend, Simmel was able to point to the need for metropolitan people to create a distance between their inner selves and the tumult of impressions with which the city dweller is confronted. On a number of occasions, Simmel draws attention to the social distance that is preserved on public transport systems, a largely absent interaction – apart from glances – with adjacent passengers, perhaps made more striking by the rapidity and confined space of underground carriages. In his essays on social space, rather than the more famous essay on the metropolis, Simmel mentions the social space between social classes, the boundaries of social interaction. In his own interactions, Simmel occasionally was confronted with the need to create a distance, most notably in the attempt to shoot the young Simmel in 1886 by a recalcitrant tenant of one of his uncle's properties administered by Simmel. The tenant, being unable to pay rent arrears, 'pulled out a revolver from the pocket of his overcoat and, from a *distance* of only one pace, fired a shot at Simmel which missed him and then fired two further shots at Simmel who had turned to flee. One bullet pierced the latter's hat and grazed the head of the fleeing figure . . .'[16] Here, and perhaps subsequently, Simmel was made aware of the acute need for distance and the dangers attached to a mature money economy when circulation and exchange break down.

III

In 1903 Simmel published two articles on the sociology of space: 'The Sociology of Space' and 'On the Spatial Projections of Social Forms'. This second essay was reviewed by Emile Durkheim in *L'année sociologique*.[17] As was so often the case, Durkheim applauded Simmel's 'souplesse d'esprit' but, as was also not uncommon, castigated the lack of precision in his conceptualization. Indeed, Durkheim detected 'une elasticité excessive' in Simmel's use of concepts. As a cryptic conclusion to his review, Durkheim noted that the subject of the frontiers or borders between peoples discussed by Simmel had been dealt with more profoundly by the geographer Friedrich Ratzel in his *Politische Geographie*, 'which M. Simmel does not cite'.[18] Be that as it may, the two essays were reworked into a substantial chapter of Simmel's major *Soziologie* (1908), as simply 'The Sociology of Space', but accompanied by three revealing appendices on 'The Social Boundary', 'The Sociology of the Senses' and 'The Stranger'. All three analyse various spatial dimensions of social interaction, and, more specifically, forms of social *distance*, all involving forms of social, physical and psychological *differentiation*. It should again be noted that Simmel's essay 'The Stranger' has led a quasi-autonomous existence, divorced in many of its interpretations from the original context in which it appeared.

The two original essays on the sociology of space do not deal exclusively with social space in the metropolis. Rather, only occasionally is the metropolis touched upon. None the less, it is possible to draw out their relevance for the metropolis. The same is also true of the three appendices on the social boundary, the senses and the stranger. In none of these cases is the metropolis a central focus of attention. Indeed, Simmel's sociology of space can be understood in a different context, as part of his incomplete study of the formal preconditions for human sociation that would include space but also time, mass, number, etc.

'The Sociology of Space' and 'On the Spatial projections of Social Forms' examine respectively 'the significance which the spatial preconditions of a sociation possess for its other determination and developments from a sociological perspective'[19] and 'the effect which the spatial determinations of a group experience through its social forms and energies'.[20] Of the two essays, the first is probably of greater significance. The interaction of human beings is experienced as different ways of filling in space. Thus, Kant's definition of space as the possibility of being together *(Beisammkeit)* does not exclude other possibilities in human sociation. However, in order to examine the social preconditions for sociation more closely, Simmel concentrates attention upon some basic qualities – five in all – of spatial forms that are confronted in social interaction. These comprise the exclusiveness or uniqueness of space, the boundaries of space, the fixing of social forms in space, spatial proximity and distance and the movement of space. Hence, what Simmel wishes to demonstrate is that it is social interaction which makes what was previously empty and negative into something meaningful for us. Sociation fills in space.

Every part of space possesses an *exclusiveness* or uniqueness. Particular social formations may be identified with particular spaces, such as states or districts of cities, although in different ways. The interaction between individuals and groups in states is closely identified with a specifically demarcated territory, whereas the city's 'sphere of significance and influence' extends in various differentiated functional 'waves' – economic, cultural, political – into the hinterland. Indeed, within the city there has often been a functional rather than a quantitative filling out of space, as in the medieval city with its differentiated guilds or corporations.

Space possesses, too, the characteristic that it may be *broken into pieces* and subdivided for our purposes. In other words, it can be *framed in by boundaries*. Here Simmel specifically draws upon the analogy with the picture frame in so far as framing has a similar significance for social groups as for works of art. Spatial framing has a wider importance that Simmel does not draw out, namely in our constitution of social experience. None the less, he does indicate that a society, and forms of sociation, possess a sharply demarcated existential space in which the extensiveness of space coincides with the intensity of social relationships. This is in contrast to nature where the setting of boundaries appears arbitrary. The social boundary, however, constitutes a unique interaction in so far as each element affects the other by setting a boundary but without wishing to extend the effects to the other element. Hence, 'the boundary is not a spatial fact with sociological consequences but a sociological fact that is formed spatially'.

Therefore, the sociological boundary signifies a quite unique inter-action, in which what is significant is the interactions woven on either side of the boundary. In contrast to forms of boundary maintenance, both political and social, Simmel draws out the relationship in the city between the impulsiveness of crowds in open spaces that gives them a sense of freedom and the tension of a crowd in an enclosed space. The indeterminacy of boundaries may also be seen in the spatial frame-work of darkness, in which the narrowness and breadth of the framework merge together to provide scope for fantasy – a not insignificant theme in the literary genres of the thriller and detective novel.

A third spatial feature in social formations is the capacity for *fixing or localizing of social interaction in space*. Here Simmel indicates four possibilities. First, the existence of a continuum from the completely local binding together of individuals (as in the medieval town) to a situation of complete freedom. Second, the fixing of a social form at a focal point, as in economic transactions (though Simmel points out that this derives not from the substantive immobility of a particular place but from the functions connected with the place). Third, the bringing together of otherwise independent elements around a particular space (the religious community's focus around the church). Here, Simmel draws attention to the rendezvous whose sociological significance 'lies, on the one hand, in the tension between the punctuality and fleeting nature of the occurrence, and its spatio-temporal fixing on the other'. The rendezvous also indicates that human memory is stronger on space than on time. Finally, the individualizing of place is a significant urban development (from the earlier naming of houses to their numbering and, in the Enlightenment period, occasionally the numbering and lettering of streets).

The relationships between *proximity and distance* constitute the fourth dimension of social space. It would be possible to grade all social interactions on a scale of proximity or distance. In the metropolis it is distance, abstraction and indifference to those who are spatially adjacent, as well as close relationships to the spatially distant that are typical. The latter is a product of intellectuality which makes possible proximity to what is most remote and 'cool and often alienated objectivity between the closest individuals'. It is at this point that Simmel introduces his excursus on the sociology of the senses in his *Soziologie*, on seeing as 'perhaps the most immediate and purest reciprocal relationship that exists', and on hearing and smell, which 'remains trapped, as it were, in the human subject'.

The final dimension of space that Simmel examines is the possibility of *changing locations*. Whole groups can move their spatial determinants as in nomadic societies, but so also can individuals with particular functions (itinerant justices) or merely travellers (and here Simmel points to the temporary intimacy of interaction between travellers temporarily abstracted from their normal milieu). What Simmel does not draw attention to, but which was a marked feature of Berlin, is the substantial migration of groups to the metropolitan centre from the east. This fifth dimension is also the context in Simmel's *Soziologie* for his excursus on 'The Stranger' which opens with its spatial referent: 'If wandering, considered as a state of detachment from every given point in space, is the conceptual opposite of attachment to any point, then the sociological form of "the stranger" presents the synthesis, as it were, of both these properties . . . another indication that spatial relations are not only determining conditions of relationships among people, but are also symbolic of those relationships'.[21]

Simmel's 'On the Spatial Projections of Social Forms' examines the spatial effects and forms that emerge *through* the process of interaction itself. Here he highlights four typical spatial formations arising out of social forms themselves. These are, first, the structuring of space according to the principles of political and economic organization; second, local structure arising out of relationships of domination; third, fixed localities as the expression of social bonds (i.e. social units located in spatial forms such as the family, the club, the regiment and the trade union all have their 'house'); and, finally, empty space as the expression of neutrality, the 'no-man's land' of state borders and, more recently, of metropolitan areas.

In one of the few studies of social space in Simmel's work, Elizabeth Kornau[22] points to the disparate nature of his material and conceptualization, but also to the general thesis contained within Simmel's analysis of 'a progressive historical development towards forms of social organization increasingly detached from space'.[23] More specifically, 'space as the basis of social organization (principle of locality) signifies a stage of development that emerges between particularistic (principle of affinity) and modern (money economy) techniques of organization and domination'.[24] The development of the mature money economy results in a progressive emancipation from space. Communication techniques (e.g. the telegraph in the nineteenth century) enable spatial differences to be overcome by time. Kornau suggests that in so far as Simmel's analysis indicates the development of social formations increasingly organized according to purely rational principles (the means–ends rationality teleology), this shifts attention away from the issue of spatial location. Where this has become a more generalized thesis in social theory, it may account for the neglect of social space as a central issue. However, the past decade has surely indicated a transformation of this situation with a wealth of new studies of social space, studies that seldom refer to Simmel's early work on space.[25]

IV

The notions of distance and boundaries are important in any sociology of space. Social distance is a phenomenon of particular significance for Simmel. As Donald Levine has commented,

> nearly all of the social processes and social types treated by Simmel may be readily understood in terms of social distance. Domination and subordination, the aristocrat and the bourgeois, have to do with relations defined in terms of 'above' and 'below'. Secrecy, arbitration, the poor person, and the stranger are some of the topics related to the inside–outside dimension.[26]

We might add that forms of social distance are all the more evident where we exist in close proximity to one another. This is probably nowhere more true than in metropolitan existence.

However, we can also create a distance between ourselves and the metropolis in a number of ways. The notion of the inward retreat can take on a spatial dimension in the form of the bourgeois *interieur*; its private dimension might take the form of the salon, its quasi-public form that of café society. In a more complex manner, we can seemingly simultaneously participate and distance ourselves (although the emphasis might be on distance rather than participation), as in the figure and activity of the flâneur. In this context, Benjamin spoke of 'the flâneur who goes botanizing on the asphalt' (where the flâneur is a kind of collector of images, impressions and experiences that are subject to classification). Baudelaire spoke of the observer, the flâneur, as 'a prince who is everywhere in possession of his *incognito*'. The combination of the preservation of an *incognito* and, at the same time, the botanizing activity of a collector of vignettes and possibly much else, could, as Benjamin suggests, ensure that the flâneur 'can be turned into an unwilling detective', one who 'only seems to be indolent for behind this indolence there is the watchfulness of an observer'.[27] This might be a description of the role of a certain kind of sociologist or ethnographer, whose activity oscillates between apparent 'indolence' and 'watchfulness'. If we concur with such a characterization, we might say that whereas 'in the flâneur the joy of watching is triumphant', the results of such observations must be given a systematic form that is informed by theoretical presuppositions in order to render them sociological. In a number of respects, Simmel as an acute observer of the delicate invisible threads' of social interaction might be characterized as a sociological flâneur.[28]

Certainly we can see the detached but sensitive observer at work indicated by some of Simmel's lighter pieces for *Jugend*: 'Snapshots *sub specie aeternitatis*'. The German word current in Simmel's time for the snapshot, *Momentbild*, better captures the act of distancing ourselves momentarily from reality in order to capture a fleeting image of it for all time. Benjamin later described the activity of taking momentary images: 'A touch of the finger now sufficed to fix an event for an unlimited period of time. The camera gave the moment a posthumous shock, as it were.[29] Such a characterization must be qualified in Simmel's case given his somewhat negative response to photography. The impressionist image may be more appropriate. Simmel's essay on the picture frame suggests another analogy, that of giving a *frame* to fleeting interactions, of tearing them momentarily from a particular context. This suggests that Simmel seeks to preserve what is unique and transitory whilst simultaneously extracting from it its essential *form*, its typicality.

All this is an indication of the significance of the aesthetic dimension in Simmel's work. As he suggests in his essay 'Sociological Aesthetics', our appreciation of an object 'becomes aesthetic only as a result of increasing *distance*, *abstraction* and *sublimination*'. We can create a distance between ourselves and the metropolis by travelling to distant *landscapes*. But as Simmel maintains in his essay 'Alpine Journeys',[30] the power of the metropolis and indeed of capitalism also extends to the Alps and transforms our relationship to nature as a 'framed' landscape. The aesthetic distance implicit in the framed landscapes of experience in mass tourism are themselves aesthetic, even if merely sublime.

Such reflections may provide us with a context for the reflections of Simmel's own travel to distant cities, to Rome, Florence and Venice. They are certainly not those of the mass tourist but rather are framed by conceptions of the Italian landscape informed by travellers since Goethe's Italian aesthetic frames. Simmel's own reflections upon these cities are dramatically different from his analyses of the tumult of the metropolis, from 'the economic jungle of the metropolis'.

'Rome: an aesthetic analysis' was published in 1898.[31] It is worth noting from the outset that no such essay by Simmel exists for Berlin . Within Simmel's own milieu, however, we could point to two such essays on the aesthetic attractions of Berlin. In 1899 there appeared anonymously in *Die Zukunft*, a journal to which Simmel frequently contributed and which was edited by Maximilian Harden, an article entitled 'The Most Beautiful City in the World', whose opening section, comparing first images of London, Paris, New York and Berlin, was subtitled 'Snapshots' [*Momentbilder*].[32] Its author, Walter Rathenau, whose later works displayed the influence of Simmel, examined in a somewhat ironical manner the possibilities for Berlin as a beautiful cityscape. The second example is a longer essay, published in 1908, five years after Simmel's own metropolis essay, by August Endell, art nouveau architect and designer, entitled 'The Beauty of the Big City'.[33] It is devoted to Berlin as a big city and presents in an impressionist manner the aesthetic beauty of the metropolis. We can return later to the possibilities for Berlin as an aesthetic landscape as far as Simmel was concerned.

For the moment, what is significant is that Simmel's essay on Rome, like those on Florence and Venice, is concerned with various forms of aesthetic experience of classical Italian cities. In the essay on Rome a prominent theme is how *beauty* can emerge out of the coming together of seemingly diverse and perhaps indifferent elements. In nature, 'the mechanical fortuitousness of whose elements can form into beauty as into ugliness', can be a complement to the work of art which brings fortuitous elements together into an aesthetic totality. However, Simmel argues, in addition to nature and works of art as aesthetic objects, very seldom we confront a third: that works of human beings, created for whatever diverse purposes of life, are, over and above this to be found together in the form of beauty, so *fortuitously* in their combination as little directed by a will to beauty as are natural forms that know nothing of any purposes. It is almost always only old cities, that have developed without a preconceived plan.[34]

It is these old cities that have achieved such an aesthetic form. And the emphasis in Simmel's account is upon the fortuitousness of their creation; 'the reconciled distance between the *fortuitousness* of the parts and the aesthetic sense of the whole' is the source of their aesthetic attraction.

What we are confronted with here (and this is also true for the analyses of Florence and Venice) is the aestheticization of a feature of modernity – fortuitousness – that transcends the contradictions of modernity. In the essay on Rome, Simmel contrasts ancient and modern Rome in the following manner: 'I may leave the parts of Rome that are of uninterrupted modernity and equally uninterrupted ugliness totally aside; for happily they seldom confront the stranger who takes care'.[35] Such advice seems to complement that of Baedeker guides and corresponds with a comment made by Simmel on a holiday in 1917 which he describes as 'totally away from the railway and other such culture'. Rome exists in the aesthetic frame of antiquity and classical forms.

Florence (1906) is the city which most successfuly unifies the opposition between nature and intellect, a reconciliation of human artistic design with nature. The city in this resolution is a renaissance work of art, an aesthetic totality of these two elements. In Venice (1907) it is the architectural façades, with their 'precious game', their 'veil', that are dominant. It is 'the artificial city', full of façades in front of which individuals traverse as if on a stage. It is a city of two-dimensional surfaces in which everything moves at the same speed and rhythm. This gives our experience of it a 'dream-like' character. It possesses 'the ambiguous beauty of the adventure that swims rootlessly in life'.[36]

Although Simmel's account of Venice lays emphasis upon human artifice, it remains true that in none of these instances of classical cities viewed from the perspective of the sensitive aesthetic observer is there real contact with modernity. Simmel's aesthetic analyses of Rome, Florence and Venice raise the question as to whether the metropolis, the showplace of modernity, can, by virtue of being a *show*place itself, be aesthetically attractive. Can the metropolis be a landscape, an aesthetic cityscape? All avant-garde modernist movements since Baudelaire's declaration of the shocking beauty of the ugly metropolis have answered in the affirmative. Simmel's answer is more ambiguous. If we take his distinction between the work of art and the applied arts, in which the former is something for itself and the latter something for us, then the metropolis is something for us. It is our creation, however much it' may appear to us as an endless labyrinth whose elements are always in motion. In his essay 'The Philosophy of Landscape' (1910),[37] Simmel indicates a contrast between nature and the metropolis. With respect to elements of nature, he maintains that the fact 'that these things observable upon a piece of earth are "nature" – and not lines of streets with department stores and automobiles, this does not yet make this piece of earth into a landscape'.[38] A piece of nature, Simmel continues, is an internal contradiction, since nature can have no 'pieces'. By implication, the metropolis does have 'pieces' – of architecture, moving traffic, interactions, etc. But if the metropolis is not a landscape – or as Benjamin put it, a cityscape – it may still possess aesthetic attraction. Simmel's emphasis upon the metropolis as the focal point of the complex web or labyrinth of interactions that make up the sphere of circulation and exchange of commodities and individuals can also be viewed as a source of the sublime aesthetic experience. Webs and labyrinths are themselves both spatial and aesthetic forms. There is also another aesthetic dimension in the metropolis. The aesthetic experiences of interaction, symmetry, frames, etc. confront us every day in the metropolis, often in *forms* that we ourselves create. It may be that we do not notice them. But one of the tasks of Simmel's social analysis is surely to *reveal* the *forms* of social interaction, in the metropolis as elsewhere.

V

Let us turn, then, to Simmel's analysis of the Berlin metropolis. 'The Metropolis and Mental Life' was published in a volume of the Gehe Foundation's proceedings in Dresden in 1903. The immediate context of this essay on the metropolis was a series of lectures given in the winter of 1902–3 in connection with an exhibition on the modern metropolis in Dresden. Among other contributors to the volume in which Simmel's essay appears were Karl Bücher (the economic historian and author of *Arbeit und Rhythmus* which Simmel drew upon in the last section of *The Philosophy of Money*), Friedrich Ratzel (the geographer who, Durkheim argued, was an unacknowledged source for some of Simmel's reflections on social space), Dietrich Schäfer, and others. Five years after this volume was published, Schäfer, a historian, was the author of a completely negative, conservative, antisemitic, anonymous reference for Simmel in connection with his unsuccessful attempt to secure the second chair of philosophy at Heidelberg University in 1908. Castigating Simmel for putting '"society" in the place of state and church as the decisive organ of human coexistence', and for much else, Schäfer hardly 'comes away with much of permanent value from Simmel's writings (in so far as they have become familiar to me). It is hardly possible to treat the mental life of the metropolis in a sparser and more biased way than he did in his lecture of that title at the Gehe Foundation in Dresden.'[39] Presumably Simmel's analysis of metropolitan 'society' was devoid of references to church and state. At all events, even Simmel's reflections upon the metropolis proved to be as dangerous as some of his experiences of it.

The Dresden exhibition on the modern metropolis was significant in that it gave a positive impetus to further examination of a whole range of dimensions of modern metropolitan existence as well as the physical conditions of major cities in Germany. As Howard Woodhead informs us, in a detailed four-part survey of the 1903 Dresden exhibition published in the *American Journal of Sociology*[40] in the following year, it was the first German municipal exhibition of its kind. It covered metropolitan traffic, streets, railways; metropolitan expansion of worker and suburban housing; metropolitan public charities, welfare institutions and employment offices; metropolitan public health; education; metropolitan cultural facilities; and so on.

This positive public exhibition of the problems of metropolitan urban existence is in marked contrast to the long-established traditions of cultural pessimism associated with urban life in Germany.[41] The city as the source of all social problems, the site of 'society', in contrast to small town and rural existence was already a common theme in German literature and had taken on in rudimentary form some of the ideological dimensions that were to be capitalized upon subsequently by Nazi ideology. Simmel's essay on the metropolis also stands in dramatic contrast to such illusions of a questionable *Gemeinschaft* existence. In Simmel's essay there is no negative contrast with past forms of existence; metropolitan life is our present and future.

When we turn to Simmel's analysis we find that, in contrast to his formal treatment of social space, the essay-lecture on the metropolis is animated by an immediacy that is lacking in his spatial analysis. None the less, within this context we can see that the city is 'not a spatial entity with sociological consequences, but a sociological entity that is formed spatially'. The metropolis is not merely the focal point of social differentiation and complex of social networks – a theme in Simmel's work at least since 1890 and his study of social differentiation – but also the location of indefinite collectivities such as crowds. The city's openness, which provides for the intersection of diverse social strata, contrasts with the relative isolation and social distance that is manifested in the 'concentrated minority' of the ghetto. Hence, the spatial constellations of the metropolis also provide for the possibility of total indifference to one's fellow human beings. The development of boundaries and social distance in the metropolis is of fundamental significance in understanding patterns of social interaction and network in the city. Important too is the transcendence of such boundaries and distance in so far as the metropolis is the focal point of the mature money economy whose functional specialization enables it to transcend its own physical location and creates a distinctive kind of trans-spatial community. Money does facilitate 'an interaction and therefore a unification of people who, because of their spatial, social, personal and other discrepancies in interests, could not possibly be integrated into any other group formation'.[42] Yet, as David Harvey comments in this connection, it is also true that,

> by the same token, money creates an enormous capacity to concentrate social power in space, for unlike other use values it can be accumulated at a particular place without restraint. And these immense concentrations of social power can be put to work to realize massive but localized transformations of nature, the construction of built environments, and the like.[43]

It is indeed one of the virtues of Harvey's more recent analyses of urbanization that he draws upon both Simmel and Marx in order to bring together time, space and the money economy. As he persuasively argues, 'the very existence of money as a mediator of commodity exchange radically transforms and fixes the meanings of space and time in social life and defines limits and imposes necessities upon the shape and form of urbanization'.[44] Yet for all the plausibility of such arguments, this is not quite the focus of Simmel's essay on the metropolis, however much Simmel maintains that the origin of many of the features of metropolitan existence can be traced back to the money economy.

In *The Philosophy of Money*, Simmel makes a passing reference to 'the economic jungle of the metropolis'. In his essay on the metropolis, the connections between the money economy and the metropolis are developed more fully. The metropolis as 'the seat of the money economy' is dominated by 'the multiplicity and concentration of economic exchange'. The preponderance of exchange values negates 'the individuality of phenomena' and focuses upon 'the objective measurable achievement'. It follows that production is overwhelmingly for the market, the money economy having 'displaced the last survivals of domestic production and the direct barter of goods' by production 'for entirely unknown purchasers who never personally enter the producer's actual field of vision'.[45]

The metropolis is thus not merely the focal point of the money economy but also 'of the highest economic division of labour', with a huge diversity of specialized products and services. The metropolis is the site of antagonistic competition and specialization of function, of 'an inter-human struggle for gain'. In turn this is associated with the creation of ever-new needs:

> The seller must always seek to call forth new and differentiated needs of the enticed customer. In order to find a source of income which is not yet exhausted, and to find a function which cannot readily be displaced, it is necessary to specialize in one's services. This process promotes differentiation, refinement, and the enrichment of the public's needs, which obviously must lead to growing personal differences within this public.[46]

The extent of the division of labour in the metropolis therefore is associated with increasing differentiation of products, functions, individuals and their tastes. Such differentiation and diversity call for the emergence of distinctive occupations whose function is to act as mediators. Indeed, Nietzsche maintained that the domination of the mediator (*Vermittler*) was one of the primary characteristics of modernity.

The increasing differentiation requires a highly developed system of distribution and communications. The complexity of interactions of all kinds in the metropolis are such that

> without the strictest punctuality in promises and services the whole structure would break down into an inextricable chaos . . . this necessity is brought about by the aggregation of so many people with such differentiated interests who must integrate their relations and activities into a highly complex organism.[47]

The result is that 'punctuality, calculability, exactness are forced upon life by the complexity and extension of metropolitan existence'.

Viewed in this way, the metropolis is the focal point of the division of labour, distribution, communications, the money economy, commodity exchange and consumption. It is a huge network of interactions, and not merely economic ones. The main focus of Simmel's essay is, however, upon the subjective consequences of metropolitan existence. The economic characteristics of the metropolis outlined above call forth important phenomena that transform individual experience. They can be summarized as intellectual rationality, calculability, indifference, objectivity, anonymity and levelling. However, we should not imagine that individuals fully integrate themselves into the phemonena of the 'supra-individual contents of life' which confront them in the metropolis. It is true that the individual appears overwhelmed by the culture of things, by 'the rapid crowding of changing images, the sharp discontinuity in the grasp of a single glance, and the unexpectedness of onrushing impressions'. The urban individual response is the development of the protective organ of the intellect, of intellectuality in order 'to preserve subjective life against the overwhelming power of metropolitan life'. The particular form of intellectuality appropriate to metropolitan existence is one which reacts with indifference to external shocks and a whole field of possible interactions. This indifference manifests itself in the personality type of the blasé person who experiences 'the meaning and differing value of things . . . as insubstantial'. A levelling of our experience goes along with this process. The economic interactions in the metropolis, for their part, require precision and calculability, a regard to the functions of other participants, who may well remain anonymous. The protective mechanism of reserve in social interaction can lead to aversion and hostility. As Simmel suggests, 'dissociation' is an elementary form of sociation; we relate to one another as strangers – 'lonely and lost . . . in the metropolitan crowd'.

There are other responses to metropolitan existence which Simmel draws attention to in various places. A dedication to fashion, for instance, is concentrated in the metropolis. It can be seen as a reaction against indifference and levelling, an assertion of subjectivity.[48] So too can personal extravagances and eccentricities, not merely in Dandyism but in the accentuation of personal foibles. A subjective response to which Simmel refers in another context is the interest in spiritualism for instance, as a counter-explanatory world view to the scientific, calculating and objective world view.[49] More positively, and despite the concentration of the culture of things and our distance from an expanding objective culture, Simmel sees the metropolis as providing the social space for the development of individual independence and individuality.

If we return to the connection between this essay and Berlin then we can concur with the recent judgement relating to discussion of images of Berlin that 'Simmel was interested in Germany's metropolis not primarily as the location of political decision, not as the national centre, but as the exemplary location of the development of diversity and contradiction, as the place where a new "quantity of conscious- ness" and a new "rhythm of sensual–intellectual life" emerged'.[50] It was precisely such a neglect of the national and political and emphasis upon the cosmopolitan that conservatives such as Schäfer found so intolerable.

IV

Simmel's interest in the city has been examined at three different levels: most abstractly and formally in the work towards a sociology of space, aesthetically with respect to his treatment of Rome, Florence and Italy, and finally as the labyrinth of modernity that is also the centre of the culture of indifference. In the discussions of social space and the metropolis the dialectics of differentiation are much in evidence. Differentiation is a central theme of Simmel's social theory; it is also often taken to be a vital feature of modernity. Simmel's treatment of differentiation in this context is one which is not especially concerned with social class differentiation or the differentia- tion of public and private space. In the analysis of the metropolis, the *destruction* of social space, highlighted in Benjamin's[51] or Harvey's[52] studies of Paris in the nineteenth century, is absent from Simmel's discussion. The massive rebuilding of Berlin in order to create one of the most highly developed public transport networks in Europe is not part of Simmel's focus, even though that which the new communica- tions system facilitated, the rapid circulation of commodities and individuals, is surely one of the key features of *The Philosophy of Money*. Similarly, the correlation of metropolitan existence and the sphere of circulation and exchange does not necessarily lead directly to an examination of social class differentiation in an urban context.

The metropolis as a labyrinth, a web that extends its functional effects into the hinterland, is highlighted by Simmel. Yet the essays on the Italian cities give few indications of the dialectical relationship between the metropolis and the transformation of natural settings, though Simmel's early discussion of the Alps does precisely that. Indeed, if the metropolis is a focal point of the culture of things, cities in their classical form, where the fortuitous is a virtue, are viewed from an aesthetic distance. These cities do constitute a landscape, whereas in the hectic of metropolitan existence 'what we survey with a glance or within a momentary horizon is not yet landscape but rather, at most, the material for it'.[53]

7 Leisure and modernity

> The mere possibility of happiness, even if its realization is sparse
> and fragmentary in actual life, englobes our existence in light.
>
> Georg Simmel, *Schopenhauer and Nietzsche*

> Just as it has been said that the history of women has the peculiar
> characteristic that it is not the history of women but of men, so one
> can say that, viewed more closely, the history of recreations, of play,
> of enjoyments is the history of work and of the serious side of life.
>
> Georg Simmel, 'Infelices possidentes'

I

In the late nineteenth century, the theme of consumption can be
detected as of growing importance in a number of areas. In literature,
the commodification of aesthetic activities had already been dramatically problematized in Charles Baudelaire's confrontation with the
search for a market for his poetry, as Walter Benjamin was to argue in
the following century.[1] Later, the more recent theme of mass consumption was strikingly portrayed by Emile Zola, most noticeably in
his literary treatment of the advent of mass consumption heralded by
the development of the department store and the mass article in his
novel *The Ladies' Paradise*.[2] Indeed, Zola highlighted the pathological
form of unregulated desires in his presentation of kleptomania, a
theme which should have been of importance to Emile Durkheim in
his pathology of modernity.[3] As Rosalind Williams has shown in
Dream Worlds,[4] mass consumption was indeed a significant theme in
French social theory in the closing decades of the nineteenth century,
for Durkheim, Gabriel Tarde and others. At the very close of the
century, consumption is dealt with in a critical manner by one of
America's early critical social theorists, Thorstein Veblen in his
Theory of the Leisure Class (1899).[5] There, Veblen introduces a

significant definition of leisure related to consumption as an activity which 'does not connote indolence or quiescence. What it connotes is *non-productive consumption of time.* Time is consumed non-productively (1) from a sense of the unworthiness of productive work, and (2) as an evidence of pecuniary ability to afford a life of idleness.'[6] Such 'non-productive consumption of time' indicates both a critical stance *vis-à-vis* classical political economy and, with its emphasis upon 'consumption' rather than 'use' of time, some accord with the concerns of the economists who had heralded the 'marginalist revolution' in their discipline. That revolution in the 1870s had signalled a shift of interest from production to consumption, to the economic subject's search for the maximization of satisfaction in the realization of consumer demand.

The theme of consumption is also central to the social theory of modernity outlined in various places by Simmel. For Simmel, however, the satisfaction derived from consumption is always seriously qualified. Modern consumption takes place in a context in which we can *consume* any *thing*. It is a constituent element of what he describes in *The Philosophy of Money* and elsewhere as 'the culture of things'. As such, it is not necessarily associated with satisfaction of desires. If we examine Simmel's scattered investigations of leisure, we find that in all cases it is ultimately associated with consumption. Leisure is associated with the *possession* of things, with having rather than doing. It is also often identified with *escape*. If it is true that those who nowadays emphasize the everyday world as central sometimes fall into the error of viewing it as a closed, mundane universe, then Simmel's investigations of leisure point to the significance of the motif of the attempt to escape from the mundane everyday world, whether it be through sociability, adventure (including amorous adventure), travel and fashionability.

II

It should not surprise us that Simmel, one of the first sociological analysts of modernity and metropolitan experience, should also have concerned himself in direct and roundabout ways with the problem of modern leisure. This is not least because his social theory, grounded in the study of forms of social interaction or sociation, enabled him to view society as the totality of social interactions, as a complex web of interrelationships and social interactions, within which one could legitimately focus on any interaction, however fleeting and insignificant, and both arrive at its connection with any other interaction and view it as the locus of the meaning of the totality of interactions.[7] Simmel's aesthetic sensitivity to the tempo, rhythm and symmetry of social interactions, so distinctive a feature of much of his sociological writings – especially after his seminal article, 'Sociological Aesthetics' (1896)[8] – suggests the influence of an aesthetic distance which he himself practised in some of his writings. Was it perhaps part of the psychological defence mechanisms with which he argued metropolitan dwellers should go armed in order to withstand the tumultuous shocks of endlessly new impressions and encounters in big-city life? Certainly leisure is often seen as an escape, a distancing, either physical, social, mental or aesthetic, from the demands of external life, or as Simmel would have it, from the growing objective culture. But Simmel was a sufficiently astute social theorist to recognize that this did not mean that leisure was therefore to be located solely in what he termed subjective culture, that realm wherein genuine individuality might still be created in a context of growing materialism and individualism. The organization of leisure, however individual its form, was also permeated by the objective, material culture, by the social. Indeed, as we shall see, one of the most universal forms of leisure – sociability itself and conversation – was viewed by Simmel not merely as 'the play form of society' but also as a pure form of what he understood to be society.

Indeed, as with many of the themes of Simmel's reflections, it is impossible to view them as detached from his own activities and experiences. From what we know of Simmel's life, his own leisure activities at first sight reflect those of certain strata of the Berlin bourgeois intelligentsia at the turn of the century. In Berlin itself, Simmel valued the institutional arrangements for sociability that were soon to become anachronistic: the intellectual salons. But even here one should be careful to distinguish 'the intersecting of social circles'. When Simmel himself had become established as a leading intellectual figure after the turn of the century, the 'salons' conducted in his own home might contain figures from a variety of spheres: philosophers, poets, artists (Stefan George, Heinrich Rickert, Martin Buber, Paul Ernst, Rilke), and so on.[9] At the Simmel family's weekly 'jours', Simmel's favourite students might be in attendance, so that these 'jours' took on the atmosphere of a 'Privatisimum'.[10] But earlier in his career, in the early 1890s, Simmel probably also attended the so-called 'Red Salon' of Leo Arons – an active socialist academic dismissed from Berlin University who was also a developer of neon (whose shrill light was to illuminate the showplaces of modernity a few decades later) – where he would have come into contact with Mehring,

Kautsky and other such 'dangerous' figures.[11] Much later in his life, Simmel's own thirst for sociability was reflected in arrangements to meet and converse with friends even for an hour at railway stations and elsewhere, even in the darkened days of the First World War.

The latter suggests that Simmel was prepared to travel to meet his friends. Certainly Simmel and his wife Gertrud would visit the Webers in Heidelberg and mix with their social and intellectual circle. But even when he was academically established, Simmel did not always attend academic congresses. Perhaps his appearance to give the opening address to the first meeting of the German Sociologial Association in Frankfurt in 1910 on 'The Sociology of Sociability' was an exception.[12] Maybe that fusion of leisure and work, signalled even in its title, was too uncomfortable to be often repeated. More typical of Simmel's activities was his summer travel; for instance, in his early years, until 1887, Simmel went to work on his writing at one of his uncle's residences on the Reichenau on Lake Constance. In keeping with his strong aesthetic interests, Simmel visited art exhibitions (the subject of one of his essays, examined later in this chapter) and trade exhibitions (another theme examined in this chapter) in Berlin. In 1902, Simmel travelled to the Rodin exhibition in Prague, and in 1905 went to Paris to visit Rodin himself. His vignettes of the Alps, Rome, Florence and Venice indicate the activities of an extensive railway traveller, accompanied sometimes by his family or students such as Ernst Bloch (to Florence) or Margarete Susman. Occasionally, these visits prompted another of Simmel's leisure activities: the writing of poems, aphorisms and 'snapshots' (with intriguing titles such as 'The Metaphysics of Laziness' or 'Money Alone Doesn't Make You Happy') which usually appeared in the leading German *Jugendstil* journal, *Jugend,* and included one of his longest poems 'Autumn on the Rhine' (1897).[13]

But however compelling Simmel's aesthetic interests may have been – he was also a collector of Japanese vases at the turn of the century – and however widely he travelled to attractive rural or urban settings, his interests remained those of a cosmopolitan urban intellectual. Unlike Tönnies, for instance, who hated cities and above all Berlin, Simmel was completely at home in his native city.[14] When he was finally appointed to a chair of philosophy at Strasbourg University in 1914, he very soon felt the loss of the metropolitan context for his work. And that metropolitan context was for Simmel a crucial source of the modern search for new leisure forms, of the thirst for ever-new excitements.

III

The social space of the metropolis might well constitute a starting point for an examination of Simmel's treatment of leisure. It is both the source of the metropolitan personality type and the focal point of the money economy and the modern division of labour in production and consumption. For Simmel, the metropolis is the showplace of modernity, extending its effects – like the money economy itself, which also symbolizes the complex networks of interaction in the spheres of circulation and exchange – far into the hinterland. Indeed, the metropolis and the mature money economy together constitute a central constellation within which we can understand Simmel's reflections upon leisure.

The metropolis is 'the genuine showplace of this culture' of objectified material entities, of objective culture which Simmel saw as having advanced so rapidly in the later decades of the nineteenth century. In turn, this is related to the phenomenal growth of Berlin following German unification. Yet this complex network and labyrinth of social interactions within the ever-changing, disintegrating and reconstituting social space of the metropolis, facilitating as it does an increase in 'the material enjoyment of life', also requires the creation of new responses by human beings to the complexities of functional differentiation, to 'the most advanced economic division of labour', to the levelling effect of the money economy which 'dominates the metropolis' and, above all, to 'the tumult of the metropolis', to 'the jostling crowdedness', to 'the motley disorder of metropolitan communication'.

As 'seats of the most developed economic division of labour', in which 'city life has transformed the struggle with nature for livelihood into a struggle with other human beings for gain, which is here not granted by nature but by human beings',[15] metropolitan centres are sites of production as well as of consumption, circulation and exchange. It should be noted here that Berlin as a site of production is absent from Simmel's analysis of the metropolis. At the turn of the century, Berlin was the largest production site of finished goods in Germany, and was a centre of new industries such as electronics. Elsewhere, in a manner sometimes reminiscent of the early Marx, Simmel argues that modern production is not the site of creativity, of individuality, of pleasure. Indeed, the personality of the individual worker 'often even becomes stunted' through its fragmented specialization. The separation of the worker from the means of production and from work activity itself 'as purely objective and autonomous' indicates that 'labour now shares the same character, mode of valuation and fate with all other commodities'.[16] Since Simmel was more interested in the circulation, exchange and consumption dimensions, it is legitimate to inquire whether the sphere of consumption was any more satisfying.

The sphere of consumption and the circulation of individuals as customers or as commodities is also concentrated in the metropolis. The sphere of non-work, ostensibly that of leisure, can also be filled out by consumption and by circulation in search of what is new. Where a 'mass' of consumers has been created, commodities can be sold for their price rather than their quality. Simmel sees this as the attraction of 'the "fifty cents bazaar" ', as part of the cycle of 'the production of cheap trash', and in turn 'a broadening of consumption [which] corresponds to the specialisation of production'.[17]

The other dimension of mass consumption to which Simmel indirectly draws attention is the creation of customers' needs, since

> the seller must always seek to call forth new and differentiated needs of the enticed customer. In order to find a source of income which is not yet exhausted, and to find a function which cannot readily be displaced, it is necessary to specialise in one's services. This process promotes differentiation, refinement and the enrichment of the public's needs.[18]

It is a process which does not necessarily enrich the individual. At first sight, it seems as if, in the metropolis, 'life is made infinitely easy for the personality in that stimulations, interests, *fillings in of time and consciousness [Ausfüllungen von Zeit und Bewusstsein]* are offered to it from all sides. They carry the person, *as if in a stream*, and one needs hardly to swim for oneself.'[19] Today, we would wish to say, too, that we enter the sphere of consumption as if in a dream. Yet such passivity on the part of the individual consumer indicates 'the atrophy of individual culture through the hypertrophy of objective culture'.

What does this signify? Simmel indicates a whole range of areas of economic and social life in which subjectivity is threatened: *production* is not the sphere of 'the harmonious growth of the self'; the 'subjective aura of the *product* also disappears' in mass production; in *exchange* relations, 'subjectivity is destroyed and transposed into cool reserve and anonymous objectivity'; in the sphere of *consumption*, 'by their independent, impersonal mobility, objects complete the final stage of their separation from people. The slot machine is the ultimate example of the mechanical character of the modern economy'; as part of 'the objectivity of the *life-style*' of the modern metropolis, 'the externalities of life . . . confront us as autonomous objects' and the objectification process 'invades even the more intimate aspects of our daily life'.[20] This objectified, reified world presents itself to us 'at an ever-increasing distance'.

Not surprisingly, the impact of this reified world of the metropolis and the money economy upon individuals is all the greater because human subjects are themselves compelled to respond to their 'particularly abstract existence' only by attempting to distance themselves from it (as we shall see, individuals in fact take this existence with them). Above all, they must respond to the shock of 'the rapid and unbroken change in external and internal stimuli' that is experienced 'with every crossing of the street, with the speed and diversity of economic, professional and social life', as 'the rapid crowding of changing images, the sharp discontinuity in the grasp of a single glance, and the unexpectedness of onrushing impressions'.[21] This accounts, Simmel argues, for the 'increase in nervous life', the neurasthenia of modern human beings, including its pathological forms of agoraphobia and hyperaesthesia, and the 'psychological distance' created by the intellect as a defence mechanism for the emotions against the endless shock experience of urban existence. Similarly, the heightening of intellectual defence mechanisms is matched by an acceleration and heightening of emotional responses that remain unsatisfied by the 'stimulations, interests, fillings-in of time and consciousness' that are offered. The permanent 'feeling of tension, expectation and unreleased intense desires', the 'secret restlessness' results in our endless neurotic search for

> momentary satisfaction in ever-new stimulations, sensations and external activities . . . we become entangled in the instability and helplessness that manifests itself as the tumult of the metropolis, as the mania for travelling, as the wild pursuit of competition and as the typical modern disloyalty with regard to taste, style, opinions and personal relationships.[22]

By implication, then, 'the inner barrier . . . between people . . . that is indispensable for the modern form of life', 'the mutual reserve and indifference', 'the specifically metropolitan excesses of aloofness, caprice and fastidiousness' are ultimately ineffective against the experience of modernity as the discontinuity and disintegration of the modes of experiencing time, space and causality (including the teleology of means and ends). Alienated forms of existence become the objective forms within which we exist.

The most typical form of existence, 'unreservedly associated with the metropolis' and the mature money economy dominated by commodity circulation and exchange, is that which is dominated by the blasé attitude resulting from 'the rapidly changing and closely compressed contrasting stimulations of the nerves' and culminating in 'an incapacity to react to new sensations with the appropriate energy'. Where individuals themselves circulate as commodities and where all values have been reduced to exchange values, the blasé individual 'experiences all things as being of an equally dull and grey hue, as not worth getting excited about'.[23] This does not remove the thirst for more amusement and excitement since it has not been satisfied. Hence, 'the craving today for excitement, for extreme impressions, for the greatest speed in its change . . . for "stimulation" as such in impressions, relationships and information – without thinking it important for us to find out why these stimulate us'.[24]

It is against this background that we can now examine those 'fillings-in of time and consciousness' that ostensibly lie outside the sphere of work and constitute 'leisure'. Where the stimulations and distractions of leisure are directly located in the sphere of the consumption of commodities – and Simmel already posited the extension of commodification to the personal sphere, to the sale of 'experiences' as commodities – it is difficult to see how they can rise beyond this sphere and contribute to the realization of the elusive creative subjectivity and individuality which Simmel sought. And, as we shall see, even when the stimulations and distractions of leisure seemed to be distanced from this sphere, it was not always the case that they were truly satisfying as far as the promulgation of subjective culture was concerned.

Since Simmel produced no elaborate treatise on leisure, what is offered in the first case is a series of vignettes illustrating the phenomenal life of the commodity in the consumption sphere: the pursuit of fashion (the commodity's new face), places of entertainment or enjoyment (*Vergnügungstätten*) and prostitution, the exhibition of aesthetic and commercial commodities (art exhibitions and trade exhibitions). As instances of those forms of leisure activity which are apparently distanced from the commodity sphere, Simmel offers us sociability and the adventure.

IV

The 'immense abundance . . . of machines, products and supra-individual organisations of contemporary culture' offers us 'endless habits, endless distractions and endless superficial needs'.[25]

Individuals, however, wish to assert their individuality and differentiation, to set themselves apart from the mass, whilst at the same time adhering to the style of life of their social group. Following fashion may also be seen as offering a qualified form of resistance to the 'trite everyday world', most dramatically in Dandyism.[26] Simmel sees this tension between differentiation and imitation in the pursuit of fashion and style. The 'individualistic fragmentation' typical of modernity requires its counterpart in the homogeneity of fashions and styles. But one feature of adherence to fashion in contemporary society, as an instance of the filling-in of time and consciousness, is the increasing rapidity of the 'turnover-time' of fashions themselves, a reflection of 'the specific "impatient" tempo of modern life', of the breaking-up of the rhythm of life into ever-shorter fragments:

> The fact that fashion takes on an unprecedented upper hand in contemporary culture – breaking into hitherto untouched areas, becoming more obsessive in existing ones, i.e. incessantly increasing the speed of changes in fashion – is merely the coalescing of a contemporary psychological trait. Our internal rhythm requires increasingly shorter pauses in the change of impressions; or, expressed differently, the accent of attraction is transferred to an increasing extent from its substantive centre to its starting and finishing points.[27]

Fashion is then an instance of the transitory pursuit which 'gives us such a strong sense of presentness' but is at the same time a reflection of 'the fleeting and changeable elements of life'. Its dedicated followers are those individuals 'who are inwardly lacking in independence and needing support', who use fashion as a means of expressing their absent individuality and content. And although 'each individual fashion to a certain extent emerges as if it wishes to live for eternity', its 'illusory nature' manifests itself in the rapidity with which each fashion disappears. Yet the 'seed of death' that is contained in fashion's moment of appearance is not some autonomous, organic process but rather arises out of the process of the production and circulation of commodities, in which 'articles' are produced for the express purpose of being fashionable. At certain intervals of time, 'a new fashion is required a priori and now there exist creators and industries which exclusively carry out this task'.[28]

New fashions for old distractions and stimulations constitute an essential part of leisure-time consumption. In 1893 (under the pseudonym of Paul Liesegang), Simmel published a short essay entitled 'Infelices possidentes' (Unhappy Dwellers)[29] which reflects upon Berlin

'places of entertainment' (*Vergnügungstätten*), devoted to 'the titilla-
tion of the senses and intoxication of the nerves'. The entertainment
which they provide must stimulate the nerves: 'It requires glamour for
the eyes, in which the establishments breathlessly excel in providing,
while the bourgeois sits by and waits, with the ease of the spectator at
the gladiators' match or of the owner of a harem, to see which of his
slaves to pleasure amuses him the most and, at the same time, makes
him the most comfortable.' Such entertainment as is offered requires
both 'the removal of any deeper content' and that everything remain
on the level of superficiality. This amusement or play is the obverse of
the 'dreadful, shocking, tragic' nature of modern life. If modern
human beings are pushed to and fro 'between the passion to gain
everything and the fear of losing everything' in 'the feverish pursuit of
daily labours', then 'what does the evening look like?'

> What inner forces still remain after the day has used up what was
> available in activity, tension and concentration? . . . Because every-
> day life has completely exhausted the individual's energy, only that
> may be offered to the individual as relaxation which lays claim to
> absolutely no energy for its assimilation; the nerves, exhausted by
> the bustle and anxiety of the day, no longer react any more to
> stimulations, except to those which are, as it were, directly
> physiological, to which the organism itself still responds if all its
> sensitivities have been blunted: the attractions of light and of
> colourful glamour, light music, finally and above all the excitement
> of sexual feelings.[30]

In this context, then, the history of forms of leisure is the history of
labour and the serious things in life. The exhaustion of our mental and
physical energies in work leads us to require only one thing of our
leisure: 'We must be made comfortable'; 'We only wish to be amused'.
This Simmel sees as 'the complete poverty of the nature of our
entertainment'. We must relax, enjoy our leisure, 'according to the
principle of energy-saving'.

This ban upon seriousness in the leisure sphere can also have a
political motivation. Simmel reports in the same year (1893) upon the
restriction on staging Gerhart Hauptmann's *The Weaver*, initially
forbidden to the public and subsequently shown only to a restricted
audience. In contrast, the police

> allow the Berlin Residenztheatre year after year to present the basest
> French burlesques which, by the titillation of sexual feelings and the
> emphatic concentration of all life-interests upon these particular

pleasures, may exercise their educational effect upon our people; in the Panoptikum a series of waxworks of bloody deeds is offered to the public under the title 'For those with strong nerves!'[31]

In contrast, a play such as Hauptmann's, challenging the illusions of the day, is not viewed as part of the 'aesthetic education' of the people. Simmel's critical response in this instance to the banning of Hauptmann's play should be contrasted perhaps with his later refusal to support the public performance of Arthur Schnitzler's 'Reigen' in 1914 on the grounds that 'our public is in no way mature enough for it'.[32]

This official hypocrisy manifest in relation to Hauptmann's work is also highlighted in Simmel's earliest treatment of prostitution (1892). The moral indignation of 'good society' at the widespread prostitution of the late nineteenth century is expressed, Simmel argues, as if it were not the result of social and economic conditions that are the consequences of that same good society's own interests. It also, of course, treats 'elegant and impoverished prostitution' in a different manner and hides its negative response to the latter in mystifying forms of description:

> There exists no more false expression than when one terms this impoverished creature 'joy girl' [*Freudenmädchen*] and hence believes that she lives out enjoyment; perhaps the joy of others, but certainly not her own. Or does one believe that it is a pleasure to wander the streets evening after evening, regardless of whether it is hot, raining or cold in order to serve as the spoils of some particular man, perhaps a repulsive one, to serve as an ejaculation mechanism?[33]

Leisure for some is thus labour for others. As in Simmel's other discussions of leisure, he also highlights prostitution's connection with the money economy. For this 'completely fleeting inconsequential relationship' between prostitute and client, 'only money . . . is the appropriate equivalent to the fleetingly intensified and just as fleetingly extinguished sexual appetite that is served by prostitution'.[34]

If prostitution serves as Simmel's crucial instance of the commodification of human values, then perhaps the exhibition of material commodities indicates a social location for leisure that is equally exemplary. The display of the phantasmagoria of commodities had become increasingly popular ever since the first World Exhibition of 1851 in London. The marvel of the serialized display of 'dead' commodities to which the visitor was passively to respond merely by observation did, of course, hide a further intention beyond this mesmerized response, namely to be brought back to life again through their purchase.

Such exhibitions were therefore also trade exhibitions and Simmel himself responded to 'The Berlin Trade Exhibition' (1896),[35] which many saw as signifying Berlin's elevation to a world metropolis (from *Grossstadt* to *Weltstadt*). The effect of the concentration of a world of commodities in a confined space is similar to that of the effect of the tumult of the metropolis. The visitor 'will be overpowered and feel disorientated by the mass effect of what is offered here', whilst the wealth and colourfulness of the impressions is itself 'appropriate to over-excited and exhausted nerves' need for stimulation'. The overall effect is that of entering a dream world since 'the close proximity within which the most heterogeneous industrial products are confined produces a paralysis in the capacity for perception, *a true hypnosis*'. In addition, 'in its fragmentation of weak impressions, there remains in the memory the notion that *one should amuse oneself here*'. This impression is accentuated by the arrangement of the exhibition into smaller galleries with entrance fees, so that the excitement and anticipation is constantly renewed and the amusement effect is both heightened and toned down.

Such exhibitions were housed in newer architectural forms which, in keeping with the fleeting life of the commodity, also reflected this transitoriness. Indeed, 'the conscious negation of the monumental style' was complemented by giving the building structures 'the character of a creation for transitoriness'. The layout of such exhibitions enhanced their 'aesthetic productivity' through 'the increase in what one might term the shop-window quality of things that is evoked by exhibitions . . . one must attempt to excite the interest of the buyer by means of the external attraction of the object, even indeed by means of the form of its arrangement'.

At the end of the previous decade, Simmel had reflected upon an earlier leisure activity which was achieving greater popularity and which possessed many common features to the world exhibitions, namely visits to art exhibitions. If the architecture of the trade exhibition became an important symbol of houses of commodities from the second half of the nineteenth century, then so too did the huge growth of museums and galleries, as houses of culture. In 'On Art Exhibitions' (1890),[36] Simmel views the art exhibition as a symbolic microcosm of 'the colourfulness of metropolitan life on the street and in the salon' which brings together for the viewer, in a series of small spaces and 'in the same concentration, the whole wealth of feelings that art as a whole can awaken in him'. However, this very wealth of impressions and images induces two modern responses to such concentrated diversity: 'the blasé attitude and superficiality'. The 'overburdening' of impressions and the 'fleeting character of art exhibitions' that resides in 'the immediately consecutive viewing of that which is contradictory' produces only a superficial overview of the whole. In place of recognition of the individuality of works of art there emerges 'more and more influence of the mass'. Later, in 'Berlin Art Report' (1896), Simmel was to point to the monotony of 'recognised' masters 'that were already antiquated at their birth'. The Berlin National Gallery appealed to those who seek 'satisfaction in the sunlit surface of things'.[37] In short, the display of works of art does not escape the developing features of modern metropolitan existence. In this respect, the structure and organization of art exhibitions fails to realize what for Simmel is one of the crucial features of the work of art: 'art brings us closer to reality; it places us in a more immediate relationship to its distinctive and innermost meanings . . . In addition, however, all art brings about a distancing from the immediacy of things; it allows the concreteness of stimuli to recede and stretches a veil between us and them just like the fine bluish haze that envelops distant mountains'.[38]

And yet we cannot escape to 'distant mountains' either in order to recover our genuine individuality. Although the flight from the present can take a spatial as well as a temporal form – an idea which Simmel examines in 'The Adventure' – a return to nature as a crucial dimension of leisure activity is also already deeply compromised. Travel in general is one instance of the attempted escape from 'the trite everyday world', from the metropolis, or as Simmel himself reports in a letter in 1917, 'totally away from the railway and other such culture'. In 'Alpine Journeys' (1895),[39] – discarding his interest in yodeling from over a decade earlier[40] – Simmel examines the consequences of opening up remoter areas of country for leisure by the extension of railways 'to destinations that were otherwise only accessible to solitary wandering'. The Swiss Alps were undergoing changes that had earlier taken place in the Black Forest: the extension of tourism to previously inaccessible places and, within tourist resorts themselves, the further extension of railways and other forms of communication up the mountains themselves. This particular form of the process of the human domination of nature creates a new environment, a new nature for the tourist: 'In more than a merely external analogy to our economic development, one could term it the large-scale enterprise of the enjoyment of nature.' The romantic solitary communion with nature (which was also a social construct, as is the ruin as an archetypical symbol of the romantic landscape, whose features are analysed in Simmel's essay 'The Ruin') is now replaced by a 'colourless mass' experiencing a 'standardized' enjoyment of nature. This 'socialising large-scale enterprise, compared with the individual enterprise of alpinism', does open up nature to many more people. But 'the power of capitalism also extends over concepts', such as that of the creative formation (*Bildung*) of individuals which was associated with the image of communion with nature. As Simmel declares more fully: 'It is said that part of our formative education is viewing the Alps . . . the power of capitalism also extends itself over concepts; it is rich enough to appropriate a once so refined a concept as creative formation (*Bildung*) as its own private property.' Instead of an effect upon the total personality – physical, intellectual and moral – Simmel detects a fragmentation of the personality into differentiated elements associated with 'subjective–egoistic enjoyment'. The latter replaces any formative and moral value of our relationship to nature and is to be found in alpine sports and the ideology of the alpine clubs which assume that overcoming dangerous physical difficulties is morally meritorious. The egoistic risk to one's life, the gamble with the forces of nature, does bring excitement, but an excitement that is intimately associated with the modern drive towards greater stimulations.

V

Are there any forms of leisure activity which escape the reduction to forms of empty filling-in of time and consciousness? Apart, perhaps, from total idleness, which Simmel satirizes in his 'Metaphysics of Laziness' (1900)[41] as the total saving of energy, there are two, almost ideal–typical instances of leisure activity which are removed from the contents of everyday existence: sociability and the adventure.

At first sight, sociability seems to be the mere filling-in of time. Yet as 'the play form' of society it has a much greater significance. It is 'the pure form, the free-playing interacting interdependence of individuals' that is 'freed of substance' and 'spared the frictional relations of real life; but out of its formal relations to real life, sociability . . . takes on a symbolically playing fullness of life . . . it alone presents the pure, abstract play of form'.[42] The activity of sociability, then, 'plays at the forms of society', a 'social game' with whose help 'people actually "play" society'. This is only possible because sociability possesses 'no ulterior end, no content, and no result outside itself, it is oriented completely around personalities', but without any excessive emphasis upon individuality and egoism which would destroy sociability as a form. Sociability, then, is 'a pure interaction', 'an ideal sociological world, for in it . . . the pleasure of the individual is always contingent on the joy of others' and each participant '"acts" as though all were equal'.

The social game of sociability is found in various forms. At a universal level, it is to be found 'in that most extensive instrument of all human common life, *conversation*', in which 'talking is an end in itself', indeed 'a legitimate end in itself'. In interaction between the sexes, too, 'eroticism has elaborated a form of play: *coquetry*, which finds in sociability its highest, most playful, and yet its widest realisation'. Just as 'sociability plays at the forms of society, so coquetry plays out the forms of eroticism'. But where the play forms of sociability become too rigid, as in over elaborated forms of *etiquette*, they become a caricature of themselves and sociability dissolves.

If sociability as the play form of society is, in principle, a universal form, especially as conversation, in everyday existence, then Simmel's typification of the experience of the adventure[43] is a form of experience which is dissociated from everyday existence. Indeed, 'the most general form of adventure is its dropping-out of the continuity of life', 'the exclave of the life-context, that which has been torn away [*das Abgerissene*]', 'something alien, untouchable, out of the ordinary', 'an island in life which determines its beginning and end according to its own formative powers'.

In the adventure, we experience the synthesis of activity and passivity, 'we forcibly pull the world into ourselves'. Simmel contrasts this experience with work which

> has an organic relation to the world. In a conscious fashion, it develops the world's forces and materials toward their culmination in the human purpose, whereas in adventure we have a non-organic relation to the world. Adventure has the gesture of the conqueror, the quick seizure of opportunity, regardless of whether the portion we carve out is harmonious or disharmonious with us, with the world, or with the relation between us and the world. On the other hand, however, in the adventure we abandon ourselves to the world with fewer defenses and reserves than in any other relation.[44]

Like sociability, the adventure is '*a form of experiencing*. The *content* of the experience does not make the adventure.' It is a 'closed entity' which is momentarily detached from the reified everyday existence. The adventurer gives himself or herself to the moment, to 'a fragmentary incident'. Hence the time-consciousness within which the adventure is lived out is that of

> unconditional presentness, the quickening of the process of life to a point that possesses neither past nor future and therefore contains life within itself with an intensity that, compared with the content of what has gone before, is often relatively indifferent.[45]

When the adventure is recalled in our memory it takes on 'the nuance of dreaming'; the character of 'a remembrance which is connected with fewer strands than other experiences to the unified and continuous process of life . . . The more "adventurous" an adventure is . . . the more "dream like" it will be for our memory.[46] The more the adventure accords with its concept, the more it comes to stand 'over and above life'. In so far as this is the case, it has an affinity with the work of art:

> Precisely because the work of art and the adventure stand juxtaposed to life . . . the one and the other are analogous to the totality of life itself, as it is presented in the brief outline and the condensation of the dream experience. Thereby, *the adventurer is also the most powerful example of the unhistorical person, of the contemporary essence. On the one hand, he is determined by no past* . . . *on the other, the future does not exist for him.*[47]

The ambiguity of the adventure is present here in its encapsulation of the experience of modernity as immediate presentness and in its promise of an eternal presentness. Somewhat cryptically, Simmel wishes to see it as 'admixed with all practical human existence' whilst at the same time recognizing that 'so much of life is hostile to adventure'.

VI

Were Simmel able to look forward to the images of sociability and the adventure that are so central to the marketing strategies of the leisure and tourist industries today, he would have no difficulty in recognizing that their ideologically permeated forms have also been incorporated into the world of the commodity.[48] Forms of sociability and the adventure are central, for instance, to modern advertising of the leisure form of nicotine addiction. Indeed, had Simmel been reflecting upon sociability and the adventure a decade earlier (both essays were written in 1910), his presentation might well have been closer to those which appeared in that earlier decade. At all events, Simmel's earlier reflections on leisure, on 'the fillings-in of time and consciousness', would find accord with more recent judgements such as that of David Harvey that 'the social spaces of distraction and display become as vital to urban culture as the spaces of working and living'.[49]

Thus, although Simmel produced no systematic treatise on modern leisure, he was none the less one of the first social theorists for whom leisure is a significant object of investigation. There are a number of inferences and insights which can be drawn from Simmel's discussions of leisure. First, leisure can be viewed as an ideological denotation for the emptier 'fillings-in of time and consciousness'. In other words, leisure as a concept requires the same kind of deconstruction as did the nineteenth-century notion of 'recreation'. Second, Simmel insists that leisure is not an autonomous sphere that can be examined without reference to work, to 'the serious things in life'. Third, leisure is never associated a priori with creativity, with creative subjectivity. 'Free' time is not necessarily 'creative' time. One reason which Simmel draws to our attention is that forms of leisure can be and usually are commodified, and the 'activity' of consumption is a passive one. Finally, to take up a current theme, Simmel indicates that leisure viewed in the context of our relation to *nature* involves the transformation of nature into that which is no longer an escape from society. Indeed, nature itself is available for consumption. Nature is *framed* for us as a landscape that becomes an essential feature of the aesthetics of modern life. As Simmel notes elsewhere, it is not merely the picture which has a frame; so too does society. And in the present context, so too does nature, where our time and consciousness are 'filled in' and framed by a constructed constellation of that form of sociation which we term the holiday, our leisure 'activity'.

8　The aesthetics of modern life

> . . . the culture of things as a culture of human beings . . .
>
> G. Simmel, *The Philosophy of Money*

> All sense interest connects with the perceptible, with what is real or whose reality we wish; all moral interest with that which *should* really exist, however unlikely it will be realised. *Aesthetic judgement, however, connects with the mere image of things, with their appearance and form, regardless of whether they are supported by an apprehendable reality.*
>
> G. Simmel, *Kant*

I

After the completion of *The Philosophy of Money* in 1900, Simmel wished to write a comprehensive philosophy of art or aesthetics – something which never came to fruition. None the less, Simmel's contribution to the understanding and interpretation of the aesthetic dimension of life and of the social world permeates many of his writings (and not merely his explicit essays on aesthetics or monographs and essays on artists such as Rembrandt, Rodin, Michelangelo, Böcklin and others). In his teaching too, Simmel lectured on aesthetics and culture almost every year from 1902 to 1915 (1903 is the only exception). A full analysis of his treatment of the aesthetic dimension would also have to deal with his often critical relationship to major modern aesthetic movements, such as naturalism, impressionism, symbolism, art nouveau and expressionism.[1]

More significantly for our theme, however, it can be argued that Simmel's emphasis upon the *forms* of interaction (*Wechselwirkung*) or sociation (*Vergesellschaftung*) in his programme for sociology – first tentatively announced in 1890[2] – indicates an interest in revealing an aesthetic dimension of all social interaction that we do not immediately perceive in our everyday life, composed as it is of a multiplicity of diverse and intersecting interactional frames. In other words, and without diminishing Simmel's major contribution to establishing sociology as an independent social science disipline, the sociologist can reveal and analyse aesthetic constellations and configurations that both exist in and are originally hidden in 'the flat surface of everyday life'.

What are the facets of the aesthetic dimension of social life which interest Simmel? In the fifteenth lecture devoted to Kant's aesthetics in his book on *Kant*,[3] Simmel announces that we enjoy what is beautiful because it is valuable; this enjoyment, however, 'depends not on the existence but on the qualities or *forms* of the thing which we must judge to be valuable'.[4] Indeed, following Kant, 'only the form of things bears its beauty'.[5] Aesthetic judgement applies to things themselves 'and not their significance for ends and values'.[6] The work of art constitutes a unity out of diversity 'and its fundament therefore lies in the interaction of its parts'; it '*is form*' for this is what relates the elements to one another. Art is the representation of that which one characterizes as the formation of things.

This crucial dimension of form, in turn, reveals other facets of aesthetic judgement. The latter 'connects with *the mere image of things, with their appearance and form*, regardless of whether or not they are borne by a graspable reality'.[7] Whereas the reality of existence 'exhausts itself in concrete individual elements', the aesthetic dimension is felt in 'the lightness and freedom of *play*', for the latter implies that 'one exercises functions . . . purely formally' without regard to 'the reality-contents of life'.[8] Hence, beauty does not lie in the objective existence of things but rather is a *subjective* reaction which the latter arouses in us. It follows, too, that the justification for aesthetic judgment 'does not lie in definite concepts . . . but in that quite general *internally harmonious* feeling[9] which we experience. In turn, this feeling of satisfaction with respect to the work of art arises out of the latter's success in creating a totality out of the fragmentary; it is 'the feeling that the fortuitous elements of the phenomenon are dominated by a *single* meaning, that the mere facticity of the individual elements is permeated by the significance of a totality, that *the fragmentary and disintegrating dimension of existence*, at least in this single point, *has gained a living unity*'.[10]

The dialectic of the fragment and the totality is paralleled by that of the individual and the universal. Simmel suggests that 'what has recently attracted modern people so strongly to aesthetic values is *this unique play between the objective and the subjective standpoint,* between the individuality of taste and the feeling that it is indeed rooted in a supra-individual, universal'.[11] It may be that this aesthetic enjoyment is possible because it excites constellations 'that remain beneath the threshold of consciousness'. Simmel posits that 'the feeling with respect to art of being released from every detail and one-sidedness of existence perhaps emerges out of the fact that a bound-lessness of the individual element, as emanating from a central point and on which the work of art rests, is brought to life in us, and indeed *not with the confusion of fortuitous associations but rather, in each case, in typical and meaningful forms of relations, attractions and connections of conceptions'.*[12] When Simmel speaks here of the sense of release from existence he is again recalling the connection between the aesthetic of the play form and that of reality: 'Precisely the lightness of playing with which, in their indifference to all reality, aesthetic elements have their effect, makes possible this coming into being of spheres of the soul as a whole which would be restricted if the inner processes were burdened with the serious emphases of reality.'[13] This somewhat abstract formulation acquires a concrete form in Simmel's discussion of sociability (*Geselligkeit*) as the play form of society (*Gesellschaft*), as a form of sociation unburdened by any specific content.

However, returning to Simmel's representation of Kant's aesthetics, we already have the following dimensions of the aesthetic. We respond *subjectively* to the *form* of things, 'to the mere *image of things'*, to 'their *appearance* and form' with an '*internally harmonious* feeling'. The aesthetic dimension creates a *totality* out of the *fragmentary*; it *plays* with form and thereby abstracts from content; what is *individual* is transformed into the *universal*. The relationship between fragment and totality, between the particular and the universal, is more precisely formulated in Simmel's earlier essay 'Sociological Aesthetics'[14] in which he asserts that the aesthetic interpretation 'lies in the fact that the typical is to be found in what is unique, the law-like in what is fortuitous, the essence and significance of things in the superficial and transitory. It seems as if no phenomenon is able to escape from this reduction to that which is significant and eternal in it.' This is true of 'the meanest thing', 'the ugliest thing', 'the most indifferent thing'. Hence it follows that 'every point conceals the possibility of being released into absolute aesthetic significance. To the adequately trained eye, the *total* beauty, the *total* meaning of the world as a whole radiates from every single point'.[15]

But if this were the case in an absolute sense, Simmel continues, then the individual element or fragment would lose its significance as a distinctive individuality. The equal valuation of things cannot be sustained aesthetically, for all valuation requires making distinctions and creating a distance from each individual phenomenon. At this point, Simmel introduces two further dimensions of the aesthetic that are crucial to understanding his interpretation of the modern period. Aesthetic judgment requires the tension of *nearness* and *distance*, and ultimately its most modern expressions are based on distance. The second dimension to which Simmel here refers follows from the first: 'The first aesthetic step . . . leads beyond the mere acceptance of the meaninglessness of things to *symmetry*, until later refinement and enhancement once more connects the irregular, the *asymmetrical* with the most heightened aesthetic judgement.' As a modern instance of distance Simmel cites the reaction to naturalism, a 'reaction in painting that was supplied by the Scottish School [the 'Glasgow Boys'] and in literature which led from Zolaism to Symbolism'.[16] With the asymmetrical we return again to the fragment, to the aesthetic appeal of that which 'almost exclusively bears an individualistic character', to 'the rhapsodic fortuitousness' of the individual element (in contrast, as Simmel argues, to the socialistic tendency to search for symmetry and harmony and to view the ideal society itself as a totality, as a symmetrical work of art): 'Hence . . . the nowadays so lively experienced enjoyment of the fragment, of the mere impression, the aphorism, the symbol, the undeveloped artistic style.'[17] All these are appreciated as a result of their *distance* from their object.

The 'pathos of distance', which reappears in *The Philosophy of Money* as a central theme and which has its origin in the work of Nietzsche, is already important in this earlier essay on sociological aesthetics.[18] Indeed, Simmel already suggests that 'the inner significance of artistic styles reveals itself to be a consequence of *the diverse distance which they create between ourselves and things*'.[19] The subjective response to distance from the object – including the aesthetic object – is a differentiated one. For those with refined tastes, 'the whole secret attraction of distance from things lies *in the artistic formation of the object*'; for those less sensitive, the creation of the attraction of distance requires '*a greater distance of the object itself*: stylised Italian landscapes, historical dramas; the more uncultivated and childlike is the aesthetic sensibility, the more fantastic, the further from reality must the object be' in order to achieve its effect. Both cases, however, testify to the fact that 'present day artistic sensibility basically strongly emphasises the attraction of distance as opposed to the attraction of proximity'.[20]

Such a 'tendency to create a distance' in modern culture, in fact 'the tendency to *enlarge* the distance between human beings and their objects' which manifests itself in the aesthetic sphere, is symbolized in other spheres: 'the destruction of the family', arising out of the rejection of its presumed excessive closeness, extends to the rejection of contact with other intimate circles; 'the ease of transport to the furthest distant points strengthens this "anxiety with regard to contact" '; 'the "historical spirit", the wealth of inner relationships to spatially and temporally more distant interests makes us all the more sensitive to the shocks and the disorder that confront us from the immediate proximity and contact with human beings and things'. A 'major cause' of this anxiety with regard to contact is 'the ever deeper penetration of the money economy'.[21]

Like Simmel's own argument, we have begun to move from the elucidation of the aesthetic dimension to a more specific treatment of the aesthetics of modern life. In particular, it is appropriate here to examine in some detail the far-reaching consequences of the mature money economy for the aesthetic domain and for the aesthetics of everyday life.

II

We can commence this analysis by remaining for a moment with Simmel's essay on sociological aesthetics. Although admitting that the destruction of earlier economic relations is not complete, Simmel outlines the effect of the increasing influence of the mature money economy upon social relations as follows: 'Money intervenes between one human being and another, between human beings and commodities as a mediating instance, as a common denominator, to which each value must be reduced in order to be able to be translated further into other values. With the development of the money economy, the objects of economic transactions no longer confront us immediately.' Rather, we are confronted by 'this intermediate value', so much so that our intentionality comes to rest upon this intermediate stage, 'as if upon the centre of interest and the fulcrum of rest, whilst all concrete things pass by in restless flight, burdened by the contradiction that in fact they alone can secure all definite satisfactions but nonetheless acquire their degree of value and interest only after their devaluation into this characterless, qualityless standard. In this way, with the enlargement of its role, money places us at an ever more basic distance from objects; the immediacy of impressions, the sense of value, interest in things is weakened, our contact with them is broken and we experience them, as it were, only by means of a mediation that does not permit their complete, autonomous, immediate existence to gain full expression'.[22]

The increasing predominance of the mediating value announces the domination of the exchange value of things over their use value.[23] The domination of exchange value is the domination of *quantitative* valuation and therefore ostensibly signifies the impossibility of aesthetic valuation. The levelling tendency of monetary and commodity exchange is problematical in this context in so far as the equalization of exchange value removes the possibility of qualitative valuation but, at the same time, to refer to one dimension of the aesthetic, still possesses the aesthetic dimension of symmetry. Indeed, this is not the only aesthetic dimension present in the mature money economy, in the sphere of circulation and exchange of commodities. Money transactions, for instance, appear to create that distance which is a necessary prerequisite for aesthetic judgement. When, in his article 'The Seventh Ring'[24] – in fact, a review of Stefan George's poetry – Simmel declares that 'art gives unity to otherwise unrelated and unresolved elements that exist side by side',[25] has he not shown earlier in *The Philosophy of Money* that the mediating value (money) performs precisely this task in its capacity as the universal equivalent of 'unrelated and unresolved' use values? Does not the 'beautiful illusion' *(schöner Schein)* (Hegel) that is art and the aesthetic realm have its counterpart in the seemingly autonomous realm of the circulation and exchange of commodities (made possible by the mediation of money)? In the course of his reflections on the picture frame, Simmel maintains that 'the essence of the work of art . . . is to be a totality for itself, to require no relationship to an external entity, to weave each of its threads back once more into its focal point. In so far as the work of art is that which otherwise only *the world as a whole* or the soul can be: a *unity* out of individual elements – it encloses itself as *a world for itself* against all that exists external to it.[26] In *The Philosophy of Money*, Simmel seeks to demonstrate that 'the world as a whole' in the mature economy 'appears' as 'a world for itself', as 'the culture of things', as 'the objective culture' (*Die Sachkultur*) which not merely stands over against subjective culture, over against human subjects themselves, but creates the possibility of 'the culture of things *as* the culture of human beings'.[27] In order to substantiate these and other claims, which at least posit an 'elective affinity' between the aesthetic domain and the domain of the circulation and exchange of commodities, we must turn to Simmel's analysis in *The Philosophy of Money* and the insights associated with that work.

As Simmel declares in the preface to *The Philosophy of Money*, it is not intended as a work on the economics or the history of money. As well as being a major contribution to a sociology of money, its 'philosophy' of money contains at least forty references to the aesthetic domain, most of which cannot be dealt with here. But before looking at the seemingly more direct discussion of the aesthetic domain, we should recall Simmel's association of beauty with *subjective* reactions and, along with Kant, the attendant need for valuation. For Simmel the construction of his subjectivist theory of value proved most difficult. Drawing on contemporary marginal utility theorists such as Menger and von Wieser, Simmel constructs a theory of value that is grounded in subjective desire and enjoyment. The transition from value as substance in barter economies to value as function in money economies creates an unresolved tension between the subjectivist (and psychological) presuppositions of marginal utility theory (some of which were later criticized by Weber in another context) and the objectivist presuppositions of money exchange (i.e. between subjective needs and enjoyment and the objective, autonomous measurement and exchange of one object with another).[28] This significant shift in the mode of valuation and its consequences is already dealt with in Simmel's first comprehensive outline of some of the major themes in *The Philosophy of Money* in his essay 'Money in Modern Culture'.[29] There, Simmel maintains that money as the mediating instance between commodities intervenes between the individual and commodity as an 'in itself qualityless instance'. Indeed, its domination signifies a shift from qualitative to quantitative valuation (and implicitly carries with itself an attendant devaluation and levelling of value). The absolute mediator of values, objects and persons 'thus emerges as the secure fulcrum in the flight of phenomena'.[30] As the equivalent for everything, it displaces that which is exceptional – 'only what is individual is exceptional' – and replaces it with a common denominator. Furthermore, as the absolute expression of all value, it is also the ultimate means 'in this labyrinth of means' created by the universalization of exchange transactions. Ends are replaced by means and by techniques (another key to distinguishing the work of art and the product of the applied arts). Money's domination in the teleology of ends and means accounts for 'the unrest, the feverishness, the unceasing nature of modern life whose unstoppable wheel is provided by money, and which makes the machine of life into a *perpetuum mobile*'. At the same time as it penetrates everyday life, 'it elevates itself to the totally abstract heights above the whole broad diversity of objects, it becomes the centre in which the most antithetical, alienated, distant things find their common element and resting point'. This unification of the most contradictory elements is a dynamic process. The 'transition from stability to lability' is an accelerating process that manifests itself in the speed and rhythm of exchange transactions. At the elementary level, 'the divisibility of money into the smallest sums certainly contributes to the small style in the external and especially the aesthetic arrangement of modern life, to the growing number of little things with which we adorn our life'.[31] For Simmel, such seemingly fortuitous phenomena are related to the most profound currents of modern life.

The detailed analysis of the effects of the mature money economy, which this earlier outline prefigures but which is given greater depth in *The Philosophy of Money*, prompts the question as to the possible existence and survival of the aesthetic domain in the reified and alienated world which it creates. Although Simmel declares exchange to be 'a sociological phenomenon *sui generis*' that in some respects constitutes pure interaction, its reified form is the mature money economy. Money is 'the reification of the pure relationship between things as expressed in their economic motion'; it 'stands between the individual objects . . . in a realm organised according to its own norms'.[32] Such exchange relations acquire a spectral objectivity, they become 'the embodiment of a pure function' – they play with values just as the aesthetic judgement 'exercises functions . . . purely formally'. It seems, however, as if the more reification extends to social and cultural relations, the more the aesthetic dimension is stultified. But does not the world of the circulation and exchange of commodities and of money exchange relations create the same illusions as the aesthetic realm? Does not this sphere acquire an autonomy in which its individual elements achieve a reconciliation? Is there not a parallel between the aesthetic judgement associated with the image, appearance and form of things and the world of the circulation and exchange of commodities (with its creation of harmony through a pure function that is indifferent to the reality of all use values)?

We might question whether the sphere of circulation and exchange of commodities (facilitated by the universal commodity, the universal equivalent that is money) creates a 'beautiful' illusion, but, in securing the domination of exchange value, it certainly creates an illusory world of inverted value. Simmel argues that 'all concrete things drive on in restless flight' towards their monetary evaluation and, implicitly, their devaluation. As Scheible puts it, 'the exchange principle, rendered universal, brings about a genuine reversal of the poles of the static and the dynamic. That which is apparently stable, use value, declines totally into the economic dynamic, whilst the dynamic principle, exchange, because of the universality in which it prevails, becomes the ultimate "stabilizing pole"'.[33] In Marx's terms, 'circulation appears as a *simply infinite* process', 'as that which is immediately present on the surface of bourgeois society', but it exists in this manner 'only so far as it is constantly mediated . . . As immediate being it is therefore pure semblance. It is the phenomenon of a process taking place behind it.'[34] Although Simmel is seldom concerned explicitly with the production of commodities (i.e. with what lies behind this process), his examination of the phenomenal forms in which the circulation process of money exchange appears to us is consonant with this interpretation. In this respect, his theory of alienation not merely anticipates the then unknown analysis of alienation in Marx's *Paris Manuscripts* but, in some respects at least, Simmel's phenomenological analysis of the sphere of circulation and exchange goes beyond Marx's hints at such an analysis of it in the then equally unknown *Grundrisse*, which is only tangentially concerned with 'the daily traffic of bourgeois life'.

Where Simmel does dramatically extend the analysis of the everyday world of circulation (in the metropolis) and exchange (in the money economy) is in revealing its aesthetic dimension. This is announced in the title of the last chapter of *The Philosophy of Money* – 'The Style of Life', implicitly of modern life, but explicitly not the 'beauty' of modern life. Is not his aesthetics of modern life concerned not merely with the crisis in the work of art, in the possibility of the beautiful, but also with the illusion of the aesthetic realm in the sphere of the circulation and exchange of commodities?

If such an interpretation is justified, then it is all the more remarkable that Simmel does not draw upon the distinction which Kant makes between the beautiful and the sublime (*das Erhabene*).[35] In *The Critique of Judgement*, Kant draws the following pertinent distinctions between the two:

'The beautiful . . . is a question of the form of the object, and thus consists in limitation, whereas the sublime is to be found in an object even devoid of form, so far as it immediately involves, or else its presence provokes, a representation of *limitlessness*, yet with a super-added thought of its totality. Accordingly the beautiful seems to be regarded as a presentation of an indeterminate concept of understanding, the sublime as a presentation of an indeterminate concept of reason. Hence the delight is in the former case coupled with the representation of *Quality*, but in this case with that of *Quantity*'.[36]

And whereas the beautiful is associated with a sense of 'the furtherance of life', the sublime might be equally attracted and repelled by it, creating 'a negative pleasure'. The beautiful may be contained in sensuous form, whereas the sublime 'concerns ideas of reason'. The latter is associated with quantity and with a dynamic.

Only one half of this distinction between the beautiful and the sublime is explicitly and consciously thematized by Simmel, namely the beautiful in relation to the work of art. But it is surely legitimate, and possibly illuminating, to see his treatment of the sphere of exchange and circulation facilitated by the mature money economy as the other half of this juxtaposition. Such a sphere provides 'a representation of limitlessness', a notion of totality, a presentation of the concept of reason, a quantitative and dynamic sphere. In the wider context of the aesthetics of modern life, it is surely the case that the work of art and the possibilities for the beautiful are increasingly limited in a context in which the transition to the functional values of money exchange not merely relativizes all values but produces an indifference to value as such (manifested in Simmel's analysis of the domination of the blasé attitude in the mature money economy). The aesthetic viewpoint, on the other hand, is capable of transcending the indifference of things, but the problem here is that in so far as the universalization of money exchange reinforces the culture of things, the culture of human subjects (and the creation of the work of art) becomes increasingly threatened. This constitutes a central theme of his dialectic of subjective and objective culture, in fact the growing gap between the two. There exists within the context of the mature money economy an antagonism between an aesthetic tendency and money interests which is that of form versus quantitative valuation. For Simmel, this makes all the more important the investigation of the possibilities for the aesthetic, for 'the feeling of liberation, which is part of the aesthetic mood, the release from the dull pressure of things, the expansion of the joyful and free self into things, the reality of which usually oppresses it'.[37] Unfortunately, the experience of modernity that is located in the mature money economy and the metropolis is not conducive to such feelings. None the less, as Böhringer has persuasively argued, *The Philosophy of Money* can be read as an aesthetic theory, even as an analogy for modern art.[38]

III

Is it possible that the distinction between the beautiful and the sublime has its parallel in the distinction between the work of art and the applied arts, between form and style? Certainly, for Simmel, there exists a major difference between the work of art and the product of the applied arts, the stylized product. The unique work of art arouses in us an excitement that is related to its reconciliation of the growing gap between subjective and objective culture, between subject and object. The work of art embodies the talent, the uniqueness of the artist; the product of applied art signifies the domination of technique.[39] In the former case, it is creative subjectivity that is paramount, in the latter the results of an ever more sophisticated objective culture. The product of the applied arts stands closer to the claims of utility, its 'form' embodied in a generalized 'style'. Is it the fate of the products of the applied arts, including the mechanical reproduction of the work of art, to be the manifestation of a false reconciliation of subject and object? Even though Simmel argues that 'the perfection of the mechanical reproduction of phenomena' would not 'make the visual arts superfluous',[40] he elsewhere recognizes that the then still popular panoramas artificially produced the effect of the third dimension which he associated with the work of art. In the metropolis, of course, it is the applied arts in all their varied forms, including the multiplicity of ornamentation, with which we are confronted. As we shall see, however, the distinction between the work of art and the product of the applied arts addresses only part of the problem. The work of art reduced to an object of consumption, of passive appreciation, is itself so seriously compromised that it cannot stand uncritically juxtaposed to the already compromised stylized product of the applied arts.

The distinction between the work of art and the product of the applied arts is certainly a significant one for Simmel. It is true that the distinction is not a universal one, but rather one that is associated with the development of a market for cultural objects, with a money economy, and especially with the development of capitalism. However, at the turn of the century there is a heated debate on the significance of the applied arts that is, in part, associated with their machine production. It also comes to the fore in discussion of art nouveau. (For another sociological account of the distinction see Sombart's essay on the applied arts.)[41] In *The Philosophy of Money* it is already apparent in the distinction between beauty and utility: 'In those cases that offer *realistic* pleasure, our appreciation of the object is not specifically aesthetic, but practical; it becomes aesthetic only as a result of *increasing distance, abstraction and sublimation*.[42] In the same context, Simmel announces that

> the whole development of objects from utility value to aesthetic value is a process of objectification . . . *So long as objects are merely useful they are interchangeable* and everything can be replaced by anything else that performs the same service. But *when they are beautiful they have a unique individual existence* and the value of one cannot be replaced by another even though it may be just as beautiful in its own way . . . The more remote for the species is the utility of the object that first created an interest and a value and is now forgotten, the purer is the aesthetic satisfaction derived from the mere form and appearance of the object'.[43]

The distinction between the work of art and the product of the applied arts here relies upon the categorical distinctions we alluded to earlier in Simmel's general aesthetic.

When we turn to Simmel's reflections upon adornment or ornamentation, we find this same distinction is given greater precision. In his 'Psychology of Adornment[44] – and here adornment (*der Schmuck*) can be extended to the ornament (thereby giving it a broader realm of application that extends to architecture, one of the largely neglected spheres of Simmel's aesthetics of everyday life but one which is as apparent in the public sphere as adornment, jewelry, etc., is apparent in the private sphere)[45] – the distinction is made as follows: 'The work of art is something *for itself*, the product of applied art is something *for us* . . . [whose] significance is the enlargement into general accessibility and practical recognition.[46] The product of the applied arts 'because of its use value [*Gebrauchszweck*] applies to a plurality of human beings' and has a style that appeals to a plurality of people. We must return to the issue of style later, as does Simmel in his essay 'The Problem of Style'.[47]

For the moment, let us go back to the fate of the work of art itself in a society increasingly dominated by the money economy and the consumption of commodities. The work of art, in this context, also becomes the object of *passive consumption*. This can be illustrated by an examination of three of Simmel's lesser-known essays concerned with art as a passive object of consumption and the housing of the work of art. The fate of the work of art itself in modernity is associated with the fate of other things in this objectified and reified everyday world. In the earliest of the three essays, 'On Art Exhibitions',[48] Simmel views the art exhibition as a symbolic microcosm of 'the rich coloration of metropolitan life on the street and in the salon'. The all too close juxtaposition of the most diverse works of art (typical of the display techniques of nineteenth-century art galleries that are still to be found today) arouses in the observer a wealth of impressions and images. At the same time, the contradictory serialized display of works of art arouses two typically modern reactions, 'the blasé attitude and superficiality'. The arbitrary sequentiality of diverse pictures acts as a burden to the nerves of the observer and produces merely a superficial overview of the whole. Simmel suggests that in this respect the response of the observer in the building devoted to the display of modern works of art is merely a parallel or a further manifestation of the same response that we experience in the metropolis with its excessive impressions that can no longer be mastered. Just as in 'The Philosophy of Landscape'[49] Simmel virtually declares that the metropolitan 'cityscape' (Benjamin) cannot be a landscape, so in the museum devoted to the display of works of art (that are themselves framed) the totality is itself incapable of being 'framed'.

In an even more critical essay, 'Berlin Art Letter',[50] published anonymously, Simmel attacks the contents and mode of presentation of works of art in the Berlin National Gallery. In contrast to his earlier critique in which he saw the response to the exhibition of works of art as having a parallel in our response to the everyday metropolitan experience of modernity, Simmel here emphasizes the absence of an adequate expression of modernity: 'The fact that there exists something akin to a modern art, that a style strives to express the representation of a new affinity between meaningful appearance and the meaningless significance of things, that a state gallery for modern art must above all lay out such changes . . . in a wealth of attempts as it were in the form of an archive – of all this one has no inkling; rather there is amassed one trash after another of "recognized" masters, those miserable stale pictures that at their inception were antiquated.'[51] 'In these antiquated circumstances', Simmel continues, one must struggle for a living modern art. In this context, Simmel argues against an exhibition of the work of a now forgotten artist – Gustave Graef – as an instance of such *unmodern* art. Against the likes of his stylized art, Simmel insists that

> beauty is for him . . . something different from *us moderns*; he does not extract it from the genuine significance of phenomena, it does not reveal itself to him as the depths of life that lives each essence for itself, without comparison with all others, it does not accompany for

him, as it does for us, as a *character indelibilis* of the autonomous movement of things.[52]

And here we should highlight two aspects of Simmel's critique. First, Simmel is arguing against the typical stylization of images, the recourse to empty clichés. Second, we should note his extremely modern call for art to represent '*the autonomous movement of things*' as being an appropriate task of modernity. Here are faint echoes of the displaced object, the decentred subject so beloved of postmodern theorists.

And, to remain for a moment with this critique, we should recall Simmel's attack upon the *Kitsch* products of modern popular taste. Here the context is the then popular collection of Japanese woodcuts. Simmel suggests that 'Berlin at last has started to imitate Paris with the taste in Japanese art. But unfortunately we have already arrived too late, for the market is almost exclusively filled with the modern Japanese products which emerged under European influence and which thus represent such *a bastardised style of the most impure kind*'.[53]

As a third example of applied works in the broadest sense as passive objects of consumption – and for a rare commentary upon contemporary architecture – we may take Simmel's essay 'The Berlin Trade Exhibition'[54] whose analysis in part anticipates Walter Benjamin's later analysis of the 'universe of commodities'.[55] In this exhibition (which contemporaries viewed as a symbol of Berlin's elevation from a major city to a world metropolis) a profusion of commodities (and works of art and products of applied arts) were exhibited in the social context of *amusement*: 'The close proximity within which the most heterogeneous industrial products are confined produced a paralysis in the capacity for perception, a true hypnosis . . . but in its fragmentation of weak impressions there remains in the memory the notion that one should be amused here.'[56] Simmel also emphasizes the *passivity* of such consumption. As compensation for the one-sided restrictions of the labour process's extreme division of labour, people look for 'the increasing crowding together of heterogeneous impressions, . . . the increasingly hasty and colourful change in emotions. The differentiation of the active spheres of life evidently complement one another through the comprehensive diversity of their passive and receptive spheres.'[57]

A specifically aesthetic dimension of such exhibitions Simmel finds in their architecture with 'the conscious negation of the monumental style' giving them 'the character of a creation for transitoriness' (like the life of the commodities exhibited). Above all, an 'aesthetic super-additum' exists in the arrangement of such exhibitions 'just as the ordinary advertisement has advanced to the art of poster' (the poster as an aesthetic representation of the representation of use value as exchange value). Indeed, the exhibition increases 'what one can term *the shop-window quality of things.* Commodity production . . . must lead to a situation of *giving things an enticing external appearance* over and above their usefulness . . . one must attempt to *excite the interest of the buyer* by means of the external attraction of the object'. Simmel terms this process *'aesthetic productivity'.*[58]

Later, in *The Philosophy of Money* and in a somewhat different context, Simmel reflects upon the production of 'an enticing aesthetic appearance' as the production of a plurality of styles. Here he declares that 'the entire visible environment of our cultural life has disintegrated into a plurality of styles'.[59] Style is seen here as a disguise, indeed as 'a veil that imposes a barrier and a distance in relation to the recipient of the expression of these feelings'.[60] Style is capable of expressing any number and variety of contents in related forms. More generally, 'the aesthetic interest of recent times has tended towards an increase in the distance produced by *transposing objects into art'.*[61] Written in 1900, this is probably a reference to art nouveau's conception of the total work of art (*Gesamtkunstwerk*) whose aim was to transform not merely the exterior and interior of a building into an artistic whole but also the whole of its contents. This is confirmed in the essay 'The Picture Frame' in the context of Simmel's attack on 'the conviction that furniture is a work of art', on the grounds that 'the work of art is something for itself, furniture is something for us'.[62] Again there is a distinction derived from Kant's aesthetics at work here – in however muted a form – namely the distinction between two types of 'objective finality': either internal (the perfection of the object, in this case the work of art) or external (the utility of the object, in this case the product of the applied arts). What is explicitly absent from Simmel's discussion but present in this period is the heated debate on the relationship between art and industry, between craft production and mass production (hinted at in Simmel's discussion of custom production) and the long-standing debate surrounding the useful arts (e.g. the relation between architecture and engineering).

The great work of art which reconciles subject and object, which resolves the contradictions of modern experience ('the modern *transmutabilita'* of restless, fleeting movement and fragmentation and 'the impression of the supra-monetary, the timeless impression') is seldom found in everyday modern experience. Where 'salvation from the trouble and whirl of life, the peace and conciliation beyond its movements and contradiction . . . [is] the permanent goal of art',[63] then it is certainly realized only in exceptional works such as – for Simmel – Rodin's sculpture. Of course, there are, for Simmel, many instances in works of art of a false reconciliation, culminating in a 'satisfaction with the sunlit surface of things'.[64]

IV

None the less, Simmel is one of the first social theorists to examine the inner consequences for individual experience (*Erlebnis*) of the domination of the cultural things in everyday experience as the culture of human beings. His investigation of the two sites of modernity – the mature money economy and the metropolis – as the showplaces of modernity is also a study of the fragmentary objectifications and the fragments of experience that are to be found in the surface of the everyday world. This surface, as it is immediately experienced, is one of constant dissolution of forms. Where it becomes a permanent feature of everyday experience, its attendant fragmentation and disintegration threaten a crucial component of aesthetic experience. At one level, Simmel seeks to retrieve the aesthetic by revealing the wealth and diversity of forms, however fragmentary and fleeting they may be. In part, this is achieved through 'the deepening of the surface of life', 'the digging out of every intellectual stratum beneath its appearance'.[65] Where practical necessities and the division of labour seldom permit us to see life in its totality, we must have recourse to another mode of viewing its objectifications. Since life is in permanent flux, 'each moment is the whole'.[66]

The domination of the objective culture, of a reified world of things, even, in Benjamin's words, the recognition of 'the force of the extinct world of things'[67] makes the search for its aesthetic dimension all the more difficult. It has been argued here that Simmel does reveal the illusory aesthetic of the sphere of circulation and exchange, the sphere in which we normally experience the everyday world of capitalism. However, in his later writings Simmel seems to question the possibility of excavating the culture of things: 'The pessimism with which the majority of more profound thinkers seem to view the contemporary state of culture has its foundation in the ever-wider yawning abyss between the culture of things and that of human beings.'[68]

But if we reject the tragic vision of the separation of subjective and objective culture as a permanent 'fate' and start out from Simmel's earlier examination of the culture of things, of the phenomenal life of the commodity and the inner consequences of consumption, and of the aesthetic features of 'this' world and the world of everyday interaction, then we could investigate the transformations of aesthetic experience that are taking place without falling back upon the resignatory stance of cultural pessimism. If Simmel shows that the study of everyday modern life is a difficult task, then it is not an impossible one.[69]

Its starting point – and this is true also for an investigation of the aesthetics of modern life – can be 'the daily traffic of bourgeois life' (Marx), 'the flatness of daily life' (Simmel). Kracauer suggests that Simmel shows us 'how mundane everyday understanding consigns all flowing connections between phenomena to oblivion, severs the web of appearances and encloses its now isolated parts – each of them autonomous – in a single conception'.[70] Simmel himself alludes to attempts at an aesthetic flight from 'the flatness of daily life' in his investigation of the adventure and travel, and even possibly to a qualified resistance to it in fashion. Their examination would take us into Simmel's contribution to the study of modern leisure.[71] But, at all events, Simmel was surely one of the first social theorists to make us aware of the aesthetics of modern life, even in a manner that is relevant to the study of a putative postmodern culture. A 'prehistory' of postmodernity could do worse than re-examine the constellation and context of Simmel's 'modern' aesthetic concerns.

Simmel's analysis of modernity is significant in that it does highlight the aesthetic dimensions of our modern experience. In particular, if we accept the previous argument as to the affinity between the aesthetic realm and that of the circulation and exchange of commodities, then we can at least plausibly assert that the analogous aesthetic experience in this latter sphere is that of the sublime.

Part III

Since Simmel

9   Modernity, postmodernity and things

Prophecy would be rash, but it is quite possible that Post-Simmelism will prove to be a pillar in the ultimate sociology.

Albion W. Small (1924)

Il faut être absolument moderne.

Arthur Rimbaud, 'A Season in Hell' (1873)

I

In 1892 Simmel was being considered for a position at an American university. In 1893 he complained that he had wasted eighteen months in useless negotiations. We do not know, as yet, which university had made the original offer, though Simmel's contacts with the United States at that time were limited. We know, at least, that he was corresponding with the psychologist Stanley Hall – then at Clark University, Massachusetts.[1] By 1895 Simmel was publishing in the *Annals of the American Academy of Political and Social Science* (in fact a translation of his crucial essay 'The Problem of Sociology').[2] In the following year, Simmel began to contribute to the newly founded *American Journal of Sociology* based at Chicago University and edited by Albion Small.

Until his death, Simmel published fourteen pieces in this key journal, largely on the initiative of Albion Small and probably translated by him. Simmel never visited America, and yet he was in these years prior to the First World War the most published German sociologist in America – one might add, the most published European sociologist in America. The *American Journal of Sociology*, at Small's initiative, published essays that were to constitute chapters of Simmel's *Soziologie* (1908) as well as other essays, such as those on the sociology of religion, or part of a chapter from his *Philosophy of Money*. As a result of this Chicago initiative, no German sociologist was so well published in the United States in this period. In addition, Simmel published two important essays, 'Tendencies in German Life and Thought Since 1870' (1902) and 'Fashion' (1904) in, respectively, a journal originally called *International Monthly* and then – presumably as a result of lack of success – *International Quarterly*.[3] The editorial board on sociological matters of this journal, under its dual guises, included the following: Franklin Giddings (Columbia University), Gabriele Tarde (Paris), J.S. Mackenzie (Cardiff; his works on moral philosophy in the 1890s and later cited Simmel's works) and Georg Simmel (Berlin).[4] In addition, almost all of Simmel's works were reviewed in the philosophy journal *Philosophical Review* (Cornell University) during his lifetime.[5] It cannot be emphasized enough that this was true of no other European sociologist at this time.

In part, this reception was due not merely to individual initiatives but also to the wave of American students studying in German universities. In the Chicago group alone, Small, Park and Mead had all studied in Germany, Park with Simmel and Small with Schmoller.[6] Indicative of the climate at the turn of the century is Small's review of Schmoller's *Grundriss der allgemeinen Volkswirtschaftslehre* (1900) – reviewed also by Simmel – which concludes with the statement that 'Much of the material of the volume *is already in the notebooks of many Americans*. The elaborated and printed lectures will help to extend every dimension of our social conceptions.'[7]

Simmel's connections with the emergent Chicago School are, if not fully documented, at least well known.[8] If we turn to the *Annals*, which originally carried sociological material before turning to political science and giving way to the *American Journal of Sociology* for sociological publications, we find that as early as 1895, in a review by Ludwig Gumplowicz, there is already a reference to 'Simmel as instructor at the University of Berlin, [who] has likewise [in addition to Paul Barth at Leipzig] published some sociological studies'.[9] This mention is not surprising since Gumplowicz has already praised Simmel's *Über sociale Differenzierung* in an 1891 overview of sociological developments.[10] However, in 1898, in a review by Lester Ward, we find Ward referring to the fact that 'Simmel is talking about collective responsibility, Durkheim about the social division of labour, Le Bon about the psychology of crowds . . .'[11] Hence, Small, Giddings and Ward were all aware of Simmel's sociological work before the turn of the century.

Of these three figures, it is Small who contributed most by far to the early reception of Simmel's work in the United States – leaving aside for the moment the not insignificant subsequent contributions of Park and, to a lesser extent, Mead. To the translation of Simmel's 'The Problem of Sociology' (which appeared in German in 1894, and in English in 1895) there is appended a significant 'Supplementary Note', in which he declares that 'since the first publication of the preceding paper, the objection has been made that I unnecessarily limited the scope of Sociology'.[12] In the *previous* volume of the *Annals*, there is an extended note by Albion Small on ' "Social" vs. "Societary" '.[13] In this note, Small indicates that 'for the hundredth time I was trying to invent satisfactory equivalents for the terms *Sozialwissenschaft* and *Gesellschaftsinssenschaft*. These words mean, to most writers and readers, precisely the same thing.' Small recommends that 'whatever is *of or pertaining to society* is "societary". The word stands for the last abstraction of the reality "society".'[14] He reveals that

> The need of thus enlarging our vocabulary impressed me very forcibly in connection with Dr. Simmel's latest discussion of the task of sociology. That paper seemed to me to contain an important contribution to societary analysis, although *I should be sorry if the name sociology should be restricted to the application for which Simmel contends.*[15]

Small goes on to cite Simmel's essay 'The Problem of Sociology', (in the German version) and concludes with his view on the use of 'societary' as being

> not dependent at all upon agreement with or dissent from Simmel's program of a distinct science of societary geometry or morphology . . . It gets its force from perceptions that the facts about society cannot be thoroughly analyzed and correctly correlated unless, during certain parts of the process, they be viewed in their purely objective aspects, not as demonstration of motive but as forms of contact between individuals – as societary phenomena in the most general sense, distinguished on the one hand from phenomena of isolated individual activity, and on the other from phenomena of those particular orders or conditions of society which are evolved or preserved by sympathy.[16]

The reservations on the restrictive nature of Simmel's conception of sociology did not prevent Small from propagating Simmel's sociology in his journal, perhaps because, despite their differences, they shared some common aims when it came to the *foundation* of sociology as an independent discipline.[17]

It is the restrictive nature of the concept of sociology to which Small returns over a decade later in his review of Simmel's *Soziologie*. Again, Small argues that 'Simmel restricts the content of the term "sociology" to a limit which no other first-rate sociologist in Europe, with the possible exception of Professor Toennies, accepts, and no one in this country, as far as I am aware, is inclined to adopt his proposed usage'.[18] None the less, Small is confident that Simmel's *Soziologie* 'will mark a distinctive stage in the evaluation of sociology'. The *Annals'* much briefer and anonymous review opens with the conviction that 'for the ordinary student, the articles which Professor Simmel has published in the American Journal of Sociology will be a better introduction to his theories than this ponderous volume'.[19] And by the first decade of this century sociology in the United States appeared well established compared with the situation in Germany, at least in respect of the extent of courses in sociology offered and the number of faculty positions. The outbreak of the First World War saw a significant setback in the reception of German sociology. Simmel's initial open support for the German war was sharply criticized by Small in an extended letter to Simmel published in the British *Sociological Review* in 1914.[20] However, the letter is evidence of continued contact between the two sociologists, even though they had last met (possibly the only occasion) in 1903.[21]

In the post-war period after Simmel's death in 1918, Small saw what were, for him, fruitful developments in German sociology as the result, in part, of Simmel's continued influence. Thus, reviewing Theodor Litt's *Individuum und Gesellschaft* in 1924, Small refers to new movements in German sociology, in part associated with the new Cologne sociology journal *Kölner Vierteljahrshefte für Sozialwissenschaften*, as possibly 'post-, super- and neo-Simmelism . . . Tentatively, however, without pressing the question of origins, we may indicate a mere chronological zone of the movement as post-Simmelism.'[22] Reviewing the Cologne journal, Small had earlier already identified its direction as partly following Simmel's conception of sociology. In a revealing passage, Small maintains that

> investigation of the form aspects of social groups, as we argued more than once in both conversations and correspondence with Simmel, can be bad only when it is regarded as self-sufficient. Considered as an introductory procedure in sociology, implying corresponding analysis of functional and control aspects of group processes and problems, the Simmel method is both foundation-laying in itself and it is provocative of similarly penetrating investigation of the movement aspects of groups, and of the

personal values involved in arriving at norms for programs of
conscious group action.[23]

It is noteworthy that Small still maintains Simmel's methodology to be
'foundation-laying' and that its substance is already being translated
into American sociological concerns.

None the less, Small continued to plead that serious consideration
be given to Simmel's sociology by American sociologists. Small's final
assessment of Simmel's work, written the year before his death in
1926, is to be found in his review of Nicholas Spykman's *The Social
Theory of Georg Simmel* (1925) – the first study of Simmel's work to
appear in English.[24] Small relates that 'nearly thirty years ago the
editors of this *Journal* . . . wanted to stimulate social scientists in the
English-speaking world to begin with beginnings by devoting
themselves to fundamental problems of methodology. They believed
that no better center of attention could be selected than that proposed
by Simmel.'[25] However, despite publishing fourteen pieces by Simmel
and reviewing his work in the journal, this aim seems not to have been
realized. Small concludes that this failure was manifested in both
American and British circles:

> Up to the present time the Americans who have given indubitable
> evidence of having considered Simmel thoroughly might be counted
> on the fingers of one hand. Some years after the earlier numbers of
> the Simmel series had appeared in this *Journal*, the translator, while
> in London, had occasion to refer to one of them. He found the
> volumes containing them on the shelves of the library of the London
> School of Economics, but the leaves were uncut! So far as evidence
> of British attention to Simmel runs to the contrary, those leaves may
> have remained uncut to this day.[26]

Such judgements did not prevent Small from remaining critical of the
scope of Simmel's sociology. He states that 'the present writer's last
conversations with Simmel were in 1903. At that time he reiterated one
of his most famous doctrines, viz., that sociology should be "the
geometry, the morphology, the crystallography of groups." Probably
the writer would have had the support of most American sociologists
in declining to accept such delimitations for sociology.[27] None the less,
Small repeated his consistent claim that American sociology would
suffer if it did not attend to European developments. Indeed, he
argues,

> American methodology will remain provincial unless it maintains
> vital relations with the two European movements which seem likely

to be the path-breakers in continental sociology during its next stage of development. The one tendency we have ventured to call post-Simmelism . . . in Germany. The other is the reorganization of the Durkheim following in France.[28]

It must remain an open question as to whether there was a movement broadly approximating to 'post-Simmelism' in Germany.

Small was not the only member of the Chicago circle who argued for the significance of Simmel's contribution to sociology. In a letter to the editor of the University of Chicago Press to be used to promote Spykman's study, Park also lamented that

> Simmel's most important contribution to sociology has never been understood in this country. Although he has written the most profound and stimulating book in sociology, in my opinion, that has ever been written, he was not in the first instance a sociologist but a philosopher . . . When these writings are fully understood, I am convinced that much of the confusion and uncertainty that now reign in the social sciences will measurably disappear.[29]

Park's central influence upon the work of the Chicago School did not lie in a preoccupation with the foundational methodology for which he praises Simmel.[30] A more guarded judgement of Simmel's significance is to be found in an essay on Tönnies by another member of the Chicago circle and student of Park's, Louis Wirth. Wirth does concede that 'one of the central influences in modern German sociology emanates from Simmel' and that 'much of what is being done in German sociology at the present time is the direct result of his labors' and that, following Small, 'we may properly designate that aspect of contemporary German sociology as the post- or neo-Simmel movement.'[31] However, Wirth continues with an important qualification:

> Although Simmel's contribution to sociological thought bids fair to be epoch-making, it must not be supposed that present-day German sociology is wholly dominated by his spirit. There is, indeed, a school of thought which avowedly accepts him as its master, but Simmel was too little of a system builder to breed a generation of mere disciples.[32]

This was written in 1926. In many respects, this marked a high point in American evaluation of Simmel's work. A few years later, the judgements of Theodor Abel[33] and Pitrim Sorokin[34] were decidedly negative. Spykman's study did not stimulate translations of Simmel's works into English. In fact, apart from the occasional piece circulating in Chicago, there is almost a twenty-five year pause in the appearance of translations of his work, until 'The Sociology of Sociability' (translated by Everett Hughes) in 1949[35] and Kurt Wolff's major collection *The Sociology of Georg Simmel* in 1950.[36]

Wolff's collection, drawn largely from Simmel's *Soziologie*, to be followed by further translations in the 1950s, did stimulate a renewed interest in his work, both empirically and theoretically. Somewhat more spasmodically, though possibly with a more recent increased momentum, succeeding decades have witnessed a growing engagement with Simmel's social theory. However, it must be doubted whether this renewed confrontation has signified the development of the 'post-Simmelism' which Small assumed he could detect in the post-First World War period in Germany. Indeed, given the instances to which Small refers as evidence of this movement in Weimar Germany, it is doubtful whether there was a post-Simmel current of sociology in that period. Two exceptions which would require further detailed study are the sociological contributions of Max Scheler and Karl Mannheim (both, but especially Mannheim, admirers of Simmel's sociology).[37]

In fact, if we wished to look for evidence in the post-First World War period of the kind of interest in Simmel's work that could be seen as stimulating contributions to a social theory of modernity – some of which have been sketched out in previous chapters – then we would have to turn away, from both the Weimar currents in sociology (such as von Wiese's taxonomy of social relations which Small reviewed)[38] and those in the United States (including Talcott Parsons' unpublished chapter on Simmel, at one time destined for *The Structure of Social Action*).[39] We would have to focus our attention upon social theorists who combined a critical stance with regard to Simmel's social theory with a recognition of his insights into important dimensions of modernity. This often more muted and subterranean interest, carried out outside the confines of orthodox sociology as an academic discipline, can be found in the work of two of Simmel's erstwhile students, Siegfried Kracauer[40] and Ernst Bloch[41] (and leaving aside the not insignificant traces of his influence upon another student, Georg Lukács,[42] certainly in his earlier writings up to and including his *History and Class Consciousness* though not his *Destruction of Reason*, so replete with Stalinist excesses) and in the writings of Walter Benjamin[43] and, to a lesser extent, Theodor Adorno[44] (including affinities between Simmel's outline of the dialectics of subjective and objective culture and Adorno and Horkheimer's *Dialectics of Enlightenment*). The investigation of the contours of experience of modernity, an excavation of its often mundane, surface phenomena, the illumination of 'blank spots on the sociological atlas' (as Plant described Kracauer's contribution)[45] thus came from a direction that Small did not envisage. At least as far as our concerns go, is it an accident that, in however critical a form, traces of Small's anticipated 'neo-Simmelism' should have come from a varied tradition that was itself to be termed 'neo-Marxism'? An attempt to answer such a question would take us far from our present concerns, and would in fact require an investigation whose scope has only occasionally been intimated.

Instead, this may be the point at which to abandon such historiographical intentions – without denying their fruitfulness – and turn to an examination of contemporary themes that have been announced in earlier chapters. These are Simmel's continued relevance for a social theory of modernity, for an investigation of 'the culture of things', and for his possible relevance for social theories of postmodernity.

II

Whereas it is the case that some earlier figures within the broad and by no means homogeneous tradition of Critical Theory acknowledged Simmel's contributions to the study of modernity, the same is hardly true of more recent incursions into the origins, consequences and fate of modernity by that tradition's central contemporary figure, Jürgen Habermas. In his *Theories of Communicative Action*,[46] which certainly engages with theories of modernity, Habermas cites Simmel's work only twice, whilst in the more pertinent essay 'Modernity – an Incomplete Project',[47] Simmel is not referred to at all. And although his discussion in that essay of the transformation of the concepts of time and history are centrally relevant to a theory of modernity, when Habermas turns to a definition of cultural modernity, it is that of Max Weber which is highlighted. More recently Habermas has provided an introduction to a reissue of Simmel's *Philosophische Kultur* (1983) under the rubric 'Simmel as Diagnostician of the Times'.[48] And in *The Philosophical Discourse of Modernity* (1987), whose critical engagement with philosophies of modernity and postmodernity extends from Hegel to Derrida and Foucault, Simmel is referenced twice – on both occasions in the context of *Lebensphilosophie*.[49] Only in the introductory essay on 'Simmel as Diagnostician of the Times' does Habermas acknowledge Simmel's relevance to the study of modernity and his influence upon varied traditions of Critical Theory.

However, there Habermas seeks to limit Simmel's relevance for present-day concerns. Simmel is viewed as someone who stimulates investigation in philosophy and sociology rather than being 'a philosopher and sociologist solidly rooted in the scientific enterprise';[50] as 'a child of the fin de siècle' whose conception of culture is rooted in neo-Kantianism; as someone whose 'premisses are dead, only the consequences carry on'.[51] And when he declares that Simmel is both distant and close to us, it is the constellation of *Lebensphilosophie* that is seen as bringing us close to him, even though his conception of a tragedy of culture is so firmly rooted in metaphysics that it robs his diagnosis of the times of political–practical consequences. Although this is not the place to confront in detail such a conception of Simmel's relevance, it should be pointed out that he is more engaged in the scientific enterprise than Habermas concedes, that some key dimensions of the *fin de siècle* problematic remain with us today – not least in postmodern discourse, that his premisses for the foundation of sociology at least remain a fruitful starting point, and that merely to focus upon Simmel's later writings is to overemphasize assumptions that are not nearly so evident in his early writings. Our preceding analysis of dimensions of modernity has often drawn upon Simmel's writings of the 1890s and around the turn of the century which possess a richness that Habermas chooses to understate, if not to ignore. These writings indicate that Simmel, sometimes guardedly, sometimes openly and often anonymously did draw political conclusions from his social analysis. This is true of one area which Habermas acknowledges as a significant contribution to contemporary issues, namely Simmel's extensive writings on the position of women in modernity and the women's movement of his day. Simmel does articulate some of the issues surrounding the argument that modern objective culture is male dominated and the attendant possibilities for the development of an autonomous female culture.[52] This is a crucial dimension of Simmel's analysis of the culture of modernity in which the developmental tendency of increasing social differentiation confronts the widening gap between subjective and objective culture.

The broader context of Simmel's analysis of the culture of modernity, of our experience of modernity, has been developed earlier. Its interrelated focal points are the metropolis and the mature money economy. The experience of modernity is viewed by Simmel as discontinuous experience of *time* as transitory, in which both the fleeting moment and the sense of presentness converge; *space* as the dialectic of distance and proximity (associated with social distance as boundary maintenance and the removal of boundaries and spatial distance in the money economy's capacity to connect apparently distant and dissociated individuals and things); and *causality* as contingent, arbitrary and fortuitous. The rejection of historical necessity could result either in history no longer having any intelligibility ('a somewhat free game of fantasy', according to Troeltsch) or each individual event might have its own internal logic. The universalization of money exchange, and the domination of the sphere of circulation and exchange, critically transform the teleology of ends and means in the direction of the centrality of means. The discontinuity of experience in the metropolis and the mature money economy takes the form of fragmentation of experience, a constant flux of impressions and interactions. Our participation in the money economy involves a socialization into 'the indifference of things', into the substitution of quantities for qualities and into the levelling of values. Many of these processes are examined in Simmel's work in the 1890s as well as most fully in *The Philosophy of Money*. But they continue in his later writings too. Two instances that reveal Simmel's confrontation with the contradictory developments of modern culture are his opening discussion of the culture of means in *Schopenhauer and Nietzsche* (1907)[53] and his essays on the widening gap between subjective and objective culture, such as 'On the Essence of Culture' (1908).[54]

The predominance of a culture of means heightens the role of human mediators, in the form of agents, individuals as 'indirect' beings and materialized means in the form of technology. The complexity of mediations also challenges simple assumptions about the nature of the economy of means. Simmel does not draw the connection with the marginalist assumptions concerning the economy when he insists that the 'simple triad of desire–means–ends is excluded by the increasing multiplicity of complexity of higher life'.[55] Instead he goes on to emphasize other consequences of the economy of means. In a modern economy,

> Technology, which is the sum total of means of a civilized existence, becomes the essential object of struggle and evaluation. Thus, people are eventually surrounded everywhere by a criss-crossing jungle of enterprises and institutions in which the final and definitely valuable goals are missing altogether. Only in this state of culture does the need for a final goal and meaning for life appear.[56]

This 'criss-crossing jungle of enterprises and institutions' constitutes the supra-individual objective culture which confronts human subjects as autonomous:

> In highly developed epochs with an advanced division of labour, cultural achievements mature and grow together, into an auton-

omous realm, as it were, things become more complete, spiritual, to some extent following ever more obediently an inner objective logic of expediency.[57]

This takes place without human subjects being able to match this development, whilst at the same time being faced with the paradox that 'no subjective culture can exist without an objective one'. This is one of the reasons why Simmel's exploration of 'the culture of things' is a matter of urgency.

III

In Simmel's excursions into the nature of the experience of modernity, there is an emphasis upon the surface of everyday life, upon each of life's elements, upon 'the multiplicity and confusion on the surface of our existence'.[58] Simmel's response to this multiplicity and confusion of things is to examine how far the total meaning emanates from any one thing or element. In other words, Simmel takes seriously the problem faced by his own presupposition that our cultural existence manifests itself not merely in the experience of our objectifications but in the experience of a culture of things that have acquired an autonomous existence. Indeed, in *The Philosophy of Money* he posits 'the culture of things as the culture of human beings'. Simmel declares an interest in objective culture, in 'objective spirit' that does not view this culture or spirit as embodied in universal concepts but rather in everyday things, in the 'little things with which we adorn our life', in the fleeting interactions that may be associated with our interactions with things. As Klaus Köhnke has argued, this preoccupation is one that emanates from the *Völkerpsychologie* of Lazarus.[59] We might add that it may have received additional force from a reading of Nietzsche, with his emphasis upon the mundane things, the 'meanest' things as objects of philosophical reflection.[60] Further, the concern with things also finds a certain resonance in *The Philosophy of Money*, not merely from the whole discussion of the consequences of objectification (as *Sachlichkeit*), of a culture of things (as *Sachkultur*), but also from a paradox in neo-classical economics. There, on the one hand, its focus upon demand, upon the satisfaction of individual desires, upon consumption, seems to bring us closer to an economic theory grounded in *subjectivity*. On the other hand, however, the release of subjective desires moves in the direction of exchange *between* subjects, i.e. intersubjectivity. But, this world of relations between subjects manifests itself as *relations between things* and opens up the prospect of a threatening universe of things. Jevons, cited in Chapter 5, is not untypical in his formulations of this dimension of human experience. 'Every act of exchange', he states, 'presents itself to us in the form of *a ratio between two numbers*'[61] (i.e. quantities of X and Y). These ratios are indirect modes of expressing value. Value is not an 'intrinsic quality of a thing; it is an *extrinsic accident* or relation'.[62] In other words, 'value must be *a mere relation or accident of a thing* as regards other things and the persons needing them'.[63]

The consequences of a life surrounded by seemingly autonomous things and our accidental, fortuitous relations with them did not remain unreflected upon in the nineteenth century. Edgar Allan Poe could write a 'Philosophy of Furniture', Max Klinger could produce a threatening lithograph series on the autonomous existence of 'the glove', the whole genre of the detective novel could emanate from the collection of 'clues' in a pseudo-scientific manner. Such reflections were seldom the conscious object of social scientific endeavour. Sociology, for example, could be preoccupied with attempts to ground the new discipline in society as a hypostatized organic totality. Simmel's attempts to establish sociology as an independent discipline took a different direction, which encouraged the investigation of any form of interaction however fleeting and insignificant it may be. The mundane everyday things too that, like 'the purloined letter', were always there but never noticed could become the object of study for social theory.

Simmel is one of the first social theorists to examine, in however fragmentary a manner, what Benjamin was later to term 'the power of the extinct world of things'.[64] The interest in the world of mundane things was not in order to celebrate the surface of everyday existence, not to concede 'satisfaction with the sunlit surface of things' but rather, as he puts it in *Philosophische Kultur*, 'the deepening of the surface of life', 'the digging out of every intellectual stratum beneath its appearance'.[65] The exploration of the mundane surface proceeds, as he stated in his essay on the metropolis, 'from each point on the surface of existence, however closely attached to the surface alone'. From each of these points or fragments, 'one may drop a sounding into the depth of the psyche so that all the most banal externalities of life finally are connected with the ultimate decisions concerning the meaning and style of life'.[66] Through an excavation of the surface of everyday life, Simmel seeks to overcome 'the ever wider yawning abyss between the culture of things and that of human beings', to penetrate 'a purely objectively developed life [that] lives for itself, which, for the greatest part, we cannot even understand'.[67]

In his analysis of the changing perception of things in the nineteenth century, Christoph Asendorf in *Batteries of Life-force* makes a number of references to Simmel's contribution to such an investigation.[68] One such instance is Simmel's remarks on the changing nature of the bourgeois *intérieur* (later a significant theme in Benjamin's excavations of modernity). In *The Philosophy of Money* and elsewhere, Simmel draws attention to the 'attachment' of individuals to the things that surround them, often, as in the case of the heavy furniture of the historicist *Gründerjahre*, as immovable objects. This growing together of individuals and objects in the bourgeois *intérieur* is dissolved with the creation of a 'plurality of very specifically formed objects'. The 'differentiation of objects' and 'a mass of specialised things' confront the individual as autonomous entities. In contrast to the historicist interior's wealth of immobile objects, modern furniture (*Möbel*) has 'become mobile like capital'. As Asendorf comments, citing Simmel:

> Previously trusted things have become a plurality of commodities, about which one can relate nothing since they have no history. By means of money, things become exchangeable: 'Material just as much as mental objects move about independently now, without personal agents or transporters. Things and human beings have come asunder' . . . For Simmel there is suggested here a certain sense of uncanniness with regard to the 'plurality' of things – he speaks of the 'independence' of 'the surrounding throng of things', of a 'fetish function', of a feeling of 'lack of freedom in relation to objects', and thereby makes reference to the submerged physiognomy of this interior that would first be revealed by surrealism'.[69]

Of course, not all of Simmel's treatments of 'things' are threatening and uncanny (one thinks here of 'The Handle', or 'Bridge and Door'). And not all of his concern by any means was with the *intérieur*. In a little known piece 'On Spiritualism' (1892),[70] Simmel draws a significant parallel between the predominant belief in science (and calculability, rationality, etc.) and the popularity of alternative explanations of the forces in the world associated with spiritualism. Things do not have to be material things in order to achieve their effect. It is worth noting in passing that just as Simmel was drawing this connection between belief in scientific rational explanation and spiritualist explanations, his contemporary Conan Doyle, the creator of detective fiction's most 'rational' detective, Sherlock Holmes, himself later became a spiritualist. Attempts to control the world of things can take many forms.

What is important in the present context, however, is that Simmel provided a significant impetus to investigate 'the culture of things' that was acknowledged and continued in the work of Kracauer, Bloch and Benjamin. The 'traces' of the past, the 'hieroglyphics' of the past and present, the 'excavations' at the site of modernity that they investigated owe something at least to Simmel's original impetus. From another direction, Roy Pascal[71] has suggested that Simmel's desire to recognize 'a new significance of things' in *The Philosophy of Money*, in the essay on the metropolis and elsewhere, has affinities with contemporary literary attempts to come to terms with the culture of things, with the 'snowfall' of things (Kafka), the 'thing poem' (Rilke) and the like.

Simmel's own subsequent philosophical reflections upon the widening gap between subjective and objective culture, upon the conflict in modern culture and its very essence, all reveal a concern for the apparent autonomy of the culture of things. In its most extreme form, it has been suggested by Scheible that 'the total reified world is transposed into a new mystical context of meaning that brings together subject and object insofar as the object – any object – becomes the receptacle for the momentary infusion of life'.[72] At best, the world of things seems to become a self-referential system, whose own reference points we can only dimly grasp.

IV

This apparent autonomy of the cultural sphere has achieved a new significance in recent theories of postmodernity. If we wish to extend the relevance of Simmel's work for a social theory of modernity, for a study of 'the culture of things', to a social theory of postmodernity, then we may do so only on the foundations of his critique of modernity. Neither Simmel nor, for that matter, Nietzsche or Benjamin set out to develop a theory of postmodernity. If present-day commentators seek to claim them as advocates for theories of postmodernity, then this must be recognised as the activity only of contemporary commentators. The critiques of modernity that are to be found in many texts from the late nineteenth century onwards are not celebrations of postmodernity.

It would not be possible, in the present context, to outline all the attempts to develop a social theory of postmodernity that have emerged in the past decade or so. Instead, those dimensions of a putative postmodern condition will be sketched out which have to some degree been anticipated in Simmel's work. This is not intended to support the contention that Simmel is a postmodern theorist. Indeed, a brief examination of some strands of Simmel's analysis of modernity might indicate that what we take to be new dimensions of postmodernity are, in fact, an extension or accentuation of tendencies already present in this modernity itself. In other words, it would be plausible to argue that postmodernity is a new face of modernity, in a context in which the aesthetic modernisms emanating from the experience of modernity have always announced themselves as absolutely new.[73]

What, then, are some of the features of postmodernity that are advanced in recent discussions? Our present investigation is confined to three features: the centrality of the sphere of exchange and consumption, the autonomy of the cultural sphere, and the preoccupation with the aesthetic domain. At one level, it is easy to see Simmel's relevance for those theorists of postmodernity who point to its emergence around the turn of the century. For Lyotard, the post modern condition 'designates the state of our culture following the transformations which, since the end of the nineteenth century, have altered the game rules for science, literature and the arts'. The abandonment of grand narratives and their replacement by a diversity of language games is already heralded by the plurality of value spheres in neo-Kantian philosophy, and of course elaborated in Wittgenstein's (later) philosophy. Simmel certainly envisaged the fragmentation of both discourses and individuals, located in a past that 'comes down to us only in fragments', a past that 'can come to life and be interpreted only through the experiences of the immediate present'.[74] The experience of the immediate present is one of discontinuity, flux and fragmentation.

However, for many theorists of postmodernity, there is a more decidedly materialist transformation that accounts for its emergence. It is associated with a putative shift from industrial to post-industrial society, from production to post-production society, from capitalist to post-capitalist society, from the sphere of production to that of consumption. The latter shift was already heralded a century ago in the theoretical transformation in economic theory known as the Marginalist Revolution. It is a shift that animates, in part, Simmel's theory of value in *The Philosophy of Money*. Although this is not the place to engage in a critique of such presumed economic transformations, it should at least be pointed out here that a possible meaning of post-industrial, post-production society is that what was associated previously with the core of the world capitalist system now takes place elsewhere, in what was, until recently, the periphery. A post-capitalist society requires the abandonment not merely of historically variable relations between wage labour and capital but also the abandonment of the production of commodities. Simmel was aware, in a rudimentary manner, of the extension of commodification, of the commodification of leisure and human experience itself – themes that are now associated with a putatively postmodern society.

However, there are more compelling affinities between Simmel's conception of what was for him a *modern* socio-economic formation and its *postmodern* successor. Simmel's *Philosophy of Money* 'dethrones industrialism as the determining force of modern society' and replaces it with a discourse on the effects of the mature money economy – conceived largely as the spheres of circulation, exchange and consumption – but 'without discussing money as capital'. Fully in keeping with this shift of focus, 'the paratypical phenomenon of Simmel's conceptual world is the metropolis . . . , not the industrial corporation.[75] The metropolis is not merely the focal point of the money economy, the intersection of social circles and networks of the division of labour, of fashion as the 'external and unstable illusion of modernity', but also of the circulation of individuals and their fragmentary images of things. But in economic terms, the study of the universal equivalent of value and its functions was likely to engage Simmel's attention in the spheres of circulation, exchange and consumption. An investigation of the phenomenal forms of these spheres would reveal endless circulation, equivalent exchange between unequal participants and identical consumption of the same good again by unequal participants. However, Simmel points to the extent and consequences of the differentiation of consumption in the cultural as well as the material spheres (thus anticipating some of Bourdieu's concerns in *Distinction* and elsewhere).[76]

Simmel therefore explores the phenomenal forms of these economic spheres without, as in the case of Marx, searching for the essential relations which ensure that these phenomenal forms appear to us in the manner or form in which they do so. Simmel does view money as obliterating the distinctions between use values, as being the form in which value exists as autonomous exchange value. He also recognizes that the sphere of circulation appears to us as an autonomous sphere, one that seems to be guided by its own laws. This apparently autonomous sphere of circulation and exchange is one which can be characterized as an internally self-referential system. What takes place within it, each motion *within* it, appears intelligible only in terms of other movements within this system. An analysis of the sphere of circulation in this manner suggests affinities with a further dimension of postmodern existence, namely the self-referentiality of signifiers. In one respect, however, Simmel does not go so far as postmodern analysts in asserting the collapse of the distinction between signifier and referent. For Simmel, the distinction still exists, as in the realm of fashion as the ever-new face of the commodity, where the economic production of things is more than the mere production and reproduction of things, it is a co-production of their aesthetic attraction as a veil.[77] However, in so far as Simmel investigates the *symbolic* significance of money and commodities there are anticipatory echoes of postmodern theories of consumption which imply that we consume the sign or symbol of the commodity rather even than its 'spectral objectivity'. Such reflections upon Simmel's analysis of the sphere of circulation, exchange and consumption suggest that, in some respects at least, his investigations both parallel and deepen those of Marx in the latter's then unknown *Grundrisse* as well as anticipate reflections upon aspects of the postmodern economy.

Viewed more broadly, the apparent autonomy of the sphere of circulation and exchange – which for over a decade has appeared as the infinite source of fictitious capital, and whose analogous development in the metropolis has been in the creation of fictitious façades – has its parallel for Simmel in two related spheres, in objective culture and in the aesthetic sphere. With regard to objective culture, though in a different context, Marx in his early writings maintained that 'the devaluation of the human world grows in direct proportion to the increase in value of the world of things'.[78] For Simmel, the culture of things was an important component of objective culture, one that appeared to have its own internal logic. A logic of autonomous circulation was suggested earlier by Nietzsche's eternal return of the ever same, the experience of which could be transposed, as Benjamin later indicated, to the sphere of circulation and exchange.[79]

The connection between the autonomy of objective culture and the apparent autonomy of the sphere of circulation and exchange (with its attendant commodity fetishism) was drawn by Simmel himself in his essay 'The Concept and the Tragedy of Culture' (1911), where he declared that

> The 'fetishism' which Marx assigned to economic commodities represents only a special case of this general fate of contents of culture. With the increase in culture these contents more and more stand under a paradox: . . . originally created by subjects . . . in their intermediate form of objectivity . . . they follow an immanent

logic of development . . . impelled not by physical necessities, but by truly cultural ones.[80]

The contents of objective culture thus acquire an 'ominous independence', just as did the universe of commodities for Marx. Commenting upon this and related passages in Simmel's essay, Franco Moretti draws a number of inferences – though this is not his aim – that are important for some postmodern theories of culture. First, that 'the autonomization of culture, its transformation into an objective form, capable of producing meanings basically independent of the consciousness and the will of its producers, is ideology's true core: its content can change with time, but its formal nature endures'.[81] Second, that 'the attainment of autonomy by cultural forms implies . . . that they develop according to their own specific logic and, therefore, cannot be predicted and deduced from analysis of other social spheres. If they are truly autonomous they can no longer be traced back to a central and unique 'cause-aim' . . . They can no longer be deducted from it, nor do they reproduce it. They are not built upon, nor can they be explained by, the principle of homology or isomorphism'.[82] Such reflections are not those which Simmel himself elicits from the study of objective culture. Yet they do go some way to clarify his insistence upon the great work of art as the possibility for transcending this cultural problematic. Indeed, one of Simmel's pupils, the young Georg Lukács, following his teacher, located the work of art in precisely the constellation which Moretti's commentary highlights. The perfect work of art, the essence of artistic creation aims 'to cut every bond which tied it to living, concrete, moving life in order to give itself a new life, closed in as itself . . . In every artistic creation there exists a kind of *Inselhaftigkeit*, as Simmel calls it, as a result of which it is reluctant to be a part of any continuous development'.[83] In his essay on the tragedy of culture, Simmel is careful to draw the distinction between the *contents* of objective culture, developing according to their own laws, and their 'essential meaning and value', presumably revealed by their *form* at least as far as the work of art is concerned.

In Simmel's writings on culture after 1900, there is in fact an increasingly pronounced tragic vision arising out of the opposition of form and life. This opposition extends to all spheres of society and manifests itself as an ongoing resistance to form. Life generates form and struggles against that which it has created. In *The Conflict of Modern Culture* (1918)[84], Simmel detects a wide range of areas of culture in which there is a contemporary opposition to 'form *as such*, against the *principle* of form'. The opposition manifests itself in art in expressionism where 'the inner emotions of the artist are manifest in his work exactly as he experiences them; his emotions are continued, extended in the work';[85] in philosophy as Pragmatism and, more generally, 'in all thinkers who are filled with the modern feeling against closed systems' ;[86] in 'the new morality' which views marriage and prostitution as 'oppressive forms which thwart immediate and genuine life'; in religion as mysticism and, more generally, as 'a tendency for forms of religious *belief* to dissolve into modes of religious *life*, into religiosity as a purely *functional* justification of religion'.[87] In these and other areas of modern life, Simmel detects a revolt against the ideology of form. Some of these dimensions find resonance today in theories of postmodernity.[88]

There is a third dimension of Simmel's social theory which appears to accord with a tendency in postmodernism, namely the accentuation of the aesthetic domain. In Simmel's case, the aesthetic domain is one which, in the great work of art, can transcend the contradictions of modernity. However, the aesthetic sphere is present in everyday modern life. Indeed, as has been argued in connection with the development of the mature money economy, it is the experience of the sublime which predominates in this mode. The aesthetic perception of the sphere of circulation and exchange is one in which exchange value replaces value, aesthetics replaces ethics and, as Vattimo has argued for Heidegger's philosophy, Being is replaced by value (as exchange value).[89] The aesthetic viewpoint overcomes the indifference of things in the sphere of circulation and exchange. The appeal to the aesthetic mode of experiencing the world has often been seen as a response to the crisis and contradictions in modernity. Simmel, as we have seen, illuminates many aspects of the aesthetic viewpoint, both in terms of distance, symmetry and asymmetry, form and formlessness and in terms of juxtapositions of the work of art and the applied work of art, the preponderance of style as disguise, 'a *veil* that imposes a barrier and a distance', the stylization of forms of life. As Simmel puts it in *The Philosophy of Money*, 'the entire visible environment of our cultural life has disintegrated into a plurality of styles'.[90]

To view reality 'as from afar' is one response to unresolved tensions and contradictions. Simmel himself was not always preoccupied with the aesthetic mode of experience. In his early work, especially on ethics – a subject he returned to in later years – there is a dimension of Simmel's work that is only now beginning to be explored. But around the turn of the century, he did detect an increase in an aesthetic stance with regard to social reality. It has been suggested by David Harvey with regard to postmodernity as a historical condition that 'the confidence of an era can be assessed by the width of the gap between scientific and moral reasoning. In periods of confusion and uncertainty the turn to aesthetics (of whatever form) becomes more pronounced'.[91] Earlier in his study of postmodernity, Harvey had pointed to 'the continuity of the condition of fragmentation, ephemerality, discontinuity, and chaotic change in both modernist and postmodernist thought'.[92] Despite the different responses to this condition, is this what gives Simmel's theory of modernity its affinity with some dimensions at least of theories of postmodernity?

Notes

1 THE STUDY OF SOCIETY

1 See K.C. Köhnke, 'Four Concepts of Social Science at Berlin University', in M. Kaern, B.S. Phillips and R.S. Cohen (eds), *Georg Simmel and Contemporary Sociology*, Dordrecht/Boston/London, Kluwer Academic, 1990, pp.99—108.

2 See G. Simmel, *Die Probleme der Geschichtsphilosophie*, Leipzig, Duncker & Humblot, 1892, and G. Simmel, 'Zur Methodik der Sozialwissenschaft', in *Jahrbuch für Gesetzgebung, Verwaltung und Volkswirtschaft*, 20, 1896 pp.575–85.

3 See G. Simmel, *Einleitung in die Moralwissenschaft*, Berlin/Herz, 1892/1893.

4 H. Böhringer, 'Spuren von spekulativem Atomismus in Simmels formaler Soziologie', in H. Böhringer and K. Gründer (eds), *Ästhetik und Soziologie um die Jahrhundertwende*, Frankfurt, 1978, pp.105–17.

5 *Op. cit.*, p.116.

6 H. Lotze, *Mikrokosmos*, vol. 3, 2nd edn., Leipzig, 1872, pp.380–452.

7 See H. Spencer, *The Principles of Sociology*, 5th thousand, vol. 1, London, 1904, p.436.

8 See W. Dilthey, *Einleitung in die Geisteswissenschaften*, 2nd edn., Leipzig/Berlin, 1923, p.37.

9 See M. Lazarus and H. Steinthal, 'Einleitende Gedanken über Völkerpsychologie', *Zeitschrift für Völkerpsychologie und Sprachwissenschaft*, 1860, 3–4.

10 G. Simmel, *Brücke und Tür*, Stuttgart, 1957, p.1.

11 G. Simmel, *Über sociale Differenzierung*, Leipzig, Duncker & Humblot, 1890, p.13.

12 G. Simmel, 'Tendencies in German Life and thought since 1870', *International Monthly*, New York, 5 (1902) pp.93–111, 166–8, especially 103.

13 G. Simmel, 'Zur Methodik der Sozialwissenschaft', *op. cit.*, p.235.

14 G. Simmel, *Einleitung in die Moralwissenschaft*, vol.1, *op. cit.*, p.164.

15 G. Simmel, 'The Problem of Sociology', *Annals of the American Academy of Political Science*, 6, 1895, pp.52–63, especially p.52.

16 G. Simmel, *Über sociale Differenzierung, op. cit.*, p.13.
17 *Ibid.*, p.15.
18 G. Simmel, 'The Problem of Sociology', *op. cit.*, pp.415–16.
19 *Ibid*, pp.422–3.
20 G. Simmel, 'Superiority and Subordination as Subject-Matter of Sociology', *American Journal of Sociology*, 2, 1896, p.167.
21 R.Park, *Soziologische Vorlesungen von Georg Simmel*, Chicago, 1931, pp.2–3.
22 *Ibid.*, p.3.
23 G. Simmel, *The Philosophy of Money*, London, Routledge, 1990, p.175.
24 G. Simmel, 'Superiority and Subordination', *op. cit.*, p.169.
25 G. Simmel, 'The Problem of Sociology', *op. cit.*, pp.421–2.
26 G. Simmel, '*Zur Methodik der Sozialwissenschaft*', *op. cit.*, p.233.
27 *Ibid.*, pp.232–3.
28 G. Simmel, 'Superiority and subordination', *op. cit.*, p.168.
29 G. Simmel, 'The Number of Members as Determining the Sociological Form of the Group', *American Journal of Sociology*, 8, 1902, p.2.
30 G. Simmel, 'Soziologie der Sinne', *Die Neue Rundschau*, 18, 1907, 1025. My emphasis.
31 G. Simmel, 'The Problem of Sociology' in K.H. Wolff (ed.), *Essays on Sociology, Philosophy and Aesthetics by Georg Simmel et al.*, Columbus, Ohio State University Press, 1959, p.327.
32 G. Simmel, 'Soziologie der Sinne', *op. cit.*, p.1026.
33 G. Simmel, 'How is Society Possible?', in K.H. Wolff (ed.), *op. cit.*, p.338.
34 *Ibid.*, p.338.
35 *Ibid.*, p.340.
36 *Ibid.*, p.342.
37 *Ibid.*, p.351.
38 Ibid., p.353. On the significance of the 'as if' notion in Simmel's work and its relationship to Vaihinger's *Philosophy of As If* see M. Kaern, 'The World as Human Construction' in *Georg Simmel and Contemporary Sociology, op. cit.*, pp.75–98
39 M. Davis, 'Georg Simmel and the Aesthetics of Social Reality', *Social Forces*, 51, 1973, pp.320–9, especially 320. My emphasis.
40 See my *Sociological Impressionism*, London, Routledge, 1991, p.68.
41 R. Goldscheid, 'Jahresbericht Über Erscheinungen der Soziologie in den Jahren 1899-1904', *Archiv für systematische Philosophie*, 10, 1904, p.411.
42 G. Simmel, 'Soziologische Aesthetik', *Die Zukunft*, 17, 1896, pp.204–16; G. Simmel 'Sociological Aesthetics' in K.P. Etzkorn (ed. and trans.), George Simmel, *The Conflict in Modern Culture and Other Essays*, New York, Teachers Press, 1968, pp.68–80. All references are to this translation.
43 G. Simmel, 'Sociological Aesthetics', *op. cit.*, pp.71–2.
44 *Ibid.*, p.74. My emphasis.
45 *Ibid.*, p.75.
46 *Ibid.*, p.69.
47 *Ibid.*, p.78.
48 G. Simmel, 'How is Society Possible?', *op. cit.*, p.355. My emphasis.

2 GEORG SIMMEL AND SOCIAL PSYCHOLOGY

1 For an overview of Georg Simmel's influence on American social theory, see Donald N. Levine *et al.*, 'Simmel's Influence on American Sociology', in *Ästhetik und Soziologie um die Jahrhundertwende: Georg Simmel*, ed. Hannes Böhringer and Karlfried Gründer, Frankfurt, Klostermann, 1976, pp.176–228. Some examples of applications of Simmel's work are Theodor M. Mills, 'Some Hypotheses on Small Groups from Simmel', *American Journal of Sociology*, 63, 1958, pp.642–50; Theodore Caplow, *Two against One*, New Jersey, Prentice-Hall, 1968, and Lewis Coser, *The Functions of Social Conflict*, New York, Free Press, 1956.

2 Some of Simmel's early essays were published in the *American Journal of Sociology* between 1896 and 1910, often translated by the editor, Albion W. Small. In the post-World War II period, sociologists and social psychologists have relied upon K. H. Wolff, trans. and ed., *The Sociology of Georg Simmel*, Glencoe, Illinois, Free Press, 1950; Georg Simmel, *Conflict and the Web of Group Affiliations*, trans. K.H. Wolff and Reinhard Bendix, Glencoe, Illinois, Free Press, 1955; and K. H. Wolff, ed., *Georg Simmel, 1858–1918: Essays on Sociology, Philosophy and Aesthetics*, Columbus, Ohio State University Press, 1959. Although all three contain parts of Simmel's *Soziologie*, the first of these is the most comprehensive with regard to extracts from the *Soziologie*.

3 See Georg Simmel, *Soziologie: Untersuchungen über die Formen der Vergesellschaftung*, Berlin, Duncker & Humblot, 1908, 5th edn, 1968.

4 Friedrich H. Tenbruck, 'Georg Simmel (1858–1918),' *Kölner Zeitschrift für Soziologie und Sozial-Psychologie*, 10, 1958, pp.586–614. For an early version of this argument see Maria Steinhoff, 'Die Form als soziologische Grundkategorie bei Georg Simmel', *Kölner Vierteljahrshefte für Soziologie*, 4, 1925, pp.216–17. For a recent examination of the thesis see David Frisby, *Sociological Impressionism: A Reassessment of Georg Simmel's Social Theory*, London, Routledge, 1991, chap. 2. Tenbruck's argument is challenged in Heinz-Jürgen Dahme, *Soziologie als exakte Wissenschaft*, Stuttgart, Enke, 1981, vol. 1.

5 See Lazarus Schweiger, 'Philosophie der Geschichte, Völkerpsychologie und Soziologie', in *Berner Studien zur Philosophie und ihre Geschichte*, 18, 1899. Schweiger's study won the Moritz Lazarus prize for that year. It also contains a brief reference to Simmel's work.

6 See Hans Simmel, 'Auszüge aus den Lebenserinnerungen', in Böhringer and Gründer, *Ästhetik und Soziologie, op. cit.*, p.249. On the location of Moritz Lazarus and Heymann Steinthal in the development of psychology, see Kurt Danziger, 'Origins and Basic Principles of Wundt's Völkerpsychologie', *British Journal of Social Psychology*, 1985. The data on Simmel's education and career are to be found in Michael Landmann, 'Bausteine zur Biographie', in *Buch des Dankes an Simmel*, ed. Kurt Gassen and Michael Landmann, Berlin, Duncker & Humblot, 1958, pp.11–33. The book as a whole remains an invaluable source of material on Simmel's life.

7 See M.A. Tinker, 'Wundt's Doctorate Students and their Theses (1875–

1920', in *Wundt Studies: A Centennial Collection*, ed. W.G. Bringmann and R.D. Tweney, Toronto, Hogrefe, 1980, p.270. I owe knowledge of Simmel's acquaintance with Paul Radestock to Klaus C. Köhnke.

8 The submission is quoted in full in Landmann, 'Bausteine zur Biographie', *op. cit.*, pp.22–3.

9 *Ibid.*, p.22.

10 *Ibid.*, p.32. My emphasis.

11 This information is contained in section D of Kurt Gassen's excellent bibliography. See Kurt Gassen, 'Georg-Simmel-Bibliographie', in Gassen and Landmann, *Buch des Dankes an Georg Simmel, op. cit.*, pp.345–9.

12 The first mention of sociology in Simmel's course titles is in the summer semester of 1887, and the first course to be simply entitled 'Sociology' was offered in the summer semester of 1894. Subsequently Simmel offered courses on sociology every year until 1908 and thereafter only in the winter semesters of 1909–10, 1911–12, and 1917–18.

13 Georg Simmel, 'Psychologische und ethnologische Studien über Musik', *Zeitschrift für Völkerpsychologie und Sprachwissenschaft*, 13, 1882, pp.261–305. A translation is available in Georg Simmel, *The Conflict in Modern Culture and Other Essays*, trans. and ed. K. Etzkorn, New York, Teachers College Press, 1968, pp.98–140; Georg Simmel, 'Dantes Psychologie', *Zeitschrift für Völkerpsychologie und Sprachwissenschaft*, 15, 1884, pp.18–69, 239–276.

14 Georg Simmel, 'Anzeige', *Vierteljahresschrift für wissenschaftliche Philosophie*, 10, 1886, pp.487–503.

15 [Georg Simmel] 'Zur Psychologie des Pessimismus', *Baltische Monatsschrift*, 35, 1888, pp.557–66. This hitherto unknown article is cited in Klaus C. Köhnke, 'Von der Völkerpsychologie zur Soziologie – unbekannte Texte des jungen Georg Simmel', in *Georg Simmel und die Moderne*, ed. Heinz-Jürgen Dahme and Otthein Rammstedt, Frankfurt, Suhrkamp, 1984. For later essays on pessimism see Georg Simmel, 'Sozialismus und Pessimismus', *Die Zeit*, (Vienna), 22, 3 February 1900; and Simmel, 'Zur einer Theorie des Pessimismus', *Die Zeit*, Vienna, 22, 20 January 1900. Simmel also lectured on pessimism (with reference to Arthur Schopenhauer's doctrine) in the winter semesters of 1887–8, 1890–1, and 1894–5.

16 Georg Simmel, 'Notiz', *Zeitschrift für Philosophie und philosophische Kritik*, 95, 1889, pp.159–60. The brief notice summarizes the psychology programme at Johns Hopkins University, which Simmel praises as offering 'a thorough schooling in exact psychology and its ancillary sciences'.

17 Georg Simmel, 'Zur Psychologie des Geldes', *Jahrbuch für Gesetzgebung, Verwaltung und Volkswirtschaft*, 13, 1889, pp.1251–64. Simmel had presented this paper in Gustav Schmoller's seminar on political science and it was published in the journal Schmoller edited.

18 Georg Simmel, *Philosophie des Geldes*, Berlin, Duncker & Humblot, 1900.

19 Georg Simmel, 'Zur Psychologie der Frauen', *Zeitschrift für Völkerpsychologie und Sprachwissenschaft* 20, 1890, 6–46. See also

Simmel, 'Ein Jubiläum der Frauenbewegung', *National-Zeitung*, 27 November 1893, Sunday supplement 48; Simmel, 'Der Militarismus und die Stellung der Frauen', *Vossische Zeitung*, 21, 28 October 1894, Sunday supplement 42; Simmel, 'Der Frauenkongress und die Socialdemokratie', *Die Zukunft*, 17, 1896, pp.80–4; Simmel, 'Weibliche Kultur', *Neue Deutsche Rundschau*, 13, 1902, pp.504–15: Simmel, 'Bruchstücke aus einer Psychologie der Frauen', *Der Tag*, 9 July 1904. See also Lewis A. Coser, 'Georg Simmel's Neglected Contributions to the Sociology of Women', *Signs*, 2, 1977, pp.869–76.

20 Georg Simmel, *Über sociale Differenzierung: Soziologische und psychologische Untersuchungen*, Leipzig, Duncker & Humblot, 1890. Some sections are translated in Peter A. Lawrence, *Georg Simmel: Sociologist and European*, Sunbury, Middlesex, Nelson, 1976, pp.95–110, 111–38.

21 Georg Simmel, *Die Probleme der Geschichtsphilosophie*, Leipzig, Duncker & Humbolt, 1892.

22 Georg Simmel, *Einleitung in die Moralwissenschaft*, 2 vols, Berlin, Hertz, 1892, 1893. This was not merely an introduction to ethics, but rather a psychological and, to some extent, sociological analysis of moral norms.

23 Georg Simmel, 'Skizze einer Willentheorie', *Zeitschrift für Psychologie und Physiologie der Sinnesorgane* 9, 1896, pp.206–20.

24 Georg Simmel, 'G. Tarde. Les lois de l'imitation', *Zeitschrift für Psychologie und Physiologie der Sinnesorgane*, 2, 1891, pp.141–2.

25 Georg Simmel, 'Massenpsychologie', *Die Zeit*, Vienna, 5, 23 November 1895.

26 Georg Simmel, 'Psychologische Glossen zur Strafgesetznovelle', *Sozialpolitisches Zentralblatt*, 1, 1892, pp.173–4. Also significant is a review on mass criminality: see Simmel, 'über Massenverbrechen', *Die Zeit*, Vienna, 2, 2 October 1897.

27 Georg Simmel, 'Das Problem der Soziologie', *Jahrbuch für Gesetzgebung. Verwaltung und Volkswirtschaft*, 18, 1894, pp.271–7. An English translation with a 'Supplementary Note' appeared as 'The Problem of Sociology', *Annals of the American Academy of Political Science*, 6, 1895, pp.52–63. Simmel, writing to Célestin Bouglé with reference to this essay, says it is one 'upon which I myself lay the greatest value and which contains my work programme (and the essential part of my teaching programme'). (Unpublished.)

28 Georg Simmel, 'Zur Psychologie der Mode: Soziologische Studie', *Die Zeit*, Vienna, 5, 12 October 1895. See subsequently Simmel, *Philosophie der Mode*, Berlin, Pan, 1905, and Simmel, *Philosophische Kultur: Gesammelte Essais*, Leipzig, Klinkhardt, 1911, chap. 2.

29 In this same period, Simmel's work was itself reviewed in the then recently established *Psychological Review*, which even contained an announcement of his being made 'assistant professor' at Berlin University in 1900.

30 Simmel, *The Philosophy of Money*, London, Routledge, 1991, p.56. This important work was widely reviewed by many social theorists, including George H. Mead. See G.H. Mead, 'Philosophie des Geldes', *Journal of*

Political Economy, 9, 1901, pp.616–19. Mead acknowledges that it contains 'an enormous wealth of psychological illustration'.

31 Rudolf Goldscheid, 'Jahresbericht über Erscheinungen der Soziologie in den Jahren 1899–1904', *Archiv für systematische Philosophie*, 10, 1904, pp.397–8.

32 Georg Simmel, 'Die Grossstädte und das Geistesleben', *Jahrbuch der Gehe-Stiftung zu Dresden*, 9, 1903, p.187.

33 *Ibid.*, p.188. There are two English translations of this essay, 'The Metropolis and Mental Life'. The first, by Edward Shils, is available in *Georg Simmel on Sociability and Social Forms*, ed. Donald Levine, Chicago, University of Chicago Press, 1971, pp.324–39; the second, by Hans Gerth and C. Wright Mills, can be found in Wolff, *The Sociology of Georg Simmel*, *op. cit.*, pp.409–74.

34 Georg Simmel. 'Soziologie der Sinne', *Die Neue Rundschau*, 18, 1907, pp.1025–36; Simmel, 'Psychologie des Schmuckes', *Morgen*, 2, 1908, pp.454–9; Simmel, 'Über das Wesen der Sozial-Psychologie', *Archiv für Sozialwissenschaft und Sozialpolitik*, 26, 1908, pp.285–291.

35 K.C. Köhnke, 'Von der Völkerpsychologie zur Soziologie', in *Georg Simmel und die Moderne*, *op. cit.*, pp.388–429.

36 Michael Landmann, 'Georg Simmel: Konturen seines Denkens', in Böhringer and Gründer, *Ästhetik und Soziologie*, p.3.

37 Hannes Böhringer, 'Spuren von spekulativen Atomismus in Simmels formaler Soziologie', *ibid.*, pp.105–19.

38 On Gustav Fechner's use of the concept of interaction, see Kurt Lasswitz, *Gustav Theodor Fechner*, 2nd edn, Stuttgart, Fromanns Verlag, 1902, pp.126–33.

39 Böhringer, 'Spuren von spekulativen Atomismus', *op. cit.*, p.114. In rejecting the notion of a *Volksseele*, Simmel was also influenced by the work of Friedrich A. Lange. Lange advocated the development of psychology 'without a social soul'. See F.A. Lange, *Geschichte des Materialismus* (Volksausgabe), Leipzig, Kröner, n.d., p.129ff.

40 Wilhelm Dilthey, *Einleitung in die Geisteswissenschaften*, 2nd edn, Leipzig and Berlin, Teubner, 1923, p.37. On Dilthey's influence on Simmel see Tenbruck, 'Georg Simmel', *op. cit.* and U. Gerhardt, 'Immanenz und Widerspruch', *Zeitschrift für philosophische Forschung*, 25, 1971, pp.276–92.

41 *Ibid.*, p.66

42 *Ibid.*, p.37

43 Gustav Lindner, *Ideen zur Psychologie der Gesellschaft als Grundlage der Sozialwissenschaft*, Vienna, Carl Gerold's Sohn, 1871.

44 Herbert Spencer, *First Principles*, London, Williams and Norgate, 1862.

45 See Georg Simmel, 'Bemerkungen zur socialethischen Problemen', *Vierteljahrsschrift für wissenschaftliche Philosophie*, 12, 1888, pp.32–49. This article later forms the basis of the third chapter of Simmel's *Über sociale Differenzierung*.

46 Moritz Lazarus and Heymann Steinthal, 'Einleitende Gedanken über Völkerpsychologie', *Zeitschrift für Völkerpsychologie und Sprachwissenschaft*, 1860, pp.1–73.

47 Moritz Lazarus, *Das Leben der Seele*, 3rd edn, Berlin, Dummler, 1883, especially pp.323–411.
48 Lazarus and Steinthal, 'Einleitende Gedanken über Völkerpsychologie', *op. cit.*, p.3.
49 *Ibid.*, p.4.
50 *Ibid.*, p.29.
51 Danziger, 'Wundt's *Völkerpsychologie*'. Quoted from draft of unpublished ms.
52 Böhringer, 'Spuren von spekulativem Atomismus', *op. cit.*, p.112.
53 Heymann Steinthal, 'An der Leser', *Zeitschrift des Vereins für Volkskunde*, 1, 1891, pp.10–17.
54 *Ibid.*, p.16.
55 *Ibid.*
56 Simmel, *Über sociale Differenzierung*, *op. cit.*, p.3.
57 *Ibid.*, p.4.
58 *Ibid.*, p.7.
59 *Ibid.*
60 *Ibid.*, p.9.
61 *Ibid.*, p.10.
62 *Ibid.*, p.13.
63 *Ibid.*, pp.12–13.
64 *Ibid.*, p.4.
65 Simmel, 'Das Problem der Soziologie', *op. cit.*
66 Wilhelm Wundt, *Logik*, vol. 2, *Methodenlehre*, Stuttgart, Enke, 1883. On this see Willem van Hoorn and Thom Verhave, 'Wundt's Changing Conceptions of a General and Theoretical Psychology', in Bringmann and Tweney, *Wundt Studies*, *op. cit.*, pp.71–113. There is, of course, no direct reference to Wundt in Simmel's essay. Indeed, I have found no reference to Wundt in Simmel's writings as a whole. In contrast, Wundt much later attacked Simmel's sociological programme. See Wilhelm Wundt, *Völkerpsychologie*, vol. 7, part 1, Leipzig, Alfred Kröner, 1917, especially pp.36–9.
67 Simmel, 'Das Problem der Soziologie', *op. cit.*, p.272.
68 *Ibid.*, p.275.
69 *Ibid.*, pp.275–6. My emphasis.
70 See Robert A. Makkreel, *Dilthey: Philosopher of the Human Studies*, Princeton, Princeton University Press, 1975, especially pp.205–18.
71 One indication of this hostility is to be found in Dilthey's correspondence in 1896 where he speaks of possible candidates for a professorial post: 'Döring, Lasson, Simmel, Dessoir – what a list!' See W. Dilthey, *Briefwechsel zwischen Wilhelm Dilthey und dem Grafen Paul Yorck v. Wartenburg: 1877–97*, Halle, Niemeyer, 1923, p.219.
72 Simmel, 'Das Problem der Soziologie', *op. cit.*, p.276.
73 *Ibid.*, My emphasis.
74 *Ibid.*, p.275.
75 *Ibid.*, p.273.
76 Georg Simmel, 'Zur Methodik der Sozialwissenschaft', *Jahrbuch für*

Gesetzgebung, Verwaltung und Volkswirtschaft, 20, 1896, pp.227–37, especially p.232.

77 Simmel, 'G. Tarde. Les lois de l'imitation', *op. cit.*, pp.141–2.

78 *Ibid.*, p.142.

79 *Ibid.*,

80 Simmel, 'Zur Psychologie der Mode', *op. cit.*

81 Georg Simmel, 'Massenpsychologie', *op. cit.*

82 Georg Simmel, 'Über Massenverbrechen', *op. cit.*

83 *Ibid.* It is this same argument that Simmel reproduces in his essay on social psychology. See note 99.

84 See Georg Simmel, 'F. Tönnies. Der Nietzsche Kultus', *Deutsche Literaturzeitung*, 23 October 1897, columns 1645–51.

85 *Ibid.*, column 1649.

86 Georg Simmel, 'Tendencies in German Life and Thought since 1870', *International Monthly*, New York, 5, 1902, pp.93–111 and 166–84, especially p.95.

87 It is one of the few references to experimental psychology in Simmel's work. (The negative judgement must be qualified with reference to his earlier praise of G. Stanley Hall's psychology programme.) A much more famous reference to experimental psychology can be found in Simmel's defence of philosophy against the threat of experimental psychology in the universities. In 1913 Simmel was one of the signatories (along with Heinrich Rickert and many others) to a petition against the filling of chairs of philosophy by experimental psychologists. In reply to an article by Karl Lamprecht (then in Leipzig) on this petition, Simmel states that 'apart, however, from Fechner's law and its developments . . . I knew of no positive or negative significance of psychological experiments for specifically philosophical endeavors. Indeed, perhaps no other natural science in its present state has so little significance for these endeavors as experimental psychology'. Simmel goes on to warn that philosophy would be seriously threatened by the intrusion of experimental psychologists in its academic chairs. More explicitly, Simmel argues that 'philosophy has nothing to gain from psychology or, put more accurately, no more than from any other natural or human science' (see Georg Simmel, 'An Herrn Professor Karl Lamprecht', *Die Zukunft*, 83, 1913). In the same volume see Lamprecht's original article, 'Ein Gefahr für die Geisteswissenschaften', pp.16–24, and his reply to Simmel, pp.421–29. On the consequences for psychology see Mitchell G. Ash, 'Wilhelm Wundt and Oswald Külpe on the Institutional Status of Psychology: An Academic Controversy in Historical Context', in Bringmann and Tweney, *Wundt Studies*, *op. cit.*, pp.396–421. The author, having quoted Simmel, then assails him as expressing 'all of the dominant motifs of the conservative thought of the day'. This is a complete misrepresentation of Simmel's position.

88 See Ferdinand Tönnies, 'Entwicklung der Soziologie in Deutschland im 19 Jahrhundert', in Tönnies, *Soziologische Studien und Kritiken*, 2nd collection, Jena, Gustav Fischer, 1926, p.103.

89 Simmel, 'Soziologie der Sinne' *op. cit.*

90 *Ibid.*, p.1025.
91 *Ibid.*, p.1026.
92 Georg Simmel, 'The Problem of Sociology', *op. cit.*, in K. H. Wolff, *Essays on Sociology, Philosophy and Aesthetics*, p.327.
93 Simmel, 'Soziologie der Sinne', *op. cit.*, p.1026. My emphasis.
94 *Ibid.*, p.1035.
95 Simmel, 'The Problem of Sociology', *op. cit.*, pp.329–30.
96 *Ibid.*, p.332.
97 *Ibid.*, p.333.
98 *Ibid.*, p.335. In fact the second section of Simmel's *Soziologie* is entitled 'How Is Society Possible'? See Wolff, *Essays on Sociology, Philosophy and Aesthetics, op. cit.*,pp.337–56.
99 Georg Simmel, 'Über das Wesen der Sozial-psychologie', *op. cit.*, pp.285–91. This essay too was incorporated into his *Soziologie*.
100 Simmel, 'Über das Wesen der Sozial-Psychologie,' p.289.
101 *Ibid.*, p.291.
102 Heinz-Jürgen Dahme, *Soziologie als exakte Wissenschaft, op. cit.*, p.403. On Simmel's psychology as a whole, see pp.396–427. For a much earlier discussion see Walter Frost, 'Die Soziologie Simmels', Riga, *Acta Universitatis Latviensis*, 12, 1925, pp.219–313; 13, 1926, pp.149–225.
103 See Othmar Spann, *Wirtschaft und Gesellschaft*, Dresden, 1907; reprinted in Spann, *Frühe Schriften in Answahl*, Graz, 1974, especially pp.223–60.
104 Max Weber, 'Georg Simmel as Sociologist', *Social Research*, 39, 1972, pp.155–63, especially p.162. My emphasis.
105 One of the few contemporary instances of an attempt to ground social psychology in part on the basis of Simmel's social theory is an essay by Franz Eulenburg. See Eulenburg, 'Über die Möglichkeit und die Aufgaben einer Sozialpsychologie', *Jahrbuch für Gesetzgebung. Verwaltung und Volkswirtschaft*, 24, 1900, pp.201–37. Tönnies mentions this inaugural lecture as 'stimulated by Simmel and the writer of this report [namely, Tönnies]' (see Tönnies, *Soziologische Studien und Kritiken, op. cit.*, p.103.
106 Simmel, *Über sociale Differenzierung, op. cit.*, p.13.
107 Siegfried Kracauer, 'Georg Simmel', *Logos*, 9, 1920, p.314.
108 Georg Simmel, 'Anfang einer unvollendeten Selbstdarstellung', in Gassen and Landmann, *Buch des Dankes, op. cit.*, p.9.
109 Simmel, 'Soziologie der Sinne', *op. cit.*
110 Georg Simmel, 'Soziologie der Geselligkeit', *Verhandlungen des l. Deutschen Soziologentages*, (1910), Tübingen, Mohr, 1911, pp.1–16. This was the opening address to the first meeting of the German Sociological Association Congress in Frankfurt in October 1910. See Simmel, 'The Sociology of Sociability', *American Journal of Sociology*, 55, 1949, pp.254–61 (trans. E.C. Hughes, and reprinted in Levine, *Sociability and Social Forms*, pp.127–40.
111 Georg Simmel, 'Soziologie der Mahlzeit', *Berliner Tageblatt*, 10 October 1910. Reprinted in Michael Landmann, ed., *Brücke und Tür*, Stuttgart, Koehler, 1957, pp.243–50.

112 Georg Simmel, 'Der Brief', *Österreichische Rundschau*, 15, 1908, pp.334–6. Reprinted as 'Exkurs über den schriftlichen Verkehr', in Simmel, *Soziologie, op. cit.*, pp.287–8.

113 Georg Simmel, 'Das Abenteuer', *Philosophische Kultur*, Leipzig, Klinkhardt, 1911, pp.11–28. Translated in Wolff, *Essays on Sociology, Philosophy and Aesthetics, op. cit.*, pp.243–58.

114 Georg Simmel, 'Über räumliche Projektionen sozialer Formen', *Zeitschrift für Sozialwissenschaft*, 6, 1903, pp.287–302: Simmel, 'Soziologie des Raumes', *Jahrbuch für Gesetzgebung, Verwaltung und Volkswirtschaft*, 27, 1903, pp.27–71; Simmel, 'Der Raum und die räumlichen Ordnungen der Gesellschaft', in Simmel, *Soziologie, op. cit.*, pp.460–526.

115 Georg Simmel, 'Die quantitative Bestimmtheit der Gruppe', in Simmel, *Soziologie, op. cit.*, pp.32–100. Translated in Wolff, *The Sociology of Georg Simmel, op. cit.*, pp.87–174.

116 See Simmel, *The Philosophy of Money, op. cit.*, pp.235–57; 429–45.

117 Georg Simmel, 'Zur Psychologie der Scham', *Die Zeit*, Vienna, 9 November 1901. This article was prompted by a review of a study by Havelock Ellis.

118 Georg Simmel, 'Dankbarkeit', *Morgen*, 1, 1907, pp.593–8: Simmel, 'Exkurs über Treue und Dankbarkeit', in Simmel, *Soziologie, op. cit.*, pp.438–47.

3 GERMAN SOCIOLOGISTS AND MODERNITY

1 In my *Fragments of Modernity*, Oxford, Polity Press, 1986.

2 J. Habermas, 'Die Moderne – ein unvollendetes Projekt', in *Kleine Politische Schriften (I–IV)*, Frankfurt, Suhrkamp, 1981, pp.444–464.

3 J. Habermas, *Theorie des kommunikativen Handelns*, II, Frankfurt, Suhrkamp, 1981, pp.446–50.

4 See J. Habermas, 'Die Moderne', *op. cit.*, p.446, where he outlines the dimensions of modernity.

5 M. Berman, *All That is Solid Melts into Air: The Experience of Modernity*, London, Verso, 1983.

6 On modernism see E. Lunn, *Marxism and Modernism*, Berkeley, University of California Press, 1983.

7 Quoted in Berman, *op. cit.*, p.95.

8 *Ibid.*

9 K. Marx, *The Revolutions of 1848*, London, Penguin, 1973, p.70.

10 Quoted in E. Pankoke, *Sociale Bewegung – Sociale Frage – Sociale Politik*, Stuggart, 1970, pp.19–47. English transl. (by D. Frisby) published as 'Social Movement' in *Economy and Society*, 11, 2, 1982, pp.317–46.

11 F. Tönnies, *Community and Association* (trans. C.P. Loomis), London 1955, p.4. I have sometimes amended the translation by reference to F. Tönnies, *Gemeinschaft und Gesellschaft*, Leipzig, 1887.

12 F. Tönnies, 'Zur Einleitung in die Soziologie', *Zeitschrift für Philosophie und philosophische Kritik*, 115, 1899, pp.240–51, especially p.248.

13 F. Tönnies, *Gemeinschaft und Gesellschaft*, op. cit., p.294.

14 F. Tönnies, 'Gemeinschaft und Gesellschaft', *Kantstudien*, 30, 1925, pp.149–179.

15 F. Tönnies, 'Zur Einleitung in die Soziologie', *op. cit.*, p.242. My emphasis.

16 F. Tönnies, Community and Association, *op. cit.*, p.10. My emphasis.

17 *Ibid.*, p.80.

18 *Ibid.*, p.87.

19 *Ibid.*, p.89.

20 *Ibid.*, pp.95–6.

21 *Ibid.*, p.269.

22 F. Tönnies, *Gemeinschaft und Gesellschaft*, op. cit., p.288.

23 F. Tönnies, *Community and Association*, op. cit., p.274.

24 F. Tönnies, 'Historismus und Rationalismus', in *Archiv für systematische Philosophie*, 1, 1895, pp.227–52. English transl. in F. Tönnies, *On Sociology: Pure, Applied and Empirical*, Chicago/London, Chicago University Press, 1971, pp.166–87, especially pp.271–2.

25 *Ibid.*, pp.272–3.

26 G. Simmel, 'Ferdinand Tönnies. Der Nietzsche Kultus', *Deutsche Literaturzeitung*, 23 October, 1897, columns 1645–51, especially 1646.

27 G. Simmel, 'Sozialismus und Pessimismus', *Die Zeit*, Vienna, 22, 3 February 1900.

28 M. Berman, *All That is Solid Melts into Air*, op cit., p.28.

29 G. Simmel, 'Tendencies in German Life and Thought Since 1870', *International Monthly*, New York, 5, 1902, 93–111, 166–84.

30 *Ibid.*, p.93.

31 *Ibid.*, p.94.

32 *Ibid.*, p.99.

33 *Ibid.*, p.101.

34 *Ibid.*, pp.176–7.

35 *Ibid.*, p.179.

36 F. Tönnies, 'Considerations sur l'histoire moderne', *Annales de l'institut international de sociologie*, 1, 1895, pp.245–52, especially p.246.

37 G. Simmel, *Philosophie des Geldes*, Berlin, 1989, p.583.

38 See Chapter 2.

39 B. Nedelmann, 'Georg Simmel – Emotion und Wechselwirkung in intimen Gruppen', in *Kölner Zeitschrift für Soziologie und Sozial psychologie*, Sonderheft, 25, 1983, pp.174–209.

40 G. Simmel, *Philosophische Kultur* (3rd edn), Potsdam, Kiepenheuer, 1923, p.196.

41 See D. Levine, 'Subjective and Objective Rationality in Simmel's *Philosophy of Money*, Weber's account of rationalization and Parson's "Theory of Action",' paper presented to the 10th World Congress of Sociology, Session on Simmel's *Philosophy of Money*, Mexico City, 1982, and S. Kalberg 'Max Weber's Types of Rationality', *American Journal of Sociology*, 85, 1980, pp.1145–79.

42 See J. Habermas, *Theories des kommunikativen Handelns*, op. cit., pp.449–88.

43 *Ibid.*, p.488.

44 *Ibid.*, p.455.

4 SIMMEL AND THE STUDY OF MODERNITY

1 The concept of modernity in social theory is discussed in my *Fragments of Modernity: Theories of Modernity in the Work of Simmel, Kracauer and Benjamin*, Cambridge, Polity Press, 1986, chap. 1, and in chap. 3 of this volume. On Weber see S. Whimster and S. Lash (eds), *Max Weber, Rationality and Modernity*, London, Allen & Unwin, 1987; D. Sayer, *Capitalism and Modernity*, London, Routledge, 1990.

2 G. Simmel, *Philosophische Kultur*, 3rd edn, Potsdam, Kiepenheuer, 1923, p.196. My emphasis.

3 G. Simmel, *Schopenhauer and Nietzsche*, (trans. H. Loiskandl, D. & M. Weinstein), Amherst, University of Massachusetts Press, 1986, p.89.

4 G. Simmel, 'Die Grossstädte und das Geistesleben', *Jahrbuch der Gehe-Stiftung zu Dresden*, 9, 1903, p.193.

5 G. Simmel, 'Soziologie der Sinne', *Die Neue Rundschau*, 18, 1907, p.1035.

6 G. Simmel, *The Philosophy of Money*, London, Routledge, 1989, p.55.

7 G. Simmel, 'Soziologische Aesthetik', *Die Zukunft*, 17, 1896, p.206.

8 G. Simmel, The Philosophy of Money, *op. cit.*, p.510.

9 This is the title given to several pieces Simmel wrote for the Munich *Jugendstil* journal, *Jugend*. See my *Sociological Impressionism*, London, Routledge, 1991, chap. 4.

10 G. Simmel, *The Philosophy of Money*, *op. cit.*, p.511.

11 On Simmel's method see my *Fragments of Modernity*, *op. cit.*, chap. 2, and *Sociological Impressionism*, *op. cit.*, chaps. 2 and 3. More recently see B. S. Green, *Literary Methods and Sociological Theory*, Chicago, Chicago University Press, 1988, part 2.

12 G. Simmel, 'Die Grossstädte und das Geistesleben', *op. cit.*, p.204.

13 K.H. Wolff (ed.), *The Sociology of George Simmel*, 2nd edn, New York/ London, Free Press, 1950, p.420. Translation amended.

14 G. Simmel, *Philosophische Kultur*, *op. cit.*, p.59.

15 K.H. Wolff (ed.), *The Sociology of Georg Simmel*, *op. cit.*, p.410. Translation amended; my emphasis. For a fuller discussion of this passage in the context of Simmel's theory of leisure see chap. 7, this volume.

16 G. Simmel, 'Die Grossstädte und das Geistesleben', *op. cit.*, p.410.

17 K.H. Wolff (ed.), *The Sociology of Georg Simmel*, *op. cit.*, p.410.

18 G. Simmel, 'Die Grossstädte und das Geistesleben', *op. cit.*, pp.191–2. My emphasis.

19 *Ibid.*, p.189.

20 G. Simmel, 'Soziologische Aesthetik', *op. cit.*, p.78.

21 G. Simmel, 'Die Grossstädte und das Geistesleben', *op. cit.*, p.195.

22 *Ibid.*, p.199.

23 *Ibid.*, p.193.

24 G. Simmel, *The Philosophy of Money*, *op. cit.*, p.459–61.

25 *Ibid.*, p.176.

26 G. Simmel, 'Das Geld in der modernen Kultur', *Zeitschrift des Ober-schlesischen Berg-und Hüttenmännischen Vereins*, 35, 1896, pp.319–24.

27 G. Simmel, 'Berliner Gewerbe-Ausstellung', *Die Zeit*, Vienna, 8, 1896, 25 July 1896.
28 *Ibid.*
29 *Ibid.*
30 G. Simmel, 'Die Mode', in *Philosophische Kultur*, *op. cit.*, p.42.
31 H. Brunkhorst, 'So etwas angenehm frisch Geköpftes. Mode und Soziologie', in S. Bovenschen (ed.), *Die Listen der Mode*, Frankfurt, Suhrkamp, 1986, pp.404–14, especially p.408.
32 G. Simmel, 'Die Mode', *op. cit.*, p.60.
33 E. Troeltsch, 'Der historische Entwicklungsbegriff in der modernen Geistes – und Lebensphilosophie', *Historische Zeitschrift*, 124, 1921, pp.424-86, especially p.431.
34 G. Simmel, 'Das Problem des Stiles', *Dekorative Kunst*, 11, 7, 1908, p.314.
35 H. Böhringer, 'Die "Philosophie des Geldes" als ästhetische Theorie' in H. J. Dahme and O. Rammstedt (eds), *Georg Simmel und die Moderne*, Frankfurt, Suhrkamp, 1984, pp.178–82, especially p.182.
36 G. Simmel, *The Philosophy of Money*, *op. cit.*, p.449.
37 *Ibid.*, p.469.
38 G. Simmel, 'Böcklins Landschaften', *Die Zukunft*, 12, 1895, pp.272-77, especially p.273.
39 G. Simmel, 'The Concept and Tragedy of Culture' in G. Simmel, *The Conflict in Modern Culture and Other Essays*, (trans. and ed. P. K. Etzkorn), New York, Teachers Press, 1968, pp.27–46, especially p.38.
40 The Hungarian and Polish reception of Simmel's works should also be considered of importance.
41 Simmel's essays on women have now been assembled in H.-J. Dahme and K. C. Köhnke (eds), *Georg Simmel, Schriften zur Philosophie und Soziologie der Geschlechter*, Frankfurt, Suhrkamp, 1985. Some of these essays are translated in G. Oakes (trans. and introd.), *Georg Simmel: On Women, Sexuality and Love*, New Haven/London, Yale University Press, 1984. For a discussion of Simmel on women see also S. Vromen, 'Georg Simmel and the Cultural Dilemma of Women', *History of European Ideas*, 8, 4/5, pp.563-79.
42 D. Miller, *Material Culture and Mass Consumption*, Oxford, Blackwell, 1987, pp.68–82.

5 SOME ECONOMIC ASPECTS OF *THE PHILOSOPHY OF MONEY*

1 G. Simmel, *The Philosophy of Money* (trans. T.B. Bottomore and D. Frisby), 2nd edn, London/New York, Routledge, 1990, p.54.
2 G. Simmel, *Philosophie des Geldes* (ed. D.P. Frisby and K.C. Köhnke), Frankfurt, Suhrkamp, 1989, p.719.
3 G. Simmel, *The Philosophy of Money*, *op. cit.*, pp.54–5.
4 *Ibid.*, p.55.
5 *Ibid.*, p.54.
6 *Ibid.*

7   *Ibid.*, p.410. My emphasis.

8   G. Simmel, 'Zur Psychologie des Geldes', *Jarhbruch für Gesetzgebung, Verwaltung und Volkswirtschaft*, 13, 1889, pp.1251–64.

9   See G. Simmel, *The Philosophy of Money*, *op. cit.*, 'The Constitution of the Text', p.516.

10 G. Simmel, 'Das Geld in der modernen Kultur', *Zeitschrift des Oberschlesischen Berg-und Hüttenmännischen Vereins*, 35, 1896, pp.319–24.

11 G. Simmel, 'Die Bedeutung des Geldes für das Tempo des Lebens', *Neue Deutsche Rundschau*, 8, 1897, pp.111–22.

12 See *The Philosophy of Money*, *op. cit.*, p.517.

13 See G. Simmel, *Philosophie des Geldes*, *op. cit.*, 'Editorischer Bericht', pp.731–84.

14 Letter of 10 May 1898 to Heinrich Rickert, in K. Gassen and M. Landmann (eds), *Buch des Dankes an Georg Simmel*, Berlin, Duncker and Humblot, 1958 p.94.

15 G. Schmoller, 'Simmels Philosophie des Geldes', *Jahrbuch für Gesetzgebung, Verwaltung und Volkswirtschaft*, 25, 3, 1901, p.799.

16 G. Simmel, 'Einige Bemerkungen zu Schmollers "Grundriss der allgemeine Volkswirtschaftslehre" ', *Allgemeine Zeitung*, 28 October 1900.

17 Simmel's study appeared as volume 10, no. 1 of Schmoller's series, 'Staats- und Socialwissenschaftliche Forschungen' in 1890. Now in G. Simmel, *Gesamtausgabe*, vol. 2 (ed. H.J. Dahme), Frankfurt, Suhrkamp, 1981, pp.109–296.

18 Cited in K. Gassen and M. Landmann (eds), *Buch des Dankes*, *op. cit.*, p.33.

19 G.F. Knapp, *Staatliche Theorie des Geldes*, Leipzig, Duncker and Humblot, 1905, p.VI.

20 Jastrow also attended the so-called 'red salon' of Leo Arons in the 1890s.

21 G. Simmel, *The Problems of the Philosophy of History* (trans. and ed. G. Oakes), New York, Free Press, 1977.

22 This is, as yet, a largely unresearched dimension of Simmel's activities.

23 G. Schmoller, 'Simmels Philosophie des Geldes', *op. cit.*, p.813.

24 *Ibid.*, p.816.

25 C. Menger (C.M.), 'Simmel, Georg, Philosophie des Geldes', *Literarische Centralblatt*, 52, 4, 1901, columns 160–1.

26 G.H. Mead, 'Philosophie des Geldes', *Journal of Political Economy*, 9, 1901, pp.616–19.

27 *Ibid.*, p.618.

28 W. Lexis, 'Neuere Schriften über das Geldwesen', *Jahrbücher für Nationalökonomie und Statistik*, 41, 1911, p.547.

29 L. von Bortkiewicz, 'Wertrechnung und Preisrechnung im Marxschen System', *Archiv für Sozialwissenschaft und Sozialpolitik*, 23, 1906, p.27.

30 W. Sombart, 'Der natuerliche Werth', *Jahrbuch für Gesetzgebung, Verwaltung und Volkswirtschaft*, 13, 4, 1889, pp.1488–90.

31 F. Hoffman, *Kritische Dogmengeschichte der Geldwerttheorien*, Leipzig, Hirschfeld, 1909, p.291; see also pp.279–80.

32 L. Stephinger, *Die Geldlehre Adam Müllers*, Stuttgart, Enke, 1909, pp.5–6.

33 H. Döring, *Die Geldtheorien seit Knapp*, Greifswald, L. Bamberg, 1921, pp.23–4.

34 K. Soda, *Geld und Wert*, Tübingen, Mohr, 1924.

35 *Ibid.*, p.1.

36 S.P. Altmann, 'Simmel's Philosophy of Money', *American Journal of Sociology*, 9, 1903, p.48.

37 See B. Biervert and J. Wieland, 'Gegenstandsbereich und Rationalitätsform der Ökonomie und der Ökonomik', in B. Biervert, K. Held and J. Wieland (eds), *Sozialphilosophische Grundlagen ökonomischen Handelns*, Frankfurt, Suhrkamp, 1990, pp.7–32.

38 *Ibid.*, p.29.

39 F. von Wieser, *Der natürliche Werth*, Vienna, Hölder, 1889, p.3.

40 *Ibid.*, p.33.

41 G. Simmel, *The Philosophy of Money, op. cit.*, pp.60–61.

42 *Ibid.*, p.62. my emphasis.

43 *Ibid.*, p.66.

44 *Ibid.*, p.67.

45 *Ibid.*, p.69. My emphasis.

46 *Ibid.*, p.78.

47 *Ibid.*, p.79.

48 *Ibid.*, p.80. My emphasis.

49 *Ibid.*, pp.83–4.

50 *Ibid.*, p.84.

51 *Ibid.*, p.87.

52 *Ibid.*, p.90.

53 *Ibid.*, p.91.

54 *Ibid.*, p.94.

55 *Ibid.*, p.100.

56 *Ibid.*, p.101.

57 *Ibid.*, p.104.

58 *Ibid.*, p.119.

59 *Ibid.*, p.124.

60 *Ibid.*, p.129.

61 *Ibid.*, p.130.

62 *Ibid.*, p.141.

63 *Ibid.*, p.168.

64 *Ibid.*, p.175. Amended translation.

65 *Ibid.*, p.185.

66 *Ibid.*, p.211.

67 G. Schmoller, 'Simmels Philosophie des Geldes', *op. cit.*, p.16.

68 See H.J. Dahme, 'Georg Simmel und Gustav Schmoller', unpublished ms.

69 R. Goldscheid, 'Jahresbericht über Erscheinungen der Soziologie in den Jahren 1899–1904', *Archiv für systematische Philosophie*, 10, 1904, pp.397–8.

70 G. Simmel, *The Philosophy of Money, op. cit.*, p.410.

71 *Ibid.*, p.96.

72 See my 'Preface to the Second Edition' and 'Afterword: The Constitution of the Text', in *The Philosophy of Money, op. cit.*, pp.xv–xli and 513–34. See also A. Cavalli in 'Introduzione' to G. Simmel, *Filosofia del Denaro*, Turin, Utet, 1984, pp.19–31 and S.H. Frankel, *Money: Two Philosophies*, Oxford, Blackwell, 1977.

73 W.S. Jevons, *The Theory of Political Economy* (ed. R.D. Collison Black), Harmondsworth, Penguin, 1970, p.101.

74 *Ibid.*, p.137.

75 *Ibid.*, p.138. For Jevons on money see W.S. Jevons, *Money and the Mechanism of Exchange*, (8th edn), London, Kegan Paul, 1887.

76 J.-J. Goux, *Symbolic Economies* (trans. J.C. Gage), Ithaca, Cornell University Press, 1990.

77 *Ibid.*, p.198.

78 G. Simmel, *The Philosophy of Money, op. cit.*, p.56.

6 SOCIAL SPACE, THE CITY AND THE METROPOLIS

1 G. Simmel, 'Die Grossstädte und das Geistesleben', *Jahrbuch der Gehe-Stiftung zu Dresden*, 9, 1903, pp.185–206.

2 G. Simmel, 'Über räumliche Projektionen sozialer Formen', *Zeitschrift für Sozialwissenschaft*, 6, 1903, pp.287–302.

3 G. Simmel, 'Soziologie des Raumes', *Jahrbuch für Gesetzgebung, Verwaltung und Volkswirtschaft*, 27, 1903, pp.27–71.

4 R.E. Park and E.W. Burgess, *The City*, Chicago/London, Chicago University Press, 1967, p.219.

5 G. Simmel, 'Rom. Eine ästhetische Analyse', *Die Zeit*, 15, 28 May 1898.

6 G. Simmel, 'Florenz', (1906), in *Zur Philosophie der Kunst*, Potsdam, Kiepenheuer, 1922, pp.61–6.

7 G. Simmel, 'Venedig', (1907), in *Zur Philosophie der Kunst, op. cit.*, pp.67–73.

8 G. Simmel, 'Berliner Gewerbe-Ausstellung', *Die Zeit*, Vienna, 8, 25 July 1896.

9 Anon, 'Berliner Kunstbrief', *Die Zeit*, 6, 21 March 1896.

10 P. Liesegang [G. Simmel], 'Infelices Possidentes', *Die Zukunft*, 3, 1893, pp.82–4.

11 G. Simmel, 'Philosophie der Landschaft', in Brücke und Tür, Stuttgart, Koehler, 1957, pp.141–52.

12 H. Simmel, 'Auszüge aus den Lebenserinnerungen' in H. Böhringer and K. Gründer (eds), *Ästhetik und Soziologie um die Jahrhundertwende: Georg Simmel*, Frankfurt, Klostermann, 1978, pp.247–8.

13 See G. Simmel, *On Women, Sexuality and Love*, New Haven/London, Yale University Press, 1984, with introduction by G. Oakes.

14 H. Simmel, 'Auszüge aus den Lebenserinnerungen', *op. cit.*, p.258.

15 *Ibid.*, pp.259–60.

16 K.C. Köhnke, 'Murderous Attack Upon Georg Simmel', *European Journal of Sociology*, 24, 2, 1983, p.349.

17 E. Durkheim, 'Simmel', *L'année sociologique*, 7, 1902–3, pp.646–7.

18 *Ibid.*, p.647.
19 G. Simmel, 'Soziologie des Raumes', *op. cit.*, p.29.
20 G. Simmel, 'Über räumliche Projektionen sozialer Formen', *op. cit.*, p.287.
21 G. Simmel, 'The Stranger' in G. Simmel, *On Individuality and Social Forms*, Chicago, Chicago University Press, 1971, p.143.
22 E. Kornau, *Raum und soziales Handeln*, Stuttgart, Enke, 1977.
23 *Ibid.*, p.48.
24 *Ibid.*, p.51.
25 An exception is D. Harvey, *Consciousness and the Urban Experience*, Oxford, Blackwell, 1985.
26 D. Levine, 'Simmel at a Distance', *Sociological Focus*, 10, 1, 1977, p.16.
27 See D. Frisby, *Sociological Impressionism. A Reassessment of Georg Simmel's Social Theory*, 2nd edn, London/New York, Routledge, 1991, chap. 3.
28 *Ibid.*
29 *Ibid.*
30 See Chapter 7.
31 G. Simmel, 'Rom', *op. cit.*
32 Anon, 'Die Schönste Stadt der Welt', *Die Zukunft*, 26, 1899, pp.36–48.
33 A. Endell, *Die Schönheit der grossen Stadt*, (1908), Berlin, Archibook, 1984.
34 G. Simmel, 'Rom', *op. cit.*, p.21.
35 *Ibid.*, p.19.
36 G. Simmel, 'Venedig', *op. cit.*, p.73.
37 G. Simmel, 'Philosophie der Landschaft', *op. cit.*
38 *Ibid.*, p.141.
39 In L. Coser (ed.), *Georg Simmel*, Englewood Cliffs, Prentice Hall, 1965, p.39.
40 H. Woodward, 'The First German Municipal Exposition (Dresden, 1903)', *American Journal of Sociology*, 9, 1904, pp.433–58; 612–30; 812–31;10, 1905, pp.47–63.
41 See A. Lees, *Cities Perceived*, Manchester, Manchester University Press, 1985, Part 2.
42 G. Simmel, *The Philosophy of Money*, (trans. T.B. Bottomore and D. Frisby), 2nd edn, London/New York, Routledge, 1990, p.347.
43 D. Harvey, *Consciousness and the Urban Experience*, *op. cit.*, p.12.
44 *Ibid.*, p.1.
45 G. Simmel, 'The Metropolis and Mental Life', in K.M. Wolff (ed.), *The Sociology of Georg Simmel*, Glencoe Free Press, 1950 p.411.
46 *Ibid.*, p.420.
47 *Ibid.*, p.413.
48 See E. Lenk, 'Wie Georg Simmel die Mode überlistet hat' in S. Bovenschen, *Die Listen der Mode*, Frankfurt, Suhrkamp, 1986, pp.415–37.
49 G. Simmel, 'Etwas vom Spiritismus', *Vorwärts*, 12 July 1892.
50 G. Korff, "Die Stadt aber ist der Mensch" in G. Korff and R. Rürup (eds), *Berlin, Berlin*, Berlin, Nicolai, 1987, p.657.
51 On Benjamin's Arcades project see D. Frisby, *Fragments of Modernity*:

Theories of Modernity in the Work of Simmel, Kracauer and Benjamin, Oxford, Polity Press; S. Buck-Morss, *The Dialectics of Seeing*, Cambridge, Mass., MIT Press, 1990.

52 D. Harvey, *Consciousness and the Urban Experience, op. cit.*
53 G. Simmel, 'Philosophie der Landschaft', *op. cit.*, p.144.

7 LEISURE AND MODERNITY

1 See W. Benjamin, *Charles Baudelaire*, London, New Left Books, 1973.
2 E. Zola, *The Ladies' Paradise*, London, Vizitelly, 1889. On this novel and others on consumption see R. Bowlby, *Just Looking*, London, Methuen, 1985.
3 Kleptomania should belong to Durkheim's discussion of excessive individualism and anomie in his analysis of suicide. See E. Durkheim, *Suicide*, London, Routledge, 1952, pp.254–60.
4 R. Williams, *Dream Worlds: Mass Consumption in Late Nineteenth-Century France*, Berkeley/Los Angeles/London, University of California Press, 1982, especially Chaps. 6–8.
5 T. Veblen, *The Theory of the Leisure Class* (with intro. by C. Wright Mills), New York/Toronto, New American Library, 1953.
6 *Ibid.*, p.46. My emphasis.
7 On Simmel's methodology see D. Frisby, *Georg Simmel*, Chichester/London/New York, Ellis Horwood/Tavistock/Methuen Inc., 1984, Chap. 3.
8 G. Simmel (1968), 'Sociological Aesthetics', in K.P. Etzkorn (ed.), *Georg Simmel: The Conflict in Modern Culture and other Essays*, New York, Teachers College Press, pp.68–80.
9 See D. Frisby, *Georg Simmel, op. cit.*, Chap. 2. See also D. Frisby, *Sociological Impressionism*, London, Heinemann, 1981 and London, Routledge, 1991.
10 *Ibid.*
11 This corresponds to the period when Simmel was publishing in such socialist journals as *Die neue Zeit*.
12 See G. Simmel (1971), 'Sociability' in Levine, D.N. (ed.), G. Simmel, *On Individuality and Social Forms*, Chicago/London, University of Chicago Press, 1971, pp.127–40.
13 G. Simmel 'Herbst am Rhein', *Jugend*, no. 4, 1897, p.54.
14 And this despite a bizarre attack on his life. See K.C. Köhnke, 'Murderous Attack Upon Georg Simmel', *European Journal of Sociology*, 24, 2, 1983, p.349. For further discussion, see my Afterword to G. Simmel, *The Philosophy of Money*, London/New York, Routledge, 1990, pp.513–14.
15 K.H. Wolff (ed.), *The Sociology of Georg Simmel*, 2nd edn, New York/London, Free Press, 1964, p.420. Translation amended.
16 G. Simmel, *The Philosophy of Money, op. cit.*, p.456. On Simmel's theory of modernity as a whole see D. Frisby, *Fragments of Modernity*, Oxford, Polity Press, 1986, chap. 2.
17 *Ibid.*, pp.393–4 and 455.

18 K.H. Wolff (ed.), *The Sociology of Georg Simmel, op. cit.*, p.420.
19 *Ibid.*, p.422. Translation amended; my emphasis.
20 G. Simmel, *The Philosophy of Money, op. cit.*, pp.459–61.
21 K.H. Wolff (ed.), *The Sociology of Georg Simmel op. cit.*, p.410. Translation amended.
22 G. Simmel, *The Philosophy of Money, op. cit.*, p.484.
23 *Ibid.*, p.256.
24 *Ibid.*, p.257.
25 *Ibid.*, p.483.
26 See E. Lenk, 'Wie Georg Simmel die Mode überlistet hat' in S. Bovenschen (ed.), *Die Listen der Mode*, Frankfurt, Suhrkamp, 1986, pp.415–37.
27 G. Simmel, 'Die Mode', in *Philosophische Kultur*, 3rd edn, Potsdam, Kiepenheuer, 1923, p.42.
28 *Ibid.*, p.36.
29 P. Liesegang, 'Infelices Possidentes', *Die Zukunft*, 3, 1893, pp.82–4.
30 *Ibid.*, p.83.
31 G. Simmel, 'Gerhart Hauptmanns "Weber" ', *Sozialpolitisches Central-blatt*, 2, 1892–3, pp.283–4.
32 A. Schnitzler, *Briefe. 1913–1931*, Frankfurt, Fischer, 1984, pp.849–50.
33 G. Simmel, 'Einiges über die Prostitution in Gegenwart und Zukunft', in G. Simmel, *Schriften zur Philosophie und Soziologie der Geschlechter*, Frankfurt, Suhrkamp, 1985, p.60.
34 G. Simmel, *The Philosophy of Money, op. cit.*, p.376.
35 G. Simmel, 'Berliner Gewerbe-Ausstellung', *Die Zeit*, Vienna, 8, 25 July 1896.
36 G. Simmel, 'Ueber Kunstausstellungen', *Unsere Zeit*, 26 February 1890, pp.474–80.
37 G. Simmel, 'Berliner Kunstbrief', *Die Zeit*, 6, 21 March 1896.
38 G. Simmel, *The Philosophy of Money, op. cit.*, p.473.
39 G. Simmel, 'Alpenreisen', *Die Zeit*, 7, 13 July 1895.
40 See 'Questionnaire on Yodeling by George Simmel' in K.P. Etzkorn (ed.), *Georg Simmel, The Conflict in Modern Culture and Other Essays, op. cit.*, pp.134–6. The original was published in 1879.
41 G. Simmel, 'Metaphysik der Faulheit', *Jugend*, 20, 1900, pp.337–9.
42 G. Simmel, 'Sociability', in G. Simmel, *On Individuality and Social Forms, op. cit.*, p.129.
43 G. Simmel, 'The Adventure', in K.H. Wolff (ed.), *Essays on Sociology, Philosophy and Aesthetics by Georg Simmel et al*, 2nd edn, New York, Harper & Row, 1965, pp.243–58.
44 *Ibid.*, p.248. In this context, the significance of railway journeys should be emphasized. See W. Schivelbusch, *The Railway Journey*, Leamington Spa/Hamburg/New York, Berg, 1986.
45 *Ibid.*, p.254, Translation amended.
46 *Ibid.*, p.244.
47 *Ibid.*, p.245. Translation amended.
48 See D. MacCannell, *The Tourist: A New Theory of the Leisure Class*, New York, Schocken Books, 1976.

49　D. Harvey, *Consciousness and the Urban Experience*, Oxford, Blackwell, 1985, p.256.

8 THE AESTHETICS OF MODERN LIFE

1　Such a comprehensive analysis has hardly been commenced. On impressionism see my *Sociological Impressionism*, London, 1981. On *The Philosophy of Money* as a major instance of aesthetic theory see H. Böhringer, 'Die "Philosophie des Geldes" als ästhetische Theorie' and S. Hübner-Funk, 'Die ästhetische Konstituierung gesellschaftlicher Erkenntnis am Beispiel der "Philosophie des Geldes" in H.J. Dahme and O. Rammstedt (eds), *Georg Simmel und die Moderne*, Frankfurt, 1984.

2　See G. Simmel, *Über sociale Differenzierung*, Leipzig, 1890, chap. 1; now in G. Simmel, *Gesamtausgabe*, vol. 2 (ed. H.J. Dahme), Frankfurt, 1989.

3　G. Simmel, *Kant*, Leipzig, 1904. References are to the fourth edition, 1918.

4　G. Simmel, *Kant*, *op. cit.*, p.188.

5　*Ibid.*, p.189.

6　*Ibid.*, p.190.

7　*Ibid.*, p.197.

8　*Ibid.*, p.194.

9　*Ibid.*, p.197.

10　*Ibid.*, p.194.

11　*Ibid.*, p.198.

12　*Ibid.*, p.199.

13　*Ibid.*, p.199. On this theme see also G. Simmel, 'Ästhetik der Schwere', *Berliner Tageblatt*, 10 June 1901.

14　G. Simmel, 'Soziologische Aesthetik', *Die Zukunft*, 17, 1896, pp.204–16.

15　G. Simmel, 'Soziologische Aesthetik', *op. cit.*, p.205.

16　*Ibid.*, p.215.

17　*Ibid.*, p.214.

18　See K. Lichtblau, 'Das "Pathos der Distanz". Präliminarien zur Nietzsche-Rezeption bei Georg Simmel' in H.J. Dahme and O. Rammstedt (eds), *Georg Simmel und die Moderne*, *op. cit.*, pp.231–81.

19　G. Simmel, 'Soziologische Aesthetik', *op. cit.*, p.213.

20　*Ibid.*, p.214.

21　*Ibid.*, pp.215–16.

22　*Ibid.*, p.216.

23　Simmel's use of the concept of value is complex and requires a detailed examination. Simmel at times participates in the neo-Kantian discourse of value spheres and, at others, in the then not completely dissociated discourse of Nietzsche on value. Not surprisingly, it was his theory of value in the first chapter of *The Philosophy of Money* which caused him the greatest difficulties and it is there that revisions were made when he came to write the second edition that appeared in 1907. In terms of economic theory, we can see Simmel oscillating between a subjective and objective theory of value, seeking out a critical position that is, as it were, neither that of Carl Menger nor of Karl Marx. In addition, the opening section of *The Philosophy of Money* (London/New York 1990, pp.73–5) takes up aesthetic valuation too. The different nuances in the application of the concept of value are compounded by the ambiguous relationship between value and worth. This is most obvious in the fifth chapter of *The Philosophy of Money* on the money equivalent of personal values, where it would be more appropriate to use the concept of human worth.

24 G. Simmel, 'Der Siebente Ring' in *Zur Philosophie der Kunst*, Potsdam, 1922, pp.74–8.

25 G. Simmel, 'Der Siebente Ring', *op. cit.*, p.78. Simmel's argument here on art's unification of diversity and disparity and elsewhere on art's capacity to resolve contradictory tensions is a central *leitmotif* of other areas of existence. Apart from the obvious applications in *The Philosophy of Money*, a great deal of his discussion of religion revolves around a sometimes explicit analogy between God and society (a comparison with Durkheim would be instructive here) and the unification of diversity (see G. Simmel, *Die Religion*, Frankfurt, Rüten & Loening, 1906). The central conception of sociation as the social process of interaction (*Wechselwirkung*) also implies that the reciprocal effects of two elements create a third entity, the interaction itself.

26 G. Simmel, 'Der Bildrahmen' in *Zur Philosophie der Kunst*, *op. cit.*, p.46.

27 G. Simmel, *The Philosophy of Money*, London/New York, Routledge, 1989.

28 The second, enlarged edition of *The Philosophy of Money* takes up the constitution of this text. See also G. Simmel, *Philosophie des Geldes* (ed. K.C. Köhnke and D.P. Frisby), Frankfurt, 1989.

29 G. Simmel, 'Das Geld in der modernen Kultur', *Zeitschrift des Oberschlesischen Berg-und Hüttenmännischen Vereins*, 35, 1896, pp.319–24. Along with other articles published 1894–1900 see (forthcoming) G. Simmel, *Aufsätze und Abhandlungen 1894–1900* (ed. H.J. Dahme and D.P. Frisby), Frankfurt, 1992 (in press).

30 G. Simmel, 'Das Geld in der modernen Kultur', *op. cit.*, p.321.

31 *Ibid.*, p.323.

32 G. Simmel, *The Philosophy of Money*, *op. cit.*, p.176.

33 H. Scheible, 'Georg Simmel und die "Tragödie der Kultur" ', *Neue Rundschau*, 91, 2/3, 1980, p.158.

34 K. Marx, *Grundrisse*, Harmondsworth, 1973, pp.254–5.

35 In addition to Kant's *Critique of Judgement* (trans. J.C. Meredith, Oxford, 1982), his *Observations on the Feeling of the Beautiful and Sublime*, New York, Doubleday, 1960, should also be consulted on the concept of the sublime. For a recent secondary discussion in Kant's philosophy, see P. Crowther, *The Kantian Sublime*, Oxford, Clarendon, 1989. A stimulating collection of essays on the sublime is *Das Erhabene* (ed. C. Pries), Weinheim, V.C.H. Verlag, 1989.

36 I. Kant, *The Critique of Judgement*, *op. cit.*, pp.90–1.

37 G. Simmel, *The Philosophy of Money*, *op. cit.*, p.328.

38 H. Böhringer, 'Die "Philosophie des Geldes" ' als ästhetische Theorie', *op. cit.*

39 See 'Adornment' in K.H. Wolff (ed), *The Sociology of Georg Simmel*, New York, 1950, pp.338–44.

40 G. Simmel, *The Philosophy of Money*, *op. cit.*, p.53.

41 See W. Sombart, 'Probleme des Kunstgewerbes in der Gegenwart', *Neue Rundschau*, 18, 1, 1907, pp.513–36.

42 *Ibid.*, p.74.

43 *Ibid.*, pp.74–5.

44 G. Simmel, 'Psychologie des Schmuckes', *Morgen*, 2, 1908, pp.454–9. In English see n.37.

45 Simmel's work is referred to in this context in M. Müller, *Schöner Schein*, Frankfurt, 1987.

46 G. Simmel, 'Adornment', *op. cit.*, p.341.

47 G. Simmel, 'Das Problem des Stiles', *Dekorative Künst*, 16, 1908, pp.307–16.

48 G. Simmel, 'Ueber Kunstausstellungen', *Unsere Zeit*, 26 February 1890, pp.474–80.

49 G. Simmel, 'Philosophie der Landschaft', *Die Güldenkammer*, 3, 1912/13, pp.635–44. Reprinted in G. Simmel, *Brücke und Tür*, Stuttgart, 1957, pp.141–52.

50 G. Simmel, 'Berliner Kunstbrief', *Die Zeit*, Vienna, 6, 21 March 1896, no.77, pp.186–7.

51 G. Simmel, 'Berliner Kunstbrief', *op. cit.*, p.186.

52 *Ibid.*

53 *Ibid.*, p.187.

54 G. Simmel, 'Berliner Gewerbe-Ausstellung', *Die Zeit*, Vienna, 8, 25 July 1896.

55 See W. Benjamin, *Charles Baudelaire*, London, 1973.

56 G. Simmel, 'Berliner Gewerbe-Ausstellung', *op. cit.*

57 *Ibid.*

58 *Ibid.*

59 G. Simmel, *The Philosophy of Money*, *op. cit.*, p.463.

60 *Ibid.*, p.473.

61 *Ibid.*, p.474.

62 G. Simmel, 'Der Bildrahmen', *op. cit.*, p.50.

63 G. Simmel, 'Rodin' in *Philosophische Kultur* (3rd edn), Potsdam, 1923, p.197. For a discussion of this essay see my *Fragments of Modernity*, Oxford, 1986, pp.62–4.

64 G. Simmel, 'Berliner Kunstbrief', *op. cit.*, p.186.

65 G. Simmel, *Philosophische Kultur*, *op. cit.*, p.11.

66 G. Simmel, *Rembrandt*, Leipzig, 1916, p.2.

67 W. Benjamin, 'Traumkitsch' in *Gesammelte Schriften*, II, 2, Frankfurt 1972, p.620.

68 G. Simmel, 'Die Zukunft unserer Kultur' in *Brücke und Tür*, *op. cit.*, p.95.

69 See my *Fragments of Modernity*, *op. cit.*, chap. 2.

70 S. Kracauer, 'Georg Simmel' in *Das Ornament der Masse*, Frankfurt, 1963, p.220.

71 See Chapter 7.

9 MODERNITY, POSTMODERNITY AND THINGS

1 See G. Simmel, 'Notiz', *Zeitschrift für Philosophie und philosophische Kritik*, 95, 1889, pp.159—60. On Stanley Hall at Clark University, see M.M. Sokal, 'G. Stanley Hall and the Institutional Character of Psychology at Clark 1889—1920', *Journal of the History of the Behavioral Sciences*, 26, 1990, pp.114-24.

2 G. Simmel, 'The Problem of Sociology', *Annals of the American Academy of Political Science*, 6, 1895, pp.52-63.

3 The contents of these two journals cast a significant light upon the reception of European thought in the United States in the first decade of this century.

4 This advisory board remained the same for both journals.

5 *The Philosophical Review* produced not merely standard book reviews but also overview articles on recent works abroad. Taken together, Simmel's work is exceptionally well represented in these reviews.

6 On Small see V.K. Dibble, *The Legacy of Albion Small*, Chicago/London, Chicago University Press, 1975; on Park see, most recently, R. Lindner, *Die Entdeckung der Stadtkultur. Soziologie aus der Erfahrung der Reportage*, Frankfurt, Suhrkamp, 1990; on Mead see J. Joas, *G.H. Mead*, Oxford, Polity Press/Cambridge, Mass., MIT Press, 1985. More generally on the School, see M. Bulmer, *The Chicago School of Sociology*, Chicago/London, Chicago University Press, 1984.

7 See A.W.Small, 'Grundriss der allgemeinen Volkswirtschaftslehre', *American Journal of Sociology*, 6, 1900-1, pp.423-4.

8 On Simmel's reception in the United States, see D.N. Levine, E.B. Carter and E.M. Gorman, 'Simmel's Influence on American Sociology', in Böhringer, H. and Gründer, K. (eds), *Ästhetik und Soziologie um die Jahrhundertwende: Georg Simmel*, Frankfurt, Klostermann, 1976, pp.176-228

9 L. Gumplowicz, 'August Comte und seine Bedeutung', *Annals of The American Academy of Political and Social Science*, 5, 1894/5, pp.151-3, especially 152.

10 L. Gumplowicz, 'Zur neuesten soziologischen Literatur' (1891), in *Soziologische Essays. Soziologie und Politik*, Innsbruck, Wagner, 1928, pp.328-33.

11 L.F. Ward, 'The Social Mind and Education', *Annals of the American Academy of Political and Social Science*, 11, 1898, pp.264-7, especially p.264.

12 G. Simmel, 'Supplementary Note' to 'The Problem of Sociology', *op. cit.*, pp.60-3, especially p.60.

13 A.W. Small, ' "Social" vs. "Societary" ', *Annals of the American Academy of Political and Social Science*, 5, 1894-5, pp.948-53.

14 *Ibid.*, p.124.

15 *Ibid.*

16 *Ibid.*, p.125.

17 See, for example, A.W. Small, 'Methodology of the Social Problem', *American Journal of Sociology*, 4, 1898-9 especially pp.390-1.

18 A.W. Small, 'Soziologie', *American Journal of Sociology*, 14, 1908–9, pp.544–5, especially p.544.
19 Anon., 'Simmel, Georg. Soziologie', *Annals of the American Academy of Political and Social Science*, 33, 1909, p.241.
20 A.W. Small, 'Germany and American Opinion', *Sociological Review*, 7, 1914, pp.106–11. Small's letter to Simmel is dated 29 October 1914.
21 Small relates that he did meet Simmel in 1903. See n.27 below.
22 A.W. Small, 'Individuum und Gemeinschaft', *American Journal of Sociology*, 30, 1924, pp.352–3, especially p.352.
23 A.W. Small, 'Kölner Vierteljahrshefte für Sozialwissenschaften', *American Journal of Sociology*, 27, 1921–2, pp.92–4, especially p.92.
24 A.W. Small, 'The Social Theory of Georg Simmel', *American Journal of Sociology*, 31, 1925–6, pp.84–7.
25 *Ibid.*, p.84.
26 *Ibid.*
27 *Ibid.*, p.87.
28 *Ibid.*, p.86.
29 See advertisement for N.J. Spykman, *The Social Theory of Georg Simmel*, *American Journal of Sociology*, 31, 1925–6, facing p.1.
30 See Lindner on Park, n.6 above.
31 L. Wirth, 'The Sociology of Ferdinand Tönnies', *American Journal of Sociology*, 32, 1926, p.413.
32 *Ibid.*
33 T. Abel, *Systematic Sociology in Germany*, New York, Columbia University Press, 1929, chap. 1.
34 P. Sorokin, *Contemporary Sociological Theories*, New York/London, Harper, 1928, chap. 9. Simmel is located firmly within 'the Formal School' of sociology.
35 G. Simmel, 'The Sociology of Sociability' (trans. E.K. Hughes), *American Journal of Sociology*, 55, 1949/50, pp.254–61.
36 K.H. Wolff (ed.), *The Sociology of Georg Simmel*, Glencoe, Illinois, Free Press, 1950.
37 See the special issue of *Theory, Culture and Society*, 8, 2, 1991.
38 A.W. Small, 'Allgemeine Soziologie', *American Journal of Sociology*, 31, 1925–6, pp.87–9.
39 See D.N. Levine, *Simmel and Parsons. Two Approaches to the Study of Society*, New York, Arno Press, 1980.
40 On Kracauer see my *Fragments of Modernity*, Cambridge, Polity Press, 1986, chap. 3 and I. Mülder, *Siegfried Kracauer*, Metzler, Stuttgart, 1985.
41 See E. Bloch, *Heritage of Our Times*, (trans. N. and S. Plaice), Berkeley/Los Angeles, University of California Press; Cambridge, Polity Press, 1991.
42 For some initial references see my 'introduction' to G. Simmel, *The Philosophy of Money*, 2nd edn, London/New York, Routledge, 1990 pp.15–21.
43 The relation between Benjamin's work and that of Simmel has not been systematically explored. *Das Passagen-Werk*, Frankfurt, Suhrkamp, 1982,

is a fruitful source of Simmel references. See also my *Fragments of Modernity*, *op. cit.*

44 Adorno's references to Simmel are almost always critical, despite some affinities.

45 Cited in *Fragments of Modernity*, *op. cit.*, p.110.

46 J. Habermas, *Theories of Communicative Action*, 2 vols (trans. T. McCarthy), Boston, Beacon Press, 1984, 1987.

47 J. Habermas, 'Die Moderne – ein unvollendetes Projekt', *Klein Politische Schriften, (I–IV)*, Frankfurt, Suhrkamp, 1983, pp.151–3. Published in English as 'Modernity – An Incomplete Project' in H. Foster (ed.), *Postmodern Culture*, London, Pluto, 1985, pp.3–15.

48 G. Simmel, *Philosophische Kultur*, Berlin, Wagenbach, 1983, with a foreword by J. Habermas, 'Simmel als Zeitdiagnostiker', pp.7–17.

49 J. Habermas, *The Philosophical Discourse of Modernity* (trans. F. Lawrence), Cambridge, Mass., MIT Press, 1987.

50 J. Habermas, 'Simmel als Zeitdiagnostiker', *op. cit.*, p.244.

51 *Ibid.*, p.250.

52 See G. Simmel, *Schriften zur Philosophie und Soziologie der Geschlechter*, (ed. H.J. Dahme and K.C. Köhnke), Frankfurt, Suhrkamp, 1985; G. Simmel, *On Women, Sexuality and Love*, especially introduction by Oakes; S. Vromen, 'Georg Simmel and the Cultural Dilemma of Women', *History of European Ideas*, 8, 4/5, pp.563–79; M.Ulmi, *Frauenfragen. Männergedanken*, Zurich, efef Verlag, 1989.

53 G. Simmel, *Schopenhauer and Nietzsche*, Amherst, University of Massachusetts Press, 1986.

54 G. Simmel, 'Vom Wesen der Kultur', in *Brücke und Tür*, Stuttgart, Koehler, 1957, pp.86–94.

55 G. Simmel, *Schopenhauer and Nietzsche*, *op. cit.*, p.3.

56 *Ibid.*, p.4.

57 G. Simmel, 'Vom Wesen der Kultur', *op. cit.*, p.94.

58 G. Simmel (Anon).

59 K.C. Köhnke, 'Soziologie als Kulturwissenschaft', *Archiv für Kulturgeschichte*, 72, 1, 1990, pp.223–32.

60 See my *Fragments of Modernity*, *op. cit.*, chap. 1.

61 W.S. Jevons, *Money and the Mechanism of Exchange*, London, Kegan Paul, 1887, p.11.

62 *Ibid.*

63 *Ibid.*, p.12.

64 Benjamin developed his reflections on things most fully in *Das Passagen-Werk*, *op. cit.*

65 G. Simmel, *Philosophische Kultur*, Potsdam, Kiepenheuer, 1923, p.11.

66 G. Simmel, 'The Metropolis and Mental Life', in Wolff (ed.), *The Sociology of Georg Simmel*, *op. cit.* p.413.

67 G. Simmel, *Brücke und Tür*, *op. cit.*, p.95.

68 C. Asendorf, *Batterien der Lebenskräfte*, Giessen, Anabas, 1984, p.95. An English translation is forthcoming.

69 *Ibid.*

70 G. Simmel [P. Liesegang], 'Etwas vom Spiritismus', *Vorwärts*, 12 June 1892.
71 R. Pascal, 'Georg Simmel, "Die Grossstädte und das Geistesleben" ', in H. Kreuzer (ed.), *Gestaltungsgeschichte und Gesellschaftsgeschichte*, Stuttgart, Meztler, 1969, pp.450–60.
72 H. Scheible, 'Georg Simmel und die "Tragödie der Kultur" ', *Neue Rundschau*, 91, 2/3, 1980, p.160.
73 For instance, as in M. Calinescu, *Five Faces of Modernity*, Durham, Duke University Press, 1987.
74 G. Simmel, *The Philosophy of Money*, op. cit., p112.
75 P.A. Lawrence, 'Review Essay: Radicalism and the Cash Nexus', *American Journal of Sociology*, 86, 1, 1980, pp.182–6, especially pp.182 and 184.
76 P. Bourdieu, *Distinction*, (trans. R. Nice), London/New York, Routledge, 1984.
77 See E. Lenk, 'Wie Georg Simmel die Mode Überlistet hat', in S. Borenschen, *Die Listen der Mode*, Frankfurt, Suhrkamp, 1986, pp.415–37.
78 K. Marx, *Early Writings*, Harmondsworth, Penguin, 1975, pp.323–4.
79 See my *Fragments of Modernity*, op. cit., chap. 4.
80 G. Simmel 'On the Concept and Tragedy of Culture' in G. Simmel, *The Conflict in Modern Culture and Other Essays*, (trans. and ed. K.P. Etzkorn), New York, Teachers College Press, 1968, p.42.
81 F. Moretti, *Signs Taken for Wonders*, London/New York, Verso, 1988, p.152.
82 *Ibid.*, p.153.
83 *Ibid.*, p.11.
84 G. Simmel, 'The Conflict in Modern Culture' in G. Simmel, *The Conflict in Modern Culture and Other Essays*, op. cit., pp.11–26.
85 *Ibid.*, p.16.
86 *Ibid.*, p.21.
87 *Ibid.*, p.23.
88 For a fuller discussion see D. Weinstein and M.A. Weinstein, 'Simmel and the Theory of Postmodern Society' in B.S. Turner (ed.), *Theories of Modernity and Postmodernity*, London, Sage, 1989, pp.75–87.
89 G. Vattimo, *The End of Modernity*, (trans. J.R. Snyder), Oxford, Polity Press, 1988.
90 G. Simmel, *The Philosophy of Money*, op. cit., p.463. For fuller discussion of style and aesthetics see B. Nedelmann, 'Aestheticization and Stylization: Two Strategies of Lifestyle Management' in C. Mongardini and M.L. Maniscalco (eds), *Moderno e Postmoderno*, Rome, Bulzoni, 1989, pp.91–110.
91 D. Harvey, *The Condition of Postmodernity*, Oxford, Blackwell, 1989, p.327.
92 *Ibid.*, p.44.

Bibliography

Abel, T., *Systematic Sociology in Germany*, New York, Columbia University Press, 1929, chap. 1.

Altmann, S.P., 'Simmel's Philosophy of Money', *American Journal of Sociology*, 9, 1903, pp.46–68

Anon., 'Simmel, Georg. Soziologie', *Annals of the American Academy of Political and Social Science*, 33, 1909, p.241.

Asendorf, C., *Batterien der Lebenskräfte*, Giessen, Anabas, 1984.

Benjamin, W., 'Traumkitsch' in *Gesammelte Schriften*, II, 2, Frankfurt, Suhrkamp, 1972, pp.619–20.

Benjamin, W., *Charles Baudelaire*, London, New Left Books, 1973.

Benjamin, W., *Das Passagen-Werk*, Gesammelte Schriften, V, Frankfurt, Suhrkamp, 1982.

Berman, M., *All That is Solid Melts into Air: the Experience of Modernity*, London, Verso, 1983.

Biervert, B., Held, K., and Wieland, J., (eds), *Sozialphilosophische Grundlagen ökonomischen Handelns*, Frankfurt, Suhrkamp, 1990.

Bloch, E., *Heritage of Our Times* (trans. N. and S. Plaice), Berkeley/Los Angeles, University of California Press, Cambridge, Polity Press, 1991.

Böhringer, H., 'Spuren von spekulativem Atomismus in Simmels formaler Soziologie', in H. Böhringer and K. Gründer (eds), *Ästhetik und Soziologie um die Jahrhundertwende*, Frankfurt, Klostermann, 1978, pp.105–17.

Bortkiewicz, L. von, 'Wertrechnung und Preisrechnung im Marxschen System', *Archiv für Sozialwissenschaft und Sozialpolitik*, 23, 1906, pp.1–50; 25, 1907, p.10, 445.

Bourdieu, P., *Distinction*, (trans. R. Nice), London/New York, Routledge, 1984.

Bowlby, R., *Just Looking*, London, Methuen, 1985.

Bringmann, W. G. and Tweney, R.D. (eds), *Wundt Studies: A Centennial Collection*, Toronto, Hogrefe, 1980.

Brunkhorst, H., 'So etwas angenehm frisch Geköpftes. Mode und Soziologie', in Bovenschen, S. (ed.), *Die Listen der Mode*, Frankfurt, Suhrkamp, 1986.

Buck-Morss, S., *The Dialectics of Seeing*, Cambridge, Mass., MIT Press, 1990.

Bulmer, M., *The Chicago School of Sociology*, Chicago/London, Chicago University Press, 1984.

Calinescu, M., *Five Faces of Modernity*, Durham, Duke University Press 1987.

Caplow, T., *Two Against One*, New Jersey, Prentice Hall, 1968.

Coser, L., *The Functions of Social Conflict*, New York, Free Press, London, Routledge, 1956.

Coser, L., (ed.) *Georg Simmel*, Engelwood Cliffs, Prentice Hall, 1965, p.39.

Coser, L., 'Georg Simmel's Neglected Contributions to the Sociology of Women', *Signs*, 2, 1977, pp.869–76.

Crowther, P., *The Kantian Sublime*, Oxford, Clarendon, 1989.

Dahme, H.J., *Soziologie als exakte Wissenschaft*, 2 vols, Stuttgart, Enke, 1981.

Dahme, H.J. and Köhnke, K.C. (eds), *Georg Simmel, Schriften zur Philosophie und Soziologie der Geschlechter*, Frankfurt, Suhrkamp, 1985.

Dahme, H.J. and Rammstedt O. (eds), *Georg Simmel und die Moderne*, Frankfurt, Suhrkamp, 1984.

Davis, M., 'Georg Simmel and the Aesthetics of Social Reality', *Social Forces*, 51, 1973, pp.320–9.

Dibble, V.K., *The Legacy of Albion Small*, Chicago/London, Chicago University Press, 1975

Dilthey, W. *Briefwechsel zwischen Wilhelm Dilthey und dem Grafen Paul Yorck v. Wartenburg: 1877–97*, Halle, Niemeyer, 1923.

Dilthey, W., *Einleitung in die Geisteswissenschaften*, 2nd edn, Leipzig/Berlin, Teubner, 1923.

Döhring, H., *Die Geldtheorien seit Knapp*, Greifswald, L. Bamberg, 1921.

Durkheim, E., 'Simmel', *L'année sociologique*, 7, 1902-3, pp.646–7.

Durkheim, E., *Suicide*, London, Routledge, 1952.

Endell, A., *Die Schönheit der grossen Stadt*, Berlin, Archibook, 1984.

Etzkorn, K.P., (ed.), Georg Simmel: *The Conflict in Modern Culture and other Essays*, New York, Teachers College Press, pp.68–80.

Eulenburg, F., 'Über die Möglichkeit und die Aufgaben einer Sozialpsychologie', *Jahrbuch für Gesetzgebung, Verwaltung und Volkswirtschaft*, 24, 1900, pp.201–37.

Foster, H., (ed.), *Postmodern Culture*, London, Pluto, 1985.

Frankel, S.H., *Money: Two Philosophies*, Oxford, Blackwell, 1977.

Frisby, D., *Georg Simmel*, Chichester/London/New York, Ellis Horwood/Tavistock/Methuen Inc., 1984.

Frisby, D., 'Georg Simmel and Social Psychology', *Journal of the History of the Behavioral Sciences*, 20, 2, 1984, pp.107–27.

Frisby, D., *Fragments of Modernity: Theories of Modernity in the Work of Simmel, Kracauer and Benjamin*, Cambridge, Polity Press; Cambridge, Mass., MIT Press, 1986.

Frisby, D., 'Soziologie und Moderne: Ferdinand Tönnies, Georg Simmel und Max Weber', in O. Rammstedt (ed.), *Simmel, und die frühen Soziologen*, Frankfurt, Suhrkamp, 1988, pp.196–221.

Frisby, D., 'Simmel and Leisure', in C. Rojek (ed.), *Leisure for Leisure*, Basingstoke/London, Macmillan, 1989, pp.75–91.

Frisby, D., 'Georg Simmel's Concept of Society' in M. Kaern, B. Phillips and R. Cohen (eds), *Georg Simmel and Contemporary Sociology*, Dordrecht, Kluwer, 1990, pp.39–55.

Frisby, D., 'The Aesthetics of Modern Life', *Theory, Culture and Society*, 8, 3, 1991, pp. 73–93.

Frisby, D., *Sociological Impressionism. A Reassessment of Georg Simmel's Social Theory*, 2nd edn, London/New York, Routledge, 1991.

Frisby, D. and Köhnke, K.C. (eds), *Materialien zur Philosophie des Geldes*, Frankfurt, Suhrkamp, 1992.

Frisby, D. and Sayer, D., *Society*, Chichester/London/New York, Ellis Horwood/ Tavistock/ Methuen Inc., 1986.

Frost, W., 'Die Soziologie Simmels', Riga, *Acta Universitatis Latviensis*, 12, 1925, pp.219–313; 13, 1926, pp.149–225.

Gassen, K. and Landmann, M., (eds), *Buch des Dankes an Georg Simmel*, Berlin, Duncker & Humblot, 1958.

Gerhardt, U., 'Immanenz und Widerspruch', *Zeitschrift für philosophische Forschung*, 25, 1971, pp.276–92.

Goldscheid, R., 'Jahresbericht über Erscheinungen der Soziologie in den Jahren 1899–1904', *Archiv für systematische Philosophie*, 10, 1904, pp.397–413.

Goux, J.-J., *Symbolic Economies*, Ithaca, Cornell University Press, 1990.

Green, B.S., *Literary Methods and Sociological Theory*, Chicago, Chicago University Press, 1988.

Gumplowicz, L., 'August Comte und seine Bedeutung', *Annals of the American Academy of Political and Social Science*, 5, 1894–5, pp.151–3.

Gumplowicz, L., 'Zur neuesten soziologischen Literatur' (1891), in *Soziologische Essays. Soziologie und Politik*, Innsbruck, Wagner, 1928, pp.328–33.

Habermas, J., *Theorie des Kommunikativen Handelns*, II, Frankfurt, Suhrkamp, 1981.

Habermas, J., 'Die Moderne – ein unvollendetes Projekt', *Kleine Politische Schriften, (I–IV)*, Frankfurt, Suhrkamp, 1983, pp.444–64.

Habermas, J., *The Philosophical Discourse of Modernity*, (trans. F. Lawrence), Cambridge, Mass., MIT Press, 1987.

Habermas, J., *Theories of Communicative Action*, 2 vols., (trans. T. McCarthy), Boston, Beacon Press, 1984, 1987.

Harvey, D., *Consciousness and the Urban Experience*, Oxford, Blackwell, 1985.

Harvey, D., *The Condition of Postmodernity*, Oxford, Blackwell, 1989.

Hoffman, F., *Kritische Dogmengeschichte der Geldwerttheorien*, Leipzig, Hirschfeld, 1909.

Jevons, W.S., *Money and the Mechanism of Exchange*, 8th edn, London, Kegan Paul, 1887.

Jevons, W.S., *The Theory of Political Economy*, Harmondsworth, Penguin, 1970.

Joas, H., *G. H. Mead*, Cambridge, Polity Press; Cambridge, Mass., MIT Press, 1985.

Kalberg, S., 'Max Weber's Types of Rationality', *American Journal of Sociology*, 85, 1980, pp.1145–79.

Kant, I., *Observations on the Feeling of the Beautiful and the Sublime*, New York, Doubleday, 1965.

Kant, I., *The Critique of Judgement*, (trans. J.C. Meredith), Oxford, Oxford University Press, 1982.

Knapp, G.F., *Staatliche Theorie des Geldes*, Leipzig, Duncker & Humblot, 1905.

Köhnke, K.C., 'Murderous Attack Upon Georg Simmel', *European Journal of Sociology*, 24, 2, 1983, p.349.

Köhnke, K.C., 'Four concepts of Social Science at Berlin University' in M. Kaern, B. Phillips and R.S. Cohen (eds), *Georg Simmel and Contemporary Sociology*, Dordrecht, Kluwer, 1990, pp.99–108.

Köhnke, K.C., 'Soziologie als Kulturwissenschaft', *Archiv für Kulturgeschichte*, 72, 1, 1990, pp.223–32.

Korff, G., and Rürup, R. (eds), *Berlin, Berlin*, Berlin, Nicolai, 1987.

Kornau, E., *Raum und soziales Handeln*, Stuttgart, Enke, 1977.

Kracauer, S., 'Georg Simmel', *Logos*, 9, 1920, pp.307–38.

Kracauer, S., *Das Ornament der Masse*, Frankfurt, Suhrkamp, 1963.

Lange, F.A. *Geschichte des Materialismus*, (Volksausgabe), Leipzig, Kröner, n.d. p.129.

Lasswitz, K., *Gustav Theodor Fechner*, 2nd edn, Stuttgart, Fromanns Verlag, 1902.

Lawrence, P.A., *Georg Simmel: Sociologist and European*, Sunbury, Middlesex, Nelson, 1976.

Lawrence, P.A., 'Review Essay: Radicalism and the Cash Nexus', *American Journal of Sociology*, 86, 1, 1980, pp.182–6.

Lazarus, M., *Das Leben der Seele*, 3rd edn, Berlin, Dummler, 1883.

Lazarus, M. and Steinthal, H., 'Einleitende Gedanken über Völkerpsychologie', *Zeitschrift für Völkerpsychologie und Sprachwissenschaft*, 1, 1860, pp.1–73.

Lees, A., *Cities Perceived*, Manchester, Manchester University Press, 1985.

Levine, D.N. (ed.), *Georg Simmel on Sociability and Social Forms*, Chicago, Chicago University Press, 1971.

Levine, D.N., E.B. Carter and E.M. Gorman, 'Simmel's Influence on American Sociology', in Böhringer, H. and Gründer, K. (eds), *Ästhetik und Soziologie um die Jahrhundertwende: Georg Simmel*, Frankfurt, Klostermann, 1976, pp.176–228.

Levine, D., 'Simmel at a Distance', *Sociological Focus*, 10, 1, 1977, pp.15–29.

Levine, D.N., *Simmel and Parsons. Two Approaches to the Study of Society*, New York, Arno Press, 1980.

Levine, D.N., *The Flight from Ambiguity*, Chicago, Chicago University Press, 1985.

Lexis, W., 'Neuere Schriften über das Geldwesen', *Jahrbücher für Nationalökonomie und Statistik*, 41, 1911, pp.547–50.

Lichtblau, K., 'Das "Pathos der Distanz". Präliminarien zur Nietzsche – Rezeption bei Georg Simmel', in H.J. Dahme and O. Rammstedt (eds), *Georg Simmel und die Moderne*, pp.231–81.

Lindner, G., *Ideen zur Psychologie der Gesellschaft als Grundlage der Sozialwissenschaft*, Vienna, Carl Gerolds Sohn, 1871.

Lindner, R., *Die Entdeckung der Stadtkultur. Soziologie aus der Erfahrung der Reportage*, Frankfurt, Suhrkamp, 1990.

Lotze, H., *Mikrokosomos*, 3 vols, 2nd edn, Leipzig, Hirzel, 1872.

Lunn, E., *Marxism and Modernism*, Berkeley, University of California Press, 1983.

MacCannel, D., *The Tourist. A New Theory of the Leisure Class*, New York, Schocken Books, 1976.

Makkreel, R.A., *Dilthey: Philosopher of the Human Studies*, Princeton, Princeton University Press, 1975.

Marx, K., *Grundrisse*, Harmondsworth, Penguin, 1973.

Marx, K., *The Revolutions of 1848*, London, Penguin, 1973.

Marx, K., *Early Writings*, Harmondsworth, Penguin, 1975.

Mead, G.H., 'Philosophie des Geldes', *Journal of Political Economy*, 9, 1901, pp.616–19.

Menger, C. [C.M.], 'Simmel, Georg, Philosophie des Geldes', *Literarische Centralblatt*, 52, 4, 1901, columns 160–1.

Miller, D., *Material Culture and Mass Consumption*, Oxford, Blackwell, 1987.

Mills, T.M., 'Some Hypotheses on Small Groups from Simmel', *American Journal of Sociology*, 63, 1958, pp.642–50.

Moretti, F., *Signs Taken for Wonders*, London/New York, Verso, 1988.

Mülder, I., *Siegfried Kracauer*, Metzler, Stuttgart, 1985.

Müller, M., *Schöner Schein*, Frankfurt, Athenäum, 1987.

Nedelmann, B., 'Georg Simmel – Emotion und Wechselwirkung in intimen Gruppen', *Kölner Zeitschrift für Soziologie und Sozial psychologie*, Sonderheft 25, 1983, pp.174–209.

Nedelmann, B., 'Aestheticization and Stylization: Two Strategies of Lifestyle Management', in C. Mongardini and M.L. Maniscalco (eds), *Moderno e Postmoderno*, Rome, Bulzoni, 1989, pp.91–110.

Oakes, G. (ed.), *Georg Simmel: On Women, Sexuality and Love*, New Haven/London, Yale University Press, 1984.

Pankoke, E., 'Social Movement', *Economy and Society*, 11, 2, 1982, pp.317–46.

Park, R., *Soziologische Vorlesungen von Georg Simmel*, Chicago, Department of Sociology, 1931.

Park, R.E. and Burgess, E.W., *The City*, Chicago/London, Chicago University Press, 1967.

Pascal, R., 'Georg Simmel's "Die Grossstädte und das Geistesleben" ', in H. Kreuzer (ed.), *Gestaltungsgeschichte und Gesellschafts-geschichte*, Stuttgart, Metzler, 1969, pp.450–60.

Pries, C. (ed.), *Das Erhabene*, Weinheim, V.C.H. Verlag, 1989.

Rathenau, W. [Anon], 'Die schönste Stadt der Welt', *Die Zukunft*, 26, 1899, pp.36–48.

Rojek, C. (ed.), *Leisure for Leisure*, London/Basingstoke, Macmillan, 1989.

Sayer, D., *Capitalism and Modernity*, London, Routledge, 1990.

Scheible, H., 'Georg Simmel und die "Tragödie der Kultur" ', *Neue Rundschau*, 91, 2/3, 1980, pp.133–64.

Schivelbusch, W., *The Railway Journey*, Leamington Spa/Hamburg/New York, Berg, 1986.

Schmoller, G., 'Simmel's Philosophie des Geldes', *Jahrbuch für Gesetzgebung, Verwaltung und Volkswirtschaft*, 25, 3, 1901, p.799.

Schnitzler, A. *Briefe. 1913–1931*, Frankfurt, Fischer, 1984.

Simmel, G., 'Psychologische und ethnologische Studien über Musik', *Zeitschrift für Völkerpsyhologie und Sprachwissenschaft*, 13, 1882, pp.261–305.

Simmel, G., 'Dantes Psychologie', *Zeitschrift für Völkerpsychologie und Sprachwissenschaft*, 15, 1884, pp.18–69, 239–76.

Simmel, G., 'Anzeige', *Vierteljahresschrift für wissenschaftliche Philosophie*, 10, 1886, pp.487–503.

Simmel, G., 'Bemerkungen zur socialethischen Problemen', *Vierteljahresschrift für wissenschaftliche Philosophie*, 12, 1888, pp.32–49.

Simmel, G., [Anon], 'Zur Psychologie des Pessimismus', *Baltische Monatsschrift*, 35, 1888, pp.557–66.

Simmel, G., 'Notiz', *Zeitschrift für Philosophie und philosophische Kritik*, 95, 1889, pp.159–60.

Simmel, G., 'Zur Psychologie des Geldes', *Jahrbuch für Gesetzgebung, Verwaltung und Volkswirtschaft*, 13, 1889, pp.1251–64.

Simmel, G., *Über sociale Differenzierung*, Leipzig, Duncker & Humblot, 1890.

Simmel, G., 'Ueber Kunstausstellungen', *Unsere Zeit*, 26 February 1890, pp.474–80.

Simmel, G., 'Zur Psychologie der Frauen', *Zeitschrift für Völkerpsychologie und Sprachwissenschaft*, 20, 1890, pp.6–46.

Simmel, G., 'G. Tarde. Les lois de l'imitation', *Zeitschrift für Psychologie und Physiologie der Sinnesorgane*, 2, 1891, pp.141–2.

Simmel, G. [P. Liesegang], 'Etwas vom Spiritismus', *Vorwärts*, 12 July 1892.

Simmel, G., *Die Probleme der Geschichtsphilosophie*, Leipzig, Duncker & Humblot, 1892.

Simmel, G., 'Psychologische Glossen zur Strafgesetznovelle', *Sozialpolitisches Zentralblatt*, 1, 1892, pp.173–4.

Simmel, G., *Einleitung in die Moralwissenschaft*, 2 vols, Berlin, Hertz, 1892, 1893.

Simmel, G., 'Gerhart Hauptmanns "Weber" ', *Sozialpolitisches Zentralblatt*, 2, 1892–3, pp.283–4.

Simmel, G., 'Ein Jubiläum der Frauenbewegung', *National-Zeitung*, 27 November 1893.

Simmel, G., [P. Liesegang], 'Infelices Possidentes', *Die Zukunft*, 3, 1893, pp.82–4.

Simmel, G., 'Das Problem der Soziologie', *Jahrbuch für Gesetzgebung, Verwaltung und Volkswirtschaft*, 18, 1894, pp.271–7.

Simmel, G., 'Der Militarismus und die Stellung der Frauen', *Vossische Zeitung*, 21, 28 October 1894.

Simmel, G., 'Alpenreisen', *Die Zeit*, 7, 13 July 1895.

Simmel, G., 'Böcklins Landschaften', *Die Zukunft*, 12, 1895, pp.272–7.

Simmel, G., 'Massenpsychologie', *Die Zeit*, Vienna, 5, 23 November 1895.

Simmel, G., 'The Problem of Sociology', *Annals of the American Academy of Political Science*, 6, 1895, pp.52–63.

Simmel, G., 'Zur Psychologie der Mode: Soziologische Studie', *Die Zeit*, Vienna, 5, 12 October 1895.

Simmel, G., 'Superiority and Subordination as Subject-Matter of Sociology', *American Journal of Sociology*, 2, 1896, pp.167–89.

Simmel, G., 'Berliner Gewerbe-Ausstellung', *Die Zeit* Vienna, 8, 25 July 1896.

Simmel, G., [Anon], 'Berliner Kunstbrief', *Die Zeit*, 6, 21 March 1896.

Simmel, G., 'Der Frauenkongress und die Sozialdemokratie', *Die Zukunft*, 17, 1896, pp.80–4.

Simmel, G., 'Das Geld in der modernen Kultur', *Zeitschrift des Oberschlesischen Berg-und Hüttenmännnischen Vereins*, 35, 1896, pp.319–24.

Simmel, G., 'Skizze einer Willenstheorie', *Zeitschrift für Psychologie und Physiologie der Sinnesorgane*, 9, 1896, pp.206–20.

Simmel, G., 'Soziologische Aesthetik', *Die Zukunft*, 17, 1896, pp.204–16.

Simmel, G., 'Zur Methodik der Sozialwissenschaft', *Jahrbuch für Gesetzgebung, Verwaltung und Volkswirtschaft*, 20, 1896, pp.575–85.

Simmel, G., 'Herbst am Rhein', *Jugend*, 4, 1897, p.54.

Simmel, G., 'Die Bedeutung des Geldes für das Tempo des Lebens', *Neue Deutsche Rundschau*, 8, 1897, pp.111–22.

Simmel, G., 'F. Tönnies. Der Nietzsche Kultus', *Deutsche Literaturzeitung*, 23 October 1897, columns 1645–51.

Simmel, G., 'Über Massenverbrechen', *Die Zeit*, Vienna, 2, 2 October 1897.

Simmel, G., 'Rom. Eine ästhetische Analyse', *Die Zeit*, 15, 28 May 1898.

Simmel, G., 'Einige Bemerkungen zu Schmollers "Grundriss der allgemeine Volkswirtschaftslehre" ', *Allgemeine Zeitung*, 28 October 1900.

Simmel, G. [G.S.] 'Metaphysik der Faulheit', *Jugend*, 20, 1900, pp.337–9.

Simmel, G., 'Sozialismus und Pessimismus', *Die Zeit*, Vienna, 22, 3 February 1900.

Simmel, G., 'Zu einer Theorie des Pessimismus', *Die Zeit*, Vienna, 22, 20 January 1900.

Simmel, G., 'Ästhetik der Schwere', *Berliner Tageblatt*, 10 June 1901.

Simmel, G., 'Zur Psychologie der Scham', *Die Zeit*, Vienna, 9 November 1901.

Simmel, G., 'Tendencies in German Life and Thought since 1870', *International Monthly*, New York, 5, 1902, pp.93–111; 166–84.

Simmel, G., 'Weibliche Kultur', *Neue Deutsche Rundschau*, 13, 1902, pp.504–15.

Simmel, G., 'The Number of Members as Determining the Sociological Form of the Group', *American Journal of Sociology*, 8, 1902/3, pp.1–46, 158–96.

Simmel, G., 'Die Grossstädte und das Geistesleben', *Jahrbuch der Gehe-Stiftung zu Dresden*, 9, 1903, pp.185–206.

Simmel, G., 'Soziologie des Raumes', *Jahrbuch für Gesetzgebung, Verwaltung und Volkswirtschaft*, 27, 1903, pp.27–71.

Simmel, G., 'Über räumliche Projektionen sozialer Formen', *Zeitschrift für Sozialwissenschaft*, 6, 1903, pp.287–302.

Simmel, G., 'Bruchstücke aus einer Psychologie der Frauen', *Der Tag*, 9 July 1904.

Simmel, G., *Kant, Sechszehn Vorlesungen*, Leipzig, Duncker & Humblot, 1904.

Simmel, G., *Philosophie der Mode*, Berlin, Pan, 1905.

Simmel, G., *Die Religion*, Frankfurt, Rüten & Loening, 1906.

Simmel, G., 'Dankbarkeit', *Morgen*, 1, 1907, pp.593–8.

Simmel, G., 'Soziologie der Sinne', *Die Neue Rundschau*, 18, 1907, pp.1025–36.

Simmel, G., 'Das Problem des Stiles', *Dekorative Kunst*, 11, 7, 1908, pp.307–16.

Simmel, G., 'Der Brief', *Österreichische Rundschau*, 15, 1908, pp.334–6.

Simmel, G., 'Psychologie des Schmuckes', *Morgen*, 2, 1908, pp.454–9.

Simmel, G., *Soziologie: Untersuchungen über die Formen der Vergesellschaftung*, Berlin, Duncker & Humblot, 1908.

Simmel, G., 'Über das Wesen der Sozial-Psychologie', *Archiv für Sozialwissenschaft und Sozialpolitik*, 26, 1908, pp.285–91.

Simmel, G., 'Soziologie der Mahlzeit', *Berliner Tageblatt*, 10 October 1910.

Simmel, G., *Philosophische Kultur: Gesammelte Essais*, Leipzig, Klinkhardt, 1911.

Simmel, G., 'Soziologie der Geselligkeit', *Verhandlungen des 1. Deutschen Soziologentages*, (1910), Tübingen, Mohr, 1911, pp.1–16.

Simmel, G., 'An Herrn Professor Karl Lamprecht', *Die Zukunft*, 83, 1913.

Simmel, G., *Rembrandt*, Leipzig, Kurt Wolff Verlag, 1916.

Simmel, G., 'Der Bildrahmen', in *Zur Philosophie der Kunst*, Potsdam, Kiepenheuer, 1922, pp.46–54.

Simmel, G., 'Florenz', in *Zur Philosophie der Kunst*, Potsdam, Kiepenheuer, 1922, pp.61–6.

Simmel, G., 'Der Siebente Ring', in *Zur Philosophie der Kunst*, Potsdam, Kiepenheuer, 1922, pp.74–8.

Simmel, G., 'Venedig', in *Zur Philosophie der Kunst*, Potsdam, Kiepenheuer, 1922, pp.67–73.

Simmel, G., 'The Sociology of Sociability' (trans. E.K. Hughes), *American Journal of Sociology*, 55, 1949/50, pp.254–61.

Simmel, G., *Conflict and the Web of Group Affiliations*, (trans. K.H. Wolff and R. Bendix), Glencoe, Illinois, Free Press, 1955.

Simmel, G., *Brücke und Tür*, Stuttgart, Koehler, 1957.

Simmel, G., 'Philosophie der Landschaft', in *Brücke und Tür*, Stuttgart, Koehler, 1957.

Simmel, G., 'How is Society Possible?' in K.H. Wolff (ed.), *Essays on Sociology, Philosophy and Aesthetics by Georg Simmel* et al., Columbus, Ohio State University Press, 1959, pp.337–56.

Simmel, G., 'The Problem of Sociology', in K.H. Wolff (ed.), *Essays on Sociology, Philosophy and Aesthetics by Georg Simmel* et al., Columbus, Ohio State University Press, 1959, pp.310–36.

Simmel, G., *The Conflict in Modern Culture and Other Essays* (trans. and ed. K.P. Etzkorn), New York, Teachers College Press, 1968.

Simmel, G., *The Problems of the Philosophy of History* (trans. and ed. G. Oakes), New York, Free Press, 1977.

Simmel, G., *Philosophische Kulture*, Berlin, Wagenbach, 1983.

Simmel, G., *On Women, Sexuality and Love*, New Haven/London, Yale University Press, 1984, with introduction by G. Oakes.

Simmel, G., *Filosofia del Denaro*, Turin, Utet, 1984.

Simmel, G., *Schriften zur Philosophie und Soziologie der Geschlechter*, (ed. H.J. Dahme and K.C. Köhnke), Frankfurt, Suhrkamp, 1985.

Simmel, G., *Schopenhauer and Nietzsche*, Amherst, University of Massachusetts Press, 1986.

Simmel, G., *Aufsätze 1887 bis 1890, Über sociale Differenzierung, Die Probleme der Geschichtsphilosophie*, (Gesamtausgabe 2) (ed. H.-J. Dahme), Frankfurt, Suhrkamp, 1989.

Simmel, G., *Philosophie des Geldes, Gesamtausgabe* 6 (ed. D. Frisby, and K.C. Köhnke), Frankfurt, Suhrkamp, 1989.

Simmel, G., *The Philosophy of Money* (trans. T. Bottomore and D. Frisby), 2nd edn, London/New York, Routledge, 1990.

Simmel, G., *Aufsätze und Abhandlungen: 1894-1900*, (ed. H. J. Dahme, and D. Frisby), Frankfurt, Suhrkamp, 1992.

Small, A.W., ' "Social" vs. "Societary" ', *Annals of the American Academy of Political and Social Science*, 5, 1894-5, pp.948-53.

Small, A.W., 'Methodology of the Social Problem', *American Journal of Sociology*, 4, 1898-9, pp.380-94.

Small, A.W., 'Grundriss der allgemeinen Volkswirtschaftslehre', *American Journal of Sociology*, 6, 1900-1, pp.423-4.

Small, A.W., 'Soziologie', *American Journal of Sociology*, 14, 1908-9, pp.544-5.

Small, A.W., 'Germany and American Opinion', *Sociological Review*, 7, 1914, pp.106-11.

Small, A.W., 'Kölner Vierteljahrsheften für Sozialwissenschaften', *American Journal of Sociology*, 27, 1921-2, pp.92-4.

Small, A.W., 'Individuum und Gemeinschaft', *American Journal of Sociology*, 30, 1924, pp.352-3.

Small, A.W., 'Allgemeine Soziologie', *American Journal of Sociology*, 31, 1925-6, pp.87-9.

Small, A.W., 'The Social Theory of Georg Simmel', *American Journal of Sociology*, 31, 1925-6, pp.84-7.

Soda, K., *Geld und Wert*, Tübingen, Mohr, 1924.

Sokal, M.M., 'G. Stanley Hall and the Institutional Character of Psychology at Clark 1889-1920', *Journal of the History of the Behavioral Sciences*, 26, 1990, pp.114-24.

Sombart, W., 'Der natuerliche Werth', *Jahrbuch für Gesetzgebung, Verwaltung und Volkswirtschaft*, 13, 4, 1889, pp.1488-90.

Sombart, W., 'Probleme des Kunstgewerbes in der Gegenwart', *Die Neue Rundschau*, 18, 1, 1907, pp.513-36.

Sorokin, P., *Contemporary Sociological Theories*, New York/London, Harper, 1928.

Spann, O., *Wirtschaft und Gesellschaft*, Dresden, 1907.

Spencer, H., *First Principles*, London, Williams & Norgate, 1862.

Spencer, H., *The Principles of Sociology*, 1, London, Williams & Norgate, 1904.

Steinhoff, M., 'Die Form als soziologische Grundkategorie bei Georg Simmel', *Kölner Vierteljahrshefte för Soziologie*, 4, 1925, pp.214–59.

Steinthal, H., 'An der Leser', *Zeitschrift des Vereins für Volkskunde*, 1, 1891, pp.10–17.

Stephinger, L., *Die Geldlehre Adam Müllers*, Stuttgart, Enke, 1909.

Tenbruck, F.H., 'Georg Simmel (1858–1918)', *Kölner Zeitschrift für Soziologie und Sozial-psychologie*, 10, 1958, pp.586–614.

Tönnies, F., *Gemeinschaft und Gesellschaft*, Leipzig, 1887.

Tönnies, F., 'Considerations sur l'histoire moderne', *Annales de l'institut international de sociologie*, 1, 1895, pp.245–52.

Tönnies, F., 'Historismus und Rationalismus', *Archiv für systematische Philosophie*, 1, 1895, pp.227–52.

Tönnies, F., 'Zur Einleitung in die Soziologie', *Zeitschrift für Philosophie und philosophische Kritik*, 115, 1899, pp.240–51.

Tönnies, F., 'Gemeinschaft und Gesellschaft', *Kantstudien*, 30, 1925, pp.149–79.

Tönnies, F., 'Entwicklung der Soziologie in Deutschland im 19 Jahrhundert', in *Soziologische Studien und Kritiken*, 2nd collection, Jena, Gustav Fischer, 1926.

Tönnies, F., *Community and Association* (trans. C.P. Loomis), London, Routledge, 1955.

Tönnies, F., *On Sociology: Pure, Applied and Empirical*, Chicago/London, Chicago University Press, 1971.

Troeltsch, E., 'Der historische Entwicklungsbegriff in der modernen Geistes – und Lebensphilosophie', *Historische Zeitschrift*, 124, 1921, pp.424–86.

Ulmi, M., *Frauenfragen. Männergedanken*, Zurich, efef Verlag, 1989.

Vattimo, G., *The End of Modernity*, (trans. J.R. Snyder), Cambridge, Polity Press, 1988.

Veblen, T., *The Theory of the Leisure Class*, New York/Toronto, New American Library, 1953.

von Wieser, F., *Der natürliche Werth*, Vienna, Hölder, 1889, p.3

Vromen, S., 'Georg Simmel and the Cultural Dilemma of Women', *History of European Ideas*, 8, 4/5, pp.563–79.

Ward, L.F., 'The Social Mind and Education', *Annals of the American Academy of Political and Social Science*, 11, 1898, pp.264–7.

Weber, M., 'Georg Simmel as Sociologist', *Social Research*, 39, 1972, pp.155–63.

Weinstein, D. and Weinstein, M.A., 'Simmel and the Theory of Postmodern Society', in B.S. Turner (ed.), *Theories of Modernity and Postmodernity*, London, Sage, 1989, pp.75–87.

Whimster, S. and Lash, S. (eds), *Max Weber, Rationality and Modernity*, London, Allen & Unwin, 1987.

Williams, R., *Dream Worlds: Mass Consumption in Late Nineteenth Century France*, Berkeley/Los Angeles/London, University of California Press, 1982.

Wirth, L., 'The Sociology of Ferdinand Tönnies', *American Journal of Sociology*, 32, 1926, pp.412–28.

Wolff, K.H., (ed.), *The Sociology of Georg Simmel*, Glencoe, Illinois, Free Press, 1950, and 2nd edn, New York/London, Free Press, 1964.

Woodward, H., 'The First German Municipal Exposition. (Dresden, 1903)', *American Journal of Sociology*, 9, 1904, pp.433–58; 612–30; 812–31; 10, 1905, pp.47–63.

Wundt, W., *Logik*, vol. 2, *Methodenlehre*, Stuttgart, Enke, 1883.

Wundt, W., *Völkerspsychologie*, 10 vols, Leipzig, Alfred Kröner, 1917.

Zola, E., *The Ladies' Paradise*, London, Vizitelly, 1889.

Index